国际新闻“十二五”规划系列教材

International Journalism A Textbook

国际新闻报道教程

经典新闻作品深度阅读

章晓英 翟 峥 / 编著

中国传媒大学出版社

图书在版编目（CIP）数据

国际新闻报道教程：经典新闻作品深度阅读．章晓英，翟峥编著．
—北京：中国传媒大学出版社，2013.5
国际新闻“十二五”规划系列教材
ISBN 978-7-5657-1165-7

Ⅰ.①国…　Ⅱ.①章…②翟…　Ⅲ.①新闻-英语-阅读教学-高等学校-教学参考资料
Ⅳ.①H319.4
中国版本图书馆 CIP 数据核字（2014）第 205909 号

国际新闻“十二五”规划系列教材
国际新闻报道教程：经典新闻作品深度阅读

编 著 者　章晓英　翟峥
策划编辑　司马兰　姜颖昳
责任编辑　司马兰　姜颖昳
封面设计　拓美设计
责任印刷　曹　辉
出 版 人　王巧林

出版发行　中国传媒大学出版社
社　　址　北京市朝阳区定福庄东街 1 号　　邮编：100024
电　　话　86-10-64450532 或 65450528　　传真：010-65779405
网　　址　http://www.cucp.com.cn
经　　销　全国新华书店

印　　刷　北京艺堂印刷有限公司
开　　本　787mm×1092mm　1/16
印　　张　15.00
印　　次　2015 年 4 月第 1 版　2015 年 4 月第 1 次印刷

书　　号　ISBN 978-7-5657-1165-7 / H・1165
定　　价　45.00 元

目 录

前 言

一、基本理念：DRDT

该教材提倡“深度阅读和思考”（Deep Reading and Deep Thinking/DRDT）。原因如下：

第一，当前互联网环境下的“跳跃式文本阅读”导致浅显性和浮躁不安。一方面，互联网给我们带来快捷链接和精准搜索，让我们享受海量信息；但另一方面，互联网阅读方式常常造成阅读状态的中断。我们可以点击某个超链接，快速而唐突地从一个页面跳转至另一个新的页面，接受另外一个文本，因为我们总是被新的内容所吸引。由于两个超链接之间的文本内容有差异，因而往往造成阅读状态的中断。这种非连续性文本阅读很容易导致对于当前内容理解的不够深入。更严重的是，面对无数个链接时，我们往往需要花时间和精力去判断这个链接是否值得我们点击。如果觉得下一个链接可能更有价值，我们就会去点击，但打开一看，其实没有什么价值，于是接着再点。如此周而复始，人们往往不知不觉变得浮躁起来，因为其大脑始终处于选择判断模式，而非深度阅读模式。

第二，近年来，全国各高校英语专业开展批判性思维教育，强调学生的批判性思维能力，因此需要培养学生的深度阅读习惯。试想如果我们的学生连深度阅读的习惯都没有养成，怎么能够对文本进行深入分析，提出独立而有深度的见解呢？

因此，DRDT 旨在培养和提高学生的“连续性阅读习惯”和“深度阅读习惯”，为最终培养和提高学生的批判性阅读能力打下扎实的基础。

二、教材目标

教材所选文章为美国普利策获奖新闻作品，包括 10 大类新闻报道：突发新闻、专题新闻、国内新闻、国际新闻、调查性报道、解释性报道、特写、专栏评论、社论和文艺批评。文章题材广泛，涉及政治、经济、文化、教育、社会与环境等诸多重要领域。教材有三个主要目标：

（一）了解和熟悉各类英语新闻报道，并掌握其写作的基本特征或要素。

（二）学习地道、成熟的英文表达方式。

（三）体验中西文化异同，提高跨文化传播意识和能力。

三、教材结构

教材共有 10 个单元，有的单元有 A、B 和 C 三篇课文，但由于篇幅问题，有的只有一篇或两篇课文。课文 A 是重点，有详细的学习计划和步骤，其他两篇作为辅助阅读材料，只提供一些最基本的信息，希望感兴趣的学生可以多读一些，走得更远一些，有更加丰富的体验。

课文 A 由四大部分组成，建议在课堂上处理：

☆ Preparing to explore. 这部分是“暖身阶段”。其总体目标是掌握阅读必备的相关基本知识。具体内容是：一、提供该课文涉及的新闻类别的相关基本知识，如什么是调查性新闻、其意义和作用、基本写作要求等；二、就课文涉及的话题进行课前讨论，希望大家对所谈内容形成基本观点，以便阅读时可以与作者进行平等对话。

☆ Exploring the text. 这部分是“新闻能力训练”，即从新闻的角度讨论和理解课文内容。具体内容是：一、了解作者背景；二、了解报纸背景；三、了解课文背景；四、讨论和熟悉作者的主要观点或者隐含在事实描述中的观点；五、从新闻价值、新闻源、新闻采集方式、目的性、新闻结构、语言风格等新闻评价基本要素方面，对新闻作品进行讨论和评价。

☆ Further exploring the text. 这部分是“语言能力训练”。具体内容是：一、重要语言点的总结和讲解；二、对语言中文化内涵的分析，并进行中西文化比较；三、语言练习。

☆ Exploring beyond the text. 这是最后一部分，主要目的是“开阔视野”。具体内容是：一、对自己的学习过程进行反思，以进一步明确改进目标；二、扩展相关知识，引发更多思考；三、对课文进行书面评论，并开展自主写作，培养写作兴趣，发掘写作潜力。

四、教材特点

（一）新闻能力训练与英语语言能力训练有机融合。在新闻能力训练部分，学生有机会用英语讨论问题，加强口语表达能力，而在英语语言训练部分，又会通过对语言的进一步理解加深对新闻作品内容或者作者意图的理解。同时，通过模仿写作，不但能发掘自己的写作潜力，还能够提高英语的笔头表达能力。总之，该教材注重新闻与英语的结合，你中有我，我中有你。你我并进。

（二）启发思维，发展能力。在教学目标、教学内容的选择、教材结构的安排上，该教材都体现对学生思维的启发和能力的开发，特别是准确的英语口笔头表达能力、总结和归纳能力以及批判思维能力。

（三）注重培养学习方法。该教材结构合理，主线清晰，目标明确。在老师的引导下，学生不但可以循序渐进地完成各项任务，获得成就感，还可以掌握学习方法。

（四）编写语言简洁明了。无论是中文还是英文，该教材的编写语言以简洁明了为原则。

五、读者对象

高校国际新闻专业学生、中文类新闻专业学生、英语专业学生、爱好英语与新闻的大中学生，以及新闻从业人员。

Joseph Pulitzer

约瑟夫·普利策

尽管普利策是一个颇有争议的人物，但这并不影响他是美国历史上最负盛名的新闻界人物之一的事实。

普利策1847年4月10日出生于匈牙利的马科，1911年在美国去世，终年64岁。

普利策的一生具有传奇色彩。他出生于一个富裕家庭，父亲是犹太人和匈牙利人混血，经营谷物生意，母亲是德国人和奥地利人混血，笃信罗马天主教。普利策受过良好的教育，在当地私立学校和私人教师的教育下长大成人。他的性格桀骜不驯，从小就梦想能成为一名军人。17岁时，身材瘦长的普利策先后向奥地利军队、拿破仑驻墨西哥军团和英国驻印度军队申请参军，但都因其视力不佳和身体虚弱而遭到拒绝。后来，他终于得到一个机会加入了美国联邦军在法国招募的兵团，于1864年秋随同一群欧洲移民乘船到了美国波士顿，后来又独自到了纽约，加入了林肯骑兵队（Lincoln Cavalry）。这对他很合适，因为部队里有许多德国人。那时他讲一口流利的德语和法语，还不太会说英语。普利策干了1年后，离开军队，到了圣·路易斯。他到处打工，当过货运工（muleteer）、行李搬运工（baggage handler）和餐厅服务员（waiter）。在打工之余，他还经常去当地的商业图书馆（mercantile library）学习法律和英语。他事业的最大转机发生在图书馆的棋艺室里。一天，他在观看两个人下棋的时候，忍不住支了一招，没想到使对方大为吃惊，并与他攀谈起来。原来，那两个下棋的人是当时一份有名的德文报纸《西方邮报》（*Westiche Post*）的编辑，他们给了他一份工作，普利策从此踏上了职业新闻工作的道路。24岁时，普利策从濒于倒闭的《西方邮报》老板那里获得了报社控股权。25岁时，普利策成为一名出版商。30岁时，他便成为了《圣路易斯邮报》的老板。他以不知疲倦、前途辉煌的人物形象出现在新闻界。同时，他与华盛顿社会名流凯特·戴维斯（Kate Davis）女士的结合，使他很快融入圣·路易斯的上流社会。

普利策办报很成功，但是过程很坎坷，甚至付出了生命的代价。自从他执掌《圣路易斯邮报》后，他就全身心地投入工作。为了证明报纸是公众利益的最好捍卫者，他大量刊发调查性文章和社论，攻击政府的腐败行为、富人偷税漏税和赌博等各种不法行为，使报纸发行量攀升。拼命三郎式的工作方法使普利策的健康受到损害，他的视力继续下降。按照医生的要求，他与妻子准备在纽约乘船赴欧休假。然而他没有在纽约上船，而是固执己见地会见了金融家杰伊·古尔德（Jay Gould），与他谈判有关收购正面临财政困境的《纽约世界报》（*New York World*）事宜。普利策不顾严重的健康状况，又全身心地投入到寻找报纸的出路上，最终为《纽约世界报》的社论方针、内容和版面带来了革命性变化。他采用诉求平民利益的方法，反对政府和商界的腐败行为，在新闻专栏上刊登大量耸人听闻的特写，并首次采用大量插图，刊登新闻噱头。他还让《纽约世界报》的订阅者募集捐款，以在纽约港入口处搭建一个台基，使困在法国等待装船的自由女神像（Statue of Liberty）有个安放之处。在此后的 10 年里，该报成为全国发行量最大的一家报纸，但出乎意料，普利策本人却在发行量的大战中成了牺牲品。《纽约太阳报》（*New York Sun*）的出版人查尔斯·安德森·达纳（Charles Anderson Dana）由于《纽约世界报》的获胜而大受挫折，便开始对普利策进行恶毒的人身攻击，说他是"一个不承认自己种族和信仰的犹太人"。这一持续的攻击就是要让纽约的犹太人疏远《纽约世界报》。普利策的健康在这一灾难中愈加衰弱。43 岁时，他退出报纸编辑岗位，从此再未回到过编辑部。他几乎双目失明，在极度的消沉中又患上了一种痛苦的对噪音极为敏感的病。他出国苦苦寻求良医，却一无所获。在此后的 20 年里，他基本上把自己关在他称之为隔音的"地窖"里，或在他的"自由号"（Liberty）游艇上，或在缅因州巴港的度假胜地"静塔"（Tower of Silence）中，或在他的纽约私邸里。

在 1896 年至 1898 年期间，普利策卷入了一场与威廉·伦道夫·赫斯特（William Randolph Hearst）领导的《纽约新闻报》（*New York Journal*）的激烈的发行大战中。两报采取被称为"黄色新闻"（yellow journalism）的策略，几乎无节制地刊登耸人听闻或是胡编乱造的新闻报道。在古巴人反对西班牙人的统治中，普利策与赫斯特试图一争高低，煽动反西班牙人的愤怒情绪。1898 年 2 月 16 日，美国军舰"缅因号"（Maine）神秘爆炸并沉没在哈瓦那港后，双方均呼吁对西班牙宣战。国会面对强烈呼声，通过了战争决议。战争结束后，《纽约世界报》变得较为克制。历史学家认为，普利策在公共服务方面的成就要强于他滑入"黄色新闻"的过错。比如，他勇敢地声讨政府和商业腐败行为，为反垄断法的通过和保险行业的规范管理起了重要作用。1909 年，《纽约世界报》揭露了一起美国对法国巴拿马运河公司（French Panama Canal Company）支付四千万美元的舞弊案。联邦政府向报纸发动了严厉反击，控告普利策恶毒诽谤西奥多·罗斯福总统（Theodore Roosevelt）和包括银行家 J. P. 摩根（J. P. Morgan）在内的一些人。普利策没有退缩，而是继续进行调查。最后法庭撤销起诉，普利策为新闻自由取得了一场关键性胜利，从而赢得广泛赞誉。

普利策坚信新闻教育的力量。1904 年 5 月，普利策在为《北美评论》（*North American Review*）撰写的一篇建议成立一所新闻学院的文章中总结了他的信条："我们的共和国将与媒体共存亡。拥有训练有素、是非分明、有勇气的、能为正义献身的报人和有能力、公正、具有为民众服务精神的媒体，就能够维护公众品德。如果没有这样的报人和媒体，人民大众的政府既虚伪又会招人嘲笑。一个愤世嫉俗、唯利是图、蛊惑民心的媒体，最终会制造出一个像自己一样卑劣的民众。塑造共和国未来的力量掌握在未来的新闻记者手中。"为此，他向哥伦比亚大学捐款 200 万美元，呼吁创建哥伦比亚新闻学院，临终前又捐款 100 万美元，呼吁成立了一个基金会，作为优秀的新闻、历史、音乐和戏剧作品的年度奖金。1912 年，根据普利策的遗嘱，哥伦比亚新闻学院(Columbia School of Journalism)成立 ，1917 年普利策奖设立。

普利策对新闻学的贡献是无与伦比的，他不仅成功地创办了《纽约世界报》，提出了许多具有深远意义的新闻理念，并通过哥伦比亚新闻学院和普利策新闻奖将其新闻理想和追求代代相传。从这个意义上说，普利策被称为"新闻巨人"毫不为过。

Unit One　Breaking News Reporting

突发新闻报道

单元导航

本单元我们将讨论突发新闻。该单元所选的三篇课文都是围绕2004年美国新泽西州州长婚外同性恋情一事展开的报道。

Part One：Preparing to explore

一、突发新闻

1. 定义与意义

以新闻的时间性来分，新闻可分为突发性新闻和延缓性新闻。

突发新闻报道是指对出乎人们意料而突然爆发的事件的报道，例如，突然发生的自然灾害，如地震、水灾、火灾、空难、车祸等，以及突然爆发的社会事件，如战争、政变、枪杀、爆炸等。突发新闻具有时效性、不确定性和影响面广三大特点。突发新闻时效性强，记者记录下的图片和文字，不仅是当时真实有效的报道，具有新闻价值，而且往往是珍贵的历史资料，具有重要的历史价值。

突发新闻报道属于动态新闻类，要求记者以最快速度予以报道，具有新鲜感和现场感，并要求文字简洁。

2. 普利策突发新闻报道奖

普利策突发新闻报道奖于1998年开始设立，替换了此前的现场新闻报道（spot news reporting）奖项。因为在报道突发新闻时，记者不仅仅在现场进行报道，也去现场以外的地方进行采访。旧的概念已不能准确反映客观现实。

从1998年以来的突发新闻获奖作品来看，关于自然灾难报道的只有四篇，分别是森林火灾、卡特里娜飓风、四个小男孩意外溺水事件和亚拉巴马州的一场龙卷风，其余获奖作品都是关于突发社会事件的报道，包括银行抢劫案、办公室或校园枪杀案、反恐战争、政府官员的性丑闻、一家人在山上失踪的悲剧、美国联邦特工用接近军事袭击方式把古巴六岁男孩从其亲戚家带走还给其父亲的事件等。

从普利策奖评审委员会给予突发新闻报道获奖作品的赞词来看，优秀的突发新闻报道作品具有以下基本特点：

（1）在报道态度上，体现了记者过人的勇气和顽强不屈的精神以及清醒的头脑（courageous，tenacious，clear-headed）。

（2）在报道速度上，求快，求快，还是求快（swift）！

（3）在报道内容上，全面详尽，提供多方位的视角（comprehensive，multi-faceted，detailed，sweeping）。

（4）在报道手法上，坚持平衡报道原则（balanced）。

（5）在写作上，技巧纯熟老练（skillful）。

（6）在语言表达上，清晰明了（clear）。

（7）在效果上，能抓住读者的注意力（compelling，gripping）。

二、课前讨论

1. Do you accept homosexual politicians? Why or why not?

2. What would be your first reaction when you hear a politician declaring him/her to be a homosexual? Why would you react like that?

Part Two: Exploring the text

Text A McGreevey quits, admits gay affair

Governor plans to leave office Nov. 15. Ex-aide expected to sue, claiming sexual harassment.

BY Jeff Whelan and John Hassell

The Star-Ledger

Friday, August 13, 2004

Gov. James E. McGreevey announced yesterday that he will resign, citing an adulterous（通奸的）affair with a male lover and declaring, "I am a gay American."

"Shamefully, I engaged in an adult consensual（两厢情愿的）affair with another man, which violates my bonds of matrimony（婚约）," the governor said from the Statehouse（州府）as his wife Dina stood, expressionless, at his side. "It was wrong. It was foolish. It was inexcusable."

McGreevey, the state's 51st chief executive and the first to quit under the cloud of scandal, said he will step down Nov. 15 to protect the governor's office from "rumors, false allegations and threats of disclosure."

"I am removing these threats by telling you directly about my sexuality," he said in a blunt six-minute speech that threw the state political scene into turmoil. He added, "I am required... to do what is right to correct the consequences of my actions."

Although McGreevey did not name his lover, top administration officials identified him as Golan Cipel, an Israeli citizen who resigned two years ago as the governor's homeland security adviser amid questions about his qualifications for the position.

Officials said they expected Cipel to file a lawsuit today in Superior Court in Mercer County, alleging sexual harassment. Cipel, a 35-year-old former public relations professional, could not be reached for comment.

Three administration sources said that a lawyer representing McGreevey, William Lawler, called the FBI in Newark yesterday morning to say Cipel was attempting to extort(敲诈)money from the governor. It was unclear why Lawler chose to file the complaint yesterday, or if the bureau had launched an investigation.

FBI Special Agent Steve Siegel, a spokesman for the Newark division, said the office would have no comment. A source close to the U. S. Attorney's Office in Newark, however, confirmed that "they are taking the allegations very seriously and the matter is currently under investigation."

By delaying his resignation until Nov. 15, McGreevey prevents a special election this fall to replace him, and instead allows the Democratic president of the state Senate, Dick Codey, to serve as acting governor for the remainder of McGreevey's four-year term, which ends in January 2006. McGreevey said his timing was designed "to facilitate a responsible transition."

Codey, echoing the sentiments of leading Democrats, expressed sadness over McGreevey's decision. "My heart goes out to Jim McGreevey and his family during this difficult personal time," Codey said. "Jim McGreevey is a good person and a good friend."

Republicans described the delay of McGreevey's departure as a ploy(计策)to preserve Democratic control of state government. Former Gov. Christie Whitman, for one, called for McGreevey to step aside immediately, saying any postponement "smacks of politics."

McGreevey's announcement, made shortly after 4 p. m., set off widespread speculation about who would run to replace him. Many leading Democrats reached out quickly to U. S. Sen. Jon Corzine, who was traveling in California in his role as chairman of the Democratic Senatorial Campaign Committee.

Corzine released a statement later saying, "I applaud the governor's decision to acknowledge a part of his identity for which he owes no one an apology." Addressing the calls for him to run, Corzine added: "Any speculation about my own political plans in light of the governor's decision is entirely premature."

If Corzine did mount a gubernatorial(州长的)bid, his deep pockets and political connections probably would discourage many rivals, who potentially include Codey; Reps. Rob Andrews, Frank Pallone and Steve Rothman; and George Zoffinger, chairman of the state Sports and Exposition Authority.

On the Republican side, yesterday's news did little more than fan the ambitions of a large field of possible candidates. They include former Jersey City Mayor Bret Schundler; former

Rep. Bob Franks; Christopher Christie, the U. S. attorney for New Jersey; state Sens. Leonard Lance, Diane Allen and Tom Kean Jr. ; businessman and former U. S. Senate candidate Douglas Forrester; Assemblyman Paul DiGaetano; Morris County Freeholder John Murphy; and Bergen County businessman Robert Schroeder.

McGreevey's speech, 690 words long, was stunningly direct, even by the standards of a self-revelatory era in American political life. Among other things, he acknowledged the pain he has caused to his wife, Dina, his former wife, Kari Schutz, and his two daughters, 3-year-old Jacqueline and 11-year-old Morag.

"From my early days in school until the present day, I acknowledged some feelings, a certain sense that separated me from others," he said.

But because of my resolve, and also thinking that I was doing the right thing, I forced what I thought was an acceptable reality onto myself, a reality which is layered and layered with all the, quote, good things and all the, quote, right things of typical adolescent and adult behavior.

"Yet, at my most reflective, maybe even spiritual, level, there were points in my life when I began to question what an acceptable reality really meant for me. Were there realities from which I was running? Which master was I trying to serve?"

HIS OWN WORDS

The governor finalized his decision to resign with top aides yesterday in the library of Drumthwacket, the governor's mansion in Princeton. Among those gathered were chief of staff Jamie Fox, chief counsel Michael DeCotiis, state party chief executive Kevin Hagan, Casino Reinvestment Development Authority executive director Curtis Bashaw and three top political consultants—Steve DeMicco, Joel Benenson and Jim Margolis.

McGreevey presented the group with a draft of his speech, which he had written himself, and he resisted any heavy editing, several people present said. Then, shortly after 3:30, the governor and his wife joined his security detail (安保人员) in a two-vehicle motorcade to the Statehouse.

After his speech, McGreevey returned to Drumthwacket, spoke with his advisers for 10 minutes, then retired to the mansion's residential quarters with his family.

McGreevey met Cipel four years ago at a reception near Tel Aviv on a visit to Israel sponsored by the United Jewish Federation of Metro West. At the time, Cipel was working as a spokesman for the mayor of his hometown, Rishon Lezion, after a stint as chief information officer for the Israeli Consulate in New York.

Six months later, McGreevey brought Cipel to New Jersey. From the summer of 2000 through the 2001 election, Cipel earned \$30,000 a year as the Jewish outreach director for the state Democratic Party.

To supplement that salary, he also received \$30,000 a year as an associate at a development firm owned by McGreevey's top political contributor, Charles Kushner.

Attorneys for Kushner—who was arrested last month and accused of hiring prostitutes to blackmail federal witnesses—denied yesterday that the fund-raiser has been cooperating in any matter involving McGreevey.

"Charles Kushner is no way involved in the unfortunate circumstances surrounding the government's resignation," said the attorneys, Jeff Smith and Alfred DeCotiis.

When Cipel arrived in New Jersey, McGreevey assigned campaign staffers to arrange for an apartment a tenth of a mile from McGreevey's own condominium(常简写为 condo,公寓)in Woodbridge. Then, after winning the election, McGreevey took time out from his transition plans to accompany Cipel on a last-minute walk-through of the West Windsor townhouse Cipel was about to purchase.

According to the seller, Elaine Dietrich, Cipel said he wanted McGreevey to see the townhouse before he signed the contract. "I thought it was highly unusual," Dietrich said afterward. "I'm counsel to the administrative director of the courts, and I'm not going to ask(the director)to come look at my place and approve a purchase... You've got to admit, it's a little bizarre."

In January 2002, Cipel joined the governor's staff at $80,000 a year, a salary that was raised to $110,000 within six weeks with no explanation.

Hired as special counsel on homeland security, Cipel quickly encountered problems. Federal officials told *The Star-Ledger that* because Cipel was an Israeli national—a foreigner who could not have top-secret security clearance[(从事政府、军事等工作需获得的)安全等级]—they would refuse to share sensitive information with him.

Cipel resigned from the homeland security post after Republican leaders in the state Senate threatened to hold up(阻挡)key gubernatorial appointments until Cipel sat for questioning. Even so, Cipel retained the title of special counsel and his salary was unchanged.

In September 2002, McGreevey helped Cipel land a job at the prominent public relations and lobbying firm, MWW, for a salary of $120,000. The next month, just before MWW bosses planned to fire him, Cipel went to work for State Street Partners, the lobbying firm where McGreevey's best friend, Rahway Mayor James Kennedy, is a partner[(公司的)合伙人]. There Cipel got a $30,000 raise, bringing his salary to $150,000.

LEGAL DEADLINE

Cipel's expected lawsuit against McGreevey, which officials said is likely to seek $5 million in damages, would come just before the expiration of a general two-year limitation on workplace sexual harassment claims. He resigned from state government Aug. 14, 2002.

McGreevey's resignation ends a political career that has consumed him since high school. He has always followed a fast track—whether it was the quick succession of degrees from Columbia University, Georgetown University Law School and Harvard University's graduate school of education, or his early foray(冒险)into politics.

From his first, successful run for the state Assembly in 1989 to his victory in the 2001 race for governor, McGreevey, 47, has maintained a dogged pace. Friends and foes alike have marveled at his peripatetic(到处走的) travels around the state, which often began well before dawn and lasted well into the night.

According to McGreevey, his work ethic came from his parents, a former Marine Corps drill instructor and a nurse, and from his blue-collar upbringing in Jersey City and Carteret. McGreevey got his favorite motto from his father: "Plan your work and work your plan."

By the time McGreevey made his first, unsuccessful bid for governor in 1997, he had compiled an impressive political résumé, with stints as a state senator and assemblyman, mayor of Woodbridge, executive director of the state Parole Board, assistant prosecutor in Middlesex County and a government lobbyist for the pharmaceutical giant Merck.

Many of McGreevey's political connections have come to haunt him in the past couple of months, however, as his administration has been shaken by a series of high-profile scandals.

THE "MACHIAVELLI" ALLUSION("马基雅维利"典故)

In early July, one of McGreevey's top fund-raisers and friends, David D'Amiano, was indicted on charges that he extorted $40,000 in cash and political donations from a farm owner in return for his promise that the governor would help persuade county officials to double their bid for his farmland.

The indictment revealed McGreevey was secretly recorded by the FBI using the word "Machiavelli," which prosecutors said was a code word for the bribery scheme. No charges were brought against McGreevey, who was referred to in the indictment only as "State Official 1." The governor acknowledged uttering the word but said it was an innocent literary allusion. He denied any wrongdoing and accused the U. S. Attorney's Office(美国联邦检察官办公室) of mounting a smear campaign against him.

A week later, federal authorities arrested Kushner, McGreevey's one-time pick to head the powerful Port Authority. Prosecutors say Kushner's efforts to entrap witnesses with prostitutes stemmed from an inquiry into allegations that he made illegal campaign and charitable contributions.

The next day, William Watley, McGreevey's commerce secretary, resigned amid conflict-of-interest questions and a state criminal investigation into spending at his agency. Authorities are reviewing if any laws were broken when the mother, sister and two sons of Watley's chief of staff were hired by the agency.

McGreevey's poll numbers had begun to rise earlier this year, after he pushed through (促成) a plan to increase income taxes on the wealthy to pay for larger property tax rebates for most New Jersey families. But a recent poll by Quinnipiac University showed the scandals ate away at the governor's public support, and by early this month, half of the state's voters said they had serious concerns about McGreevey's integrity.

Staff writers David Kinney, John P. Martin, Robert Rudolph, Josh Margolin, Robert Gebeloff, Christine V. Baird and Vinessa Erminio contributed to this report.

一、作者背景

The Star-Ledger staffers (l to r) Josh Margolin, Jeff Whelan and Kate Coscarelli celebrate as the newsroom erupts during the announcement of the 2005 Pulitzer Prize for breaking news reporting.

Columbia University President Lee C. Bollinger (left) presents Josh Margolin (center) and Jeff Whelan (right) of *The Star-Ledger* with the 2005 Pulitzer Prize in Breaking News Reporting.

乔希·马戈林(Josh Margolin)：2005年普利策突发新闻报道奖授予了纽瓦克《明星纪事报》(*The Star-Ledger*)参与报道新泽西州时任州长詹姆斯·迈格里维(James McGreevey)辞职消息的所有记者。在这里我们简单介绍该报领奖代表之一、也是主要报道记者乔希·马戈林的情况。

马戈林1992年毕业于美国最具规模的私立综合大学之一长岛大学(Long Island University)，获得新闻学学士学位。毕业后，他曾在新墨西哥州《卡尔斯巴德时事报》(*Carlsbad Current-Argus*)供职，后又在得克萨斯、新泽西和纽约等地做过记者，1998年成为《明星纪事报》记者。2002年至2010年底，马戈林担任《明星纪事报》驻新泽西州府记者，撰写政治新闻和评论。当迈格里维州长于2004年8月12日下午4点多钟突然宣布辞职后，马戈林和他的同事们立即行动起来，在当日截稿时间之前迅速采写出9篇新闻，并在次日排发。不包括为新闻撰写提供帮助的记者，仅署名的专职记者就有

15 名，稿件总字数接近 1.2 万字。

马戈林曾在自己的学士服上写了这三个字“Pulitzer or Bust”（要么就拿普利策奖，要么就不做新闻）。这个当时被很多人认为是痴人说梦的理想竟然在他毕业十三年后成为现实！

2010 年底至 2013 年 4 月，马戈林供职于《纽约邮报》（*New York Post*），目前他是美国广播公司（ABC）的一名调查性新闻记者。2012 年，他与朋友 Ted Sherman 合作写的 *The Jersey Sting* 一书，成为当年的畅销书。

马戈林曾被评为新泽西州最有影响力的 101 位人物之一和新泽西州最有影响力的记者，《华盛顿邮报》也称他为新泽西州最好的政治新闻记者。

作为突发新闻，如何在极短的截稿时间内迅速搜集素材、查证材料至关重要，这需要记者未雨绸缪，早作准备。就迈格里维州长辞职事件而言，新闻界关于州长性取向的猜测在几年前就开始了。早在 2002 年 8 月，马戈林在一篇报道中就披露过州长亲自陪同他的同性情人 Cipel 买房的经历，并引用了房产经纪人的一句话（“I thought it was highly unusual.”），这个细节在获奖作品中再次出现。

普利策奖评选委员会用“comprehensive”（全面的）和“clear-headed”（冷静的、有条理的）来评价这组突发新闻的质量。限于教材篇幅，我们只编选了其中的三篇，但读者仍可以从以下 9 篇新闻的标题了解该报对这一事件的多种报道角度和整体报道风格：

1. McGreevey quits, admits gay affair
2. After a calm morning, a thunderbolt
3. Political landscape in turmoil
4. Right place, right time—again
5. 90-day delay avoids chaos, focuses power
6. The man who toppled a governor
7. A Jersey guy who seemed so real
8. At first, surprise and then support
9. On street, the news rates three or more “Wows”

二、新泽西州与《明星纪事报》

The Star-Ledger

STAMP WORLD IN FOR A SHOCK! THIS IS NO FAKE

U.S. prods Baghdad to include Sunnis

2006 front page of *The Star-Ledger*

新泽西州与纽约市一衣带水，面积较小，排在全美倒数第四；人口密度最大，被昵称为“花园之州”（Garden State）。该州经济实力雄厚，家庭中值收入和百万富翁人数在全美50个州中均排名第一，因此这个弹丸小州的政治地位十分重要。在选举问题上，新泽西州是“骑墙派”：选总统，历来投票给民主党候选人；选州长，却选出过好几位共和党人。该州在经济政策上强调政府少收税、少出面干预市场，倾向共和党，但在社会政策上则重视多元化，接近民主党。调查表明，该州三分之二的人口认为妇女拥有合法堕胎的权利，大多数人支持同性婚姻。2007年，新泽西州成为美国第三个可以进行同性恋民事结合（civil unions）的州（另外两个州是康涅狄格州和佛蒙特州），民事结合的伴侣可以与结婚夫妇享有同样的法律权利。

《明星纪事报》是新泽西州发行量最大的报纸，总部设在新泽西州最大的城市纽瓦克（Newark）。该报的每日发行量超过新泽西州报纸发行量排名第二、三名的发行量总和，星期日版的发行量则超过排名第二、三、四名的发行量总和。《明星纪事报》的前身是创办于1832年的《纽瓦克每日广告报》，该报虽然是一份地方报纸，但由于新泽西州的重要地位，这份报纸的影响力也不容小视。

三、课文背景

2004年8月12日，时任新泽西州州长的詹姆斯·迈格里维突然宣布将在当年11月辞职，原因是他与另一男子有婚外关系。这一事件不啻为美国政坛上的一次“晴天霹雳”。经过三十多年的努力，美国同性恋群体的政治权利已经逐渐扩大。根据美国同性恋政治活动团体“同性恋胜利基金会”（Gay and Lesbian Victory Fund）的统计，截至2013年7月，美国国内共有近800名公开自己同性恋身份的各级议员。但即便如此，像迈格里维这样身居高位的政治人物公开承认自己的性取向还是凤毛麟角，他的行为也引发了一场关于如何看待同性恋政治家的争论。

詹姆斯·迈格里维（James McGreevey）的回忆录式新书《告白》（*The Confession*）于2006年9月19日起在美国上市销售。在这本书中，迈格里维详细而坦率地记录了自己身为一个同性恋者的政坛经历。迈格里维还认为，自己是同性恋者这一事实对其担任州长职务没有什么影响。他的辞职决定不是因为自己是同性恋者，而是由于自己的婚外恋行为。

四、作者主要观点

1. By extensively quoting McGreevey's resignation speech and explaining his relationship with Cipel, the authors of this story seem to reinforce McGreevey's explanation of resignation—“I am a gay American”. Do you think it is too simplistic? Why or why not?

2. In your opinion, what is the authors' attitude toward McGreevey as a “gay American”?

五、写作风格与手法

1. What has intrigued you most about this article in terms of its writing style?

2. Study the lead of the story and identify its type. Is it effective? Why or why not?

3. Does the narrative move slowly or briskly? Why?

4. How many sources of information are provided in the story? How are they presented?

5. What other possible sources might have been consulted before writing these stories? Is there any evidence that any important facts were suppressed or that the story was colored according to the journalist's or newspaper's own agenda?

6. In what order are the events arranged in the story?

7. Examine this paragraph from Text A"The governor finalized his decision to resign with top aides yesterday in the library of Drumthwacket, the governor's mansion in Princeton. Among those gathered were chief of staff Jamie Fox, chief counsel Michael DeCotiis, state party chief executive Kevin Hagan, Casino Reinvestment Development Authority executive director Curtis Bashaw and three top political consultants—Steve DeMicco, Joel Benenson and Jim Margolis." Do you think these proper names are redundant? Why or why not? How are technical details presented in the story? Provide specific examples.

8. Do you see instances where some information or idea is repeated in the story? Are they unnecessary? Why or why not?

9. Are any of the paragraphs too long or too short? Is there variety in sentence length and sentence construction? Provide specific examples.

Part Three: Further exploring the text

一、语言点讲解

1. Cipel, a 35-year-old former public relations professional, could not be reached for comment. 在这句话中,"could not be reached for comment"可以译为"没有答复采访要求"。在涉及敏感话题时，很多新闻人物往往不愿意接受记者采访，而记者为了表明自己曾尝试采访持不同观点的人士，体现新闻报道的"平衡性"，会特别注明这一点。本文还有几处类似的表达方法，你能找出来吗?

2. If Corzine did mount a gubernatorial bid, his deep pockets and political connections probably would discourage many rivals... 根据2006年出版的《蓝登书屋足本词典》(*The Random House Unabridged Dictionary*),"gubernatorial"是美国人在1725—1735年期间造出来的一个词，词源来自拉丁语 gubernator (即 governor)，专指"州长的、与州长有关的"，是一个正式语。这句话的前半句除了使用 gubernatorial 这样的"大词"以外，还用了"mount a bid"这样的正式语(试与下面这句话比较：If Corzine did run for governor...)，但在后半句中却出现了"deep pockets"(指"拥有大量财富")这个常常在口语中使用的短语。这种句子内部语域(register)的强烈对比会给读者留下深刻印象。你认为作者为什么这样处理?

3. ...a reality which is layered and layered with all the, quote, good things and all

the, quote, right things of typical adolescent and adult behavior. Quote 是新闻常用词，主要用于引出被采访者或被引用者的直接引语。常见的表达方法如“to quote someone as saying...; someone is quoted as saying...”。Quote 除了引用别人原话以外，还可以用来表达反讽、嘲讽、轻蔑的语气，即句子中的某个字并不是字面上单纯的意思。这里，迈格里维就是用 quote 来强调“good things”和“right things”必须得加上引号理解，可以译为“所谓的好事”和“所谓的正确的事情”。这种用法多用于口语，更常见的说法是 quote-unquote，如“quote-unquote tax reforms”（“所谓的税改”）。说话者同时还常常做 air quotes 的手势，即举起双手，弯曲食指和中指，做出类似双引号形状的动作，表示强调。《纽约时报》资深评论家、语言学专家威廉·萨菲尔（William Safire）认为，用 so-called 来表示“所谓的”似乎已经过时，取而代之的则是 quote-unquote。

4. After his speech, McGreevey returned to Drumthwacket, spoke with his advisers for 10 minutes, then retired to the mansion's residential quarters with his family. 这句话连用三个动词干净利索地把情况交代清楚。在把州长辞职这一“突发事件”介绍完毕后，作者笔锋一转，开始介绍主要人物和事件的背景。这句话中的“retire”指“to break from a meeting or gathering”，可以解释为“离开……去了……”。表达同样意思的词还有 adjourn 和 withdraw 等，这些词都比较正式，常用于书面语。

5. From his first, successful run for the State Assembly in 1989 to his victory in the 2001 race for governor, McGreevey, 47, has maintained a dogged pace. 美国各州政府一般具有与联邦政府相同的结构，即每州有一名经选举产生的行政首脑（州长，governor）、独立的司法体系和一个由民选产生的立法机构。各州使用的议会名称不尽相同，大多数州称上院为参议院（Senate），但下院在有些州被称为众议院（House of Representatives），在另一些州被称为代表院（House of Delegates），还有些州则称之为州立法大会（State Assembly）。

二、中西文化比较

论“内省”和“忏悔”

在本文中，迈格里维州长的公开忏悔给人留下了深刻印象。谈到他违背了婚约誓言时，他说：“这是错误的。这是愚蠢的。这是不可饶恕的。”

所谓忏悔，就是对人坦白自己的过错、求容忍宽恕之意。忏悔意识可以说是中西文化重大的差异之一。西方人长期以来浸淫在基督教原罪意识之中，故普遍具有浓厚的忏悔情结。通过忏悔，人在灵魂的撞击震荡中寻求心灵的净化与超越，最终获得精神升华与自我完善。正如作家殷谦所说：“忏悔不是逃避而是担当，忏悔不是死亡而是再生，忏悔不是绝望而是希望”。

中国自古以来就缺少原罪感，故其忏悔意识淡薄，但我们注重时时刻刻的“内省”，即在内心省察自己的思想、言行有无过失。通过内省，避免犯错，所以中国文化更强调防范措施。《论语》中说：“吾日三省吾身”，此外，“反求诸己”、“反躬自省”和“反躬自问”等成语也是家喻户晓的道理，是中国人的重要行为准则。

三、语言练习

1. 请用英语解释下列句子。

(1)"I applaud the governor's decision to acknowledge a part of his identity for which he owes no one an apology."

(2)...yesterday's news did little more than fan the ambitions of a large field of possible candidates.

(3) McGreevey's speech, 690 words long, was stunningly direct, even by the standards of a self-revelatory era in American political life.

(4)Friends and foes alike have marveled at his peripatetic travels around the state, which often began well before dawn and lasted well into the night.

(5) The governor acknowledged uttering the word but said it was an innocent literary allusion.

2. 请将下列短语翻译成英文，并比较中英文表达方式的异同。

(1) 丑闻疑云

(2) 我对……表示同情

(3) 有点玩弄政治伎俩的味道

(4) 引起广泛猜测

(5) 以……的身份访问加州

(6) 拒绝大幅修改（讲稿）

(7) 由两辆车组成的车队

(8) 做过一阵（工作）后

(9) 在一个蓝领家庭成长的背景

(10) 令人刮目相看的政坛履历

(11) 对某人恶意抹黑

(12) 曾经的人选

3. 请将下面的句子或段落翻译成中文，并比较中英文表达方式的异同。

(1)"Any speculation about my own political plans in light of the governor's decision is entirely premature."

(2)"But because of my resolve, and also thinking that I was doing the right thing, I forced what I thought was an acceptable reality onto myself, a reality which is layered and layered with all the, quote, good things and all the, quote, right things of typical adolescent and adult behavior."

(3)Cipel's expected lawsuit against McGreevey, which officials said is likely to seek $5 million in damages, would come just before the expiration of a general two-year limitation on workplace sexual harassment claims.

(4)McGreevey's resignation ends a political career that has consumed him since high school. He has always followed a fast track—whether it was the quick succession of degrees from Columbia University, Georgetown University Law School and Harvard

University's graduate school of education, or his early foray into politics.

(5) Many of McGreevey's political connections have come to haunt him in the past couple of months, however, as his administration has been shaken by a series of high-profile scandals.

(6) The indictment revealed McGreevey was secretly recorded by the FBI using the word "Machiavelli," which prosecutors said was a code word for the bribery scheme. No charges were brought against McGreevey, who was referred to in the indictment only as "State Official 1."

Part Four: Exploring beyond the text

一、自我反思

1. 我学到了什么？我要如何改进？

2. 一篇高质量的突发新闻报道的基本标准是什么？我能清楚地告诉别人吗？该篇报道的记者乔希·马戈林等人是如何达到这些标准的？我能向别人解释清楚吗？

二、知识扩展

1. 世界各地的民众是怎样看待同性恋政治家的？收集这方面的资料并进行比较。

2. 收集有关政治丑闻的报道并仔细研读。

三、能力扩展

1. 就以上报道写一篇 500 字左右的评论。

2. 如果你周围发生了火灾，请以校报记者身份撰写一篇 500 字左右的突发新闻报道。

Text B A Jersey guy who seemed so real

With the disclosure comes a rewrite of one part of the governor's story.

BY Mary Jo Patterson

The Star-Ledger

August 13, 2004

导读：课文 A 为读者介绍了迈格里维州长辞职事件的全貌，本单元的另外两篇课文则从不同侧面让这个故事更加丰满。课文 B 类似于一篇人物传记，回顾了迈格里维的成长经历、从政前的工作经历、他的整个政治生涯，以及他的个性特点和两次婚姻。在细数迈格里维曾经陷入的各种政治丑闻的同时，记者也对其在任期间取得的成绩做了比较公允的介绍。文章的结尾还引用了一位政治观察家对迈格里维的正面评论，为读者提供了另一种视角。

For as long as he was in public office—and that was 14 years—everyone who met James E. McGreevey thought they were seeing everything there was to know.

Proud American. Devout Catholic. Workaholic. Advocate for the common man. Policy wonk(政策研究者)without any private agenda, much less a private life. A failed first marriage? The man worked too many hours. Didn't the second marriage, and the birth of a baby 14 months later, show his commitment to middle-class family life?

With all his stories—about his dad, the exacting former Marine drill sergeant; the grandfather who worked on the docks in Bayonne; the brave uncle who died at Iwo Jima—McGreevey seemed so earnest. So real. So open.

Then yesterday, at the age of 47 and for the first time, he announced to the world he has been living a lie.

"Throughout my life, I have grappled with my own identity, who I am," he said, in an unfocused and emotional statement that was anything but vintage McGreevey. "My truth is that I am a gay American."

Then he made yet another confession, admitting he had engaged in an "adult consensual affair with another man" while married. Given the circumstances surrounding the affair, he said vaguely, he must resign.

Thus began the rewrite of the history of New Jersey's 51st governor, James E. McGreevey.

Or at least the personal part.

His political career and accomplishments remain.

So do the scandals that dogged him, within months of taking office on Jan. 15, 2002. They never really stopped.

McGreevey campaigned for the New Jersey governorship by criticizing "business as usual" in Trenton(特伦顿市,新泽西州首府), but subsequent events showed that he operated very much in the same old way. He courted political bosses, raised more money from more special interests than previous governors, and—like his predecessors—used taxpayer money to advance his own popularity by starring in a series of public service announcements(公益广告,简写为PSA).

By last month, a growing pile of scandal suggested to some his political career was over.

A Cabinet official, Commerce Secretary the Rev. William Watley, had just resigned under a cloud. The U. S. attorney for New Jersey had charged Charles Kushner, McGreevey's top contributor, with trying to obstruct an investigation into his political contributions by hiring prostitutes to seduce two witnesses.

Worse, McGreevey himself had been secretly taped by the feds[指联邦调查局(FBI)] talking to someone at the heart of another investigation. That probe was focused on another Democratic fund-raiser suspected of extortion. McGreevey accused U. S. Attorney Christopher Christie, a Republican, of trying to smear him for political gain.

Things should have gotten better this month when he signed a bill to preserve the northern Highlands, a measure he considered vital to the state's future. It virtually banned development on 395,000 acres of prime watershed land(流域土地). Many people assumed the measure would guarantee him an important place in New Jersey history.

On Tuesday of this week, standing against the dramatic backdrop of the Wanaque Reservoir and the dense forests ringing it, McGreevey seemed upbeat and joyous as he signed the bill to the applause of two former governors, two troops of Girl Scouts, and a sprinkling of environmentalists.

But, despite the bright sunshine overhead, there was another dark cloud.

Most of New Jersey's key environmental groups boycotted the affair. They were mad at the governor for also signing a bill to streamline development in other parts of the state, designated as growth areas—and they broadcast their discontent far and wide.

Really, until yesterday, it did not seem things could get worse.

McGreevey was born Aug. 6, 1957, in Jersey City and raised in Carteret, a blue-collar town associated with refineries and oil tanks. His father, the ex-Marine, worked for a trucking company. His mother was a nurse. He had two sisters, both younger than he. In Carteret, he often said, he formed his core values.

One of the things people always said about McGreevey is that he was born to be a politician.

"His second-grade classmates at St. Joseph elementary school in Carteret say they were sure he would run for governor someday," a newspaper article reported after his election as governor in 2001.

He continued in parochial school(教区附属学校), graduating from St. Joseph's High School in Metuchen in 1975.

Three years later, he received his bachelor of arts degree from Columbia University. In later interviews, McGreevey always gave the impression he had spent his entire undergraduate career there.

In fact, McGreevey had collected almost half his college credits elsewhere—at Catholic University in Washington, D. C., Middlesex County College and Rutgers University.

When asked, during his 2001 run for governor, why he had never talked about those schools, McGreevey said he had not intended to mislead anyone. "I apologize for any incorrect perception," he told an interviewer who had been contacted by a former acquaintance from Catholic University.

After college McGreevey went to law school. He graduated from Georgetown in 1981 and received a master's in education from Harvard the following year.

He entered politics as soon as he returned home to New Jersey and worked a year as an assistant prosecutor in Middlesex County. One of his first acts in that job, he once told a reporter chronicling his life, was to put a poster of Robert F. Kennedy[罗伯特·F·肯尼迪(1925—1968), 美国总统约翰·肯尼迪的弟弟。] up on his office wall. Kennedy, he said, was a hard-as-nails(铁面无私的)prosecutor "driven for all the right reasons," and he worshipped him.

Still, he spent only a year in the job. At a dinner on the local political circuit, Alan Karcher, then Assembly speaker(州众议院议长), offered him a job as a lawyer for the Assembly Democrats.

From there his political career was a straight trajectory(轨迹,道路). Up.

In 1985 Gov. Thomas Kean named him executive director of the state Parole Board. There was a stint at Merck & Co. , the pharmaceutical company that hired him as a lobbyist, but his heart beat in politics.

McGreevey's career as an elected official began in 1989. He served one term in the New Jersey Assembly from 1990 to 1992. He also served in the state Senate from 1994 to 1998.

...

In 1997 he decided to run for governor against incumbent(在职的) Christie Whitman. On the campaign trail, he talked about auto insurance, rising property taxes and state bonding. Whitman, he scolded, was borrowing too much to finance the state's budget.

As things turned out, McGreevey was criticized the very same thing after becoming governor.

...

During his first run for governor, McGreevey was criticized for being too robotic. But voter discontent with Whitman, plus McGreevey's finely honed ability to tap into middle-class angst, made him a formidable candidate. Whitman was too aristocratic, he said. He almost beat her, losing by 1 percent.

McGreevey's concession speech, at Woodbridge Town Hall, was viewed as one of his best political moments. He was composed, upbeat and dignified.

Everyone assumed he would start running again the next day.

In fact, he went quietly about his work as mayor, immersing himself in municipal affairs. But he was very much in touch with Democratic Party officials.

By then his first marriage to Karie Shutz McGreevey, a Canadian woman he had met on a singles cruise(单身游轮), was over. In 1995, after four years of marriage, she had taken their young daughter on a vacation to her parents' home near Vancouver, Canada, and refused to come back. The following year, she filed for divorce, saying McGreevey was consumed by his career and neglected his family.

The mayor was now living as a single man in a bare-bones(极为简单的)condo near Woodbridge Center. He resumed his habits and reputation as the driven, detail-obsessed mayor.

He married his second wife, Dina Matos McGreevey of Newark, on Oct. 7, 2000. Four months earlier, he had let it be known that he and Matos, an administrator at

Columbus Hospital in Newark and 10 years his junior, were engaged. He said they had met at a fund-raiser three years earlier.

McGreevey, normally a publicity hound, was cagey about his wedding plans. The time and place for the ceremony was not revealed for some time. Plans seemed to keep changing. The formal announcement was made at a news conference on an unrelated topic on Aug. 1, 2000.

The next year, during his second and victorious quest for the governor's seat, McGreevey's opponent was Bret D. Schundler, the former mayor of Jersey City. The campaign, played out against the backdrop of the Sept. 11, 2001, terror attacks, did not get much media coverage.

...

McGreevey handily beat Schundler on Nov. 6, 2001. At his victory party at the East Brunswick Hilton, he blew a kiss to a television camera and said, "Dina, I love you."

His first year in office wasn't at all smooth.

First came the $75,000 billed to taxpayers from a trade mission(贸易代表团访问) to Ireland that included a $720-a-night hotel suite, a tour in a luxury car, $16,000 in cell phone bills and a $3,178 dinner for his Irish relatives.

Then came reports of his taking 14 nongovernment helicopter trips.

McGreevey called them "simple, stupid mistakes," and state Democrats repaid much of the money.

There were also some odd personnel choices. He ousted Joseph Santiago, his state police superintendent, after anonymous sources made unsubstantiated claims that the former Newark top cop had ties to the mob.

And he hired Golan Cipel, a young Israeli, as the state's $110,000-a-year antiterrorism and security adviser, even though Cipel could not get the proper security clearances. Later, amid heated criticism of appointment, Cipel resigned. McGreevey gave him a second public job, as "special counsel" at the same salary. After Cipel relinquishes(离开), he arranged for jobs in the private sector. (Cipel is the man with whom McGreevey had the affair, according to top administration sources speaking on condition of anonymity.)

On the other hand, McGreevey did some good things that year. He managed to ba lance a big hole in the budget without raising income taxes, no small feat.

But with the next year, 2003, came more missteps.

McGreevey accepted a trip to Puerto Rico to speak at a convention of the International Longshoremen's Association. The union paid for his and his family's airfare and hotel, prompting withering from Republicans and editorial writers. The governor reimbursed the union.

With his approval ratings now in the 30s and low 40s, he acknowledged having stumbled a bit. But he remained optimistic.

...

Throughout the ups and downs, he never seemed to run out of steam (失去气势). His energy levels were consistently high, his glance focused and intense, and his language was always clear and forceful.

And if he was stressed, he did not look it. McGreevey never had a hair out of a place, or a wrinkle in his jacket.

Jon Shure, former spokesman for ex-Gov. Jim Florio and now president of New Jersey Policy Perspective, said yesterday's startling developments could obscure McGreevey's record.

"On a certain level, he's accomplished a lot. The corporate tax. The Highlands protection. The millionaires tax. All of these are things that addressed long-standing problems in New Jersey. There's clearly some things where you can say he took difficult actions that moved the state ahead. That's a lot for just two and half years," Shure said.

McGreevey governed in very tough times, facing budget problems no governor would want to face, he added.

"It's hard these days to do bold things because the opposition is greater than it was. ... The ability of the opposition to find ways to attack you is sharper and quicker than it used to be," Shure said. "Judged by those standards, you can argue that a governor might serve eight years and not do any more than what he's done."

Staff writers Robert Gebeloff, Joe Donohue and Steve Chambers contributed to this report.

Text C　On street, the news rates three or more "wows"

"Only in New Jersey," says one TV watcher, but even
Garden State wasn't ready for this.

BY Joe Ryan and Rudy Larini

The Star-Ledger

August 13, 2004

导读： 课文 C 先是以一个小酒吧为场景，然后又把采访的触角进一步延伸，生动地描述了当地老百姓听到迈格里维州长辞职消息时的各种反应：有人惊诧、有人同情，还有人惋惜。这篇报道中一共出现了 14 个有名有姓的受访者，他们的性别、年龄、地区、背景各不相同，表达的观点也迥然相异。可以说，这篇报道的主体部分是由普通老百姓所说的话组成的。这样的写作方式显得非常平易近人，是"自上而下"式官方新闻源的有益补充。

At Antones Tap Room(酒吧) in Union County, the news silenced the jukebox(自动点唱机).

Once word arrived that Gov. James E. McGreevey might be resigning, the men in jeans and work boots who had gathered for pints and cheddar(切达奶酪) burgers at the tavern in Cranford didn't want to hear rock and roll.

They wanted to hear their governor. So the barkeep(酒吧招待) turned up the television, and the men put down their drinks and listened.

The words left them reeling(感到眩晕).

"Wow, wow, wow," said Al O'Neill, a 57-year-old labor leader and longtime McGreevey supporter. "I just can't believe it. I can't believe it. Wow."

Even in a state with a history of public misconduct, McGreevey's announcement that he was resigning because he's a "gay American" who had an affair with a former aide left people stunned.

The news shook New Jerseyans like a heavyweight's one-two punch(拳击术语,指左右拳几乎同时出击,非常凶狠,留下重创). First came preliminary reports of the resignation. Then McGreevey's acknowledgment of his homosexuality.

"What? Why? You've got to be kidding me! Oh my Lord!" said 31-year-old Veronica Casiano of Newark when told the news.

"Only in New Jersey," said Ted Ciesla, 56, who sat at the Antones bar and shook his head after listening to McGreevey's announcement. He said he was not a McGreevey supporter.

While the governor's bombshell put him in a tiny circle of openly gay politicians, most of the people interviewed said his sexual orientation was irrelevant.

"The fact that he's a homosexual doesn't really matter to me," said Dan Radziewicz of Somerville. "The only thing that matters to me is the job he's doing as governor."

"Everyone is entitled to their lifestyle, and I don't believe his sexual orientation matters," said Janice Peal, 26, who lives in Long Valley.

Some felt the governor was brave for coming out.

"Good for him," said Margot Garcia, 20, an accountant who was walking into a Cranford clothing boutique and wouldn't believe the news until a bystander to corroborated(确认)it.

Some expressed surprise that being gay in 2004 would force a governor to step down.

"I was surprised that he resigned," said Joe Bauer, 37, of Pompton Plains. "I understand the announcement and the implications, but I don't see any reason that he would resign. If it was truly a consensual affair, then there's no reason for him to resign."

Others, however, had heard the simmering rumors that there was more to the story than McGreevey's homosexuality.

Nakia Banister, 29, of Scotch Plains said she had heard news accounts speculating the governor was about to be accused of a sexual indiscretion(言行失检), possibly sexual harassment, "which I think forced him out of the closet sooner than he would have wanted."

"Obviously sexual harassment has a certain connotation that people just don't like," Banister said. "I know there were allegations about mishandling money, but this is a whole different aspect."

Mike Kitson, 73, of Woodbridge was sipping a soda with his wife at Cafe Paris in Cranford when he heard the news. He said it didn't shock him that McGreevey was gay.

"The rumors have been going around for years," he said.

The news didn't surprise Erin Rapp, either.

The 26-year-old Phillipsburg resident used to live in the Iselin section of Woodbridge—where McGreevey had been mayor—and said tales of his homosexuality have swirled for years.

Some said McGreevey would be missed. "New Jersey is losing a great governor," said Nusrat Ahmah, 37, of Morristown.

...

Some people compared McGreevey's plight to that of former President Bill Clinton, who was impeached for lying about his sexual escapades(越轨行为) with White House intern Monica Lewinsky.

"I don't think he needs to resign," 24-year-old Natalie Hordynsky of Springfield said of McGreevey. "I mean, the president didn't step down when he had his, you know, affair with Monica."

"Clinton had an affair and that didn't mean he was a bad person," said Carmen Salamea of Bloomfield. "I was surprised, but I respect his (McGreevey's) decision."

Such sympathy for McGreevey's forthrightness was not uncommon.

"My reaction is that he was honest, and I respect a person for his honesty," said Mel Houston, 34, of Keyport. "I have to admit that I was shocked by it, but I respect that he was honest and I just wish the best for his family."

Back at Antones, O'Neill said McGreevey's resignation is bad news for labor. "He was a fighter for working people," O'Neill said, pausing before adding, "But he's still a fighter."

Staff writers Paul Nelson and Raviya Ismail contributed to this report.

Unit Two National Reporting

国内报道

单元导航

本单元将讨论国内报道。本单元共有两篇文章，皆以全球最大的连锁零售企业沃尔玛公司（Wal-Mart）为话题。课文A探讨了沃尔玛的成功之道及围绕其经营法则的一些争论。课文B描写了中国、孟加拉国和洪都拉斯等发展中国家作为沃尔玛在全球的供货商为其商品低价而付出的辛劳和贡献。

Part One：Preparing to explore

一、国内报道

1. 普利策国内新闻报道奖

国内报道是与国际报道相对指称的新闻报道。凡本国内发生的新闻事件及新闻人物均可列入国内报道范围。

普利策国内报道奖于1948年设立。获奖作品的选题广泛，涉及美国政治、经济、社会、军事等重要领域。20世纪五六十年代，获奖作品内容涉及最多的是政治话题，包括美国总统艾森豪威尔的安全和身体状况及其影响、美国总统林顿·约翰逊的财富积累、肯尼迪遇刺、工会腐败、国会裙带关系、空军部长辞职、最高法院审理案、民权等，同时，还有商业道德、肉联厂卫生和国家公园等公共话题。20世纪七八十年代，政治话题仍然占据重要位置，如印巴战争期间的美国政策制定、国会议员的生活、尼克松的联邦收入税政策、总统选举、国防部预算、核军备竞赛、税改法案等，同时，环境和科学等新的话题开始出现。20世纪90年代，政治话题开始减少，国内报道对象逐渐转向社会弱势群体，如受虐儿童、低收入者、艾滋病患者等。进入21世纪，国内报道获奖作品涉及的话题很广泛，但有两点比较引人注目：政治话题集中在对布什总统和切尼副总统的批评上，而新出现的话题包括反恐与媒体的影响及作用等方面。

值得关注的是，在约60年的历史发展中，移民和种族问题一直是记者高度关注的问题，尤其是在20世纪80年代。这可以从国内报道获奖作品中有所体现，如1959年的获奖作品讲述了佛罗里达州一个移民劳工营的故事，1981年的文章反映非法移民问题，1986 年的报道触及美国住房部门的种族歧视问题，2001 年的国内报道获奖作品则反映了美国现代社会普遍存在的种族歧视现象。

2. 基本写作特征

从普利策奖评审委员会给予国内报道获奖作品的赞词来看，优秀国内新闻报道作品具有以下基本特征：

（1）全面性（comprehensive, balanced and informative）。对报道主题进行真实全面的报道，尽可能多地为受众提供多方位的信息。

（2）启示性（revealing）。报道内容要给人带来思考与启示。

（3）吸引力（engrossing，compelling）。文章内容要有吸引力和感染力，能满足受众的求知欲和好奇心，又能引起受众感情的共鸣。

（4）清晰性（lucid）。文章的结构组织和表达方式要清晰明了。

（5）影响力（influential）。报道要产生社会影响，使反映的问题能够得到社会关注并解决。

二、课前讨论

1. Name some top global companies of your interest. Explain your choice.

2. What do you think is the Wal-Mart way? What are its impacts?（Please analyze the economic, political, social, and cultural implications of Wal-Mart from as many angels as possible. In particular, please elaborate its influence on the U. S. and China.）

Part Two: Exploring the text

Text A　An empire built on bargains remakes the working world

Wal-Mart is so powerful that it moves the economies of entire countries, bringing profit and pain. The prices can't be beat, but the wages can.

BY Abigail Goldman and Nancy Cleeland

Los Angeles Times

November 23, 2003

LAS VEGAS—Chastity Ferguson kept watch over four sleepy children late one Friday as she flipped a pack of corn dogs(玉米狗快餐食品)into a cart at her new favorite grocery store: Wal-Mart.

The Wal-Mart Supercenter(沃尔玛购物广场), a pink stucco box(外墙经拉毛粉饰的建筑)twice as big as a Home Depot(家得宝公司), combines a full-scale supermarket with the usual discount mega-store. For the 26-year-old Ferguson, the draw is simple.

"You can't beat the prices," said the hotel cashier, who makes $400 a week. "I come here because it's cheap."

Across town, another mother also is familiar with the Supercenter's low prices. Kelly Gray, the chief breadwinner for five children, lost her job as a Raley's(美国著名连锁超市)grocery clerk last December after Wal-Mart expanded into the supermarket business here. California-based Raley's closed all 18 of its stores in the area, laying off(解雇)1,400 workers.

Gray earned \$14.68 an hour with a pension and family health insurance. Wal-Mart grocery workers typically make less than \$9 an hour.

"It's like somebody came and broke into your home and took something huge and important away from you," said the 36-year-old. "I was scared. I cried. I shook."

Wal-Mart gives. And Wal-Mart takes away.

From a small-town five-and-dime(专卖便宜货的商店), Wal-Mart Stores Inc. has grown over 50 years to become the world's largest corporation and a global economic force.

It posted(记账)\$245 billion in sales in its most recent fiscal year—nearly twice as much as General Electric Co. and almost eight times as much as Microsoft Corp. It is the nation's largest seller of toys, furniture, jewelry, dog food and scores of other consumer products. It is the largest grocer in the United States.

Wal-Mart's decisions influence wages and working conditions across a wide swath(行;列)of the world economy, from the shopping centers of Las Vegas to the factories of Honduras and South Asia. Its business is so vital to developing countries that some send emissaries(emissary:使者;特使)to the corporate headquarters in Bentonville, Ark., almost as if Wal-Mart were a sovereign nation.

The company has prospered by elevating one goal above all others: cutting prices relentlessly. U.S. economists say its tightfistedness(吝啬)has not only boosted its own bottom line, but also helped hold down the inflation rate for the entire country. Consumers reap the benefits every time they push a cart through Wal-Mart's checkout lines.

Yet Wal-Mart's astonishing success exacts a heavy price.

By squeezing suppliers to cut wholesale costs, the company has hastened the flight of U.S. manufacturing jobs overseas. By scouring the globe for the cheapest goods, it has driven factory jobs from one poor nation to another.

Wal-Mart's penny-pinching extends to its own 1.2 million U.S. employees, none of them unionized. By the company's own admission, a full-time worker might not be able to support a family on a Wal-Mart paycheck.

Then there are casualties like Kelly Gray. As Wal-Mart expands rapidly into groceries, it is causing upheaval in yet another corner of the economy. When a Supercenter moves into town, competitors often are wiped out, taking high-paying union jobs with them.

Wal-Mart's plans to enter the grocery business in California early next year have thrown the state's supermarket industry into turmoil. Fearful of Wal-Mart's ability to undercut them on price, the Ralphs, Vons and Albertsons chains have sought concessions from their unionized workers in Southern and Central California, leading to a work stoppage now entering its seventh week.

Half a century ago, the nation's largest and most emulated employer was General Motors Corp. "Today," said Nelson Lichtenstein, a history professor at UC Santa Barbara, "for better or worse, it's Wal-Mart."

GM brought prosperity to factory towns and made American workers the envy of the world. With a high-wage union job, an assembly-line worker could afford a house, a decent car, maybe even a boat by the lake.

There was a bit of truth, Lichtenstein said, to the famous assertion by Charles Wilson, General Motors chief from 1941 to 1953, that what was good for GM was good for the country.

With Wal-Mart, the calculus is considerably more complex.

"We Have Split Brains"

Glenn Miraflor used to chide(责备)his wife for shopping at Wal-Mart.

As a member of Ironworkers Local 416(钢铁工人工会 416 分会), the 50-year-old father of four is well aware of the retailer's anti-union stance. But when the family's credit card debt topped $10,000, Wal-Mart's deals suddenly looked irresistible.

"Where else are you going to find a computer for $498?" he asked, looking for a PC with his wife, Debbie, at the Supercenter on Serene Avenue, far from the glitz(浮华)of the Las Vegas Strip(拉斯维加斯大道). "Everyone I work with shops here."

Surveys by the Teamsters(卡车司机) and the United Food and Commercial Workers—the two unions most threatened by Wal-Mart—show that many of their own members shop at the discounter.

"We have split brains," said Robert Reich, U. S. secretary of Labor under President Clinton and now a professor of economic and social policy at Brandeis University in Waltham, Mass. "Most of the time, the half of our brain that wants the best deal prevails."

The connection may be lost on many, Reich said, but consumers' addiction to low prices is accelerating a shift toward a two-tiered U. S. economy, with a shrinking middle class and a growing pool of low-wage workers.

"Wal-Mart's prices may be lower," he said, "but that's small consolation to a lot of people who end up with less money to spend."

Others insist there is a net benefit whenever consumers can get more for less. "If you have lower real prices, you're saving money," said Arthur Laffer, a key advisor to President Reagan who is now an economic consultant in San Diego. "The prices' falling, in effect, raises the wages of everyone who buys their products."

That's basically the way the Miraflors saw it as they cruised the aisles of the Supercenter—Wal-Mart Store No. 2593—and snapped up deals: Ragu pasta sauce for 89 cents, Aunt Jemima pancake mix for 48 cents, pork shoulder steaks for $1.49 a pound and five cans of Del Monte vegetables for $2.

After making their way through the groceries, the Miraflors turned their attention to the housewares section, stopping in front of a 20-inch box fan(转页扇). Glenn Miraflor checked the price and made room for it in their cart.

"Ten bucks," he said. "You can't beat that. That's why we come here."

Vendors' Alley

The fan was made 1,700 miles away in Chicago at Lakewood Engineering & Manufacturing Co.. A decade ago, the same fan carried a $20 price tag.

But that wasn't low enough for Wal-Mart. So Lakewood owner Carl Krauss cut costs at every turn(处处). He automated production at the red-brick factory built by his grandfather on the city's West Side. Where it once took 22 people to put together a product, it now takes seven. Krauss also badgered(烦扰;迫使)his suppliers to knock down their prices for parts.

In 2000, he took the hardest step of all: He opened a factory in Shenzhen, China, where workers earn 25 cents an hour, compared with $13 in Chicago. About 40% of his products now are made in China, including most heaters and desktop fans(台式风扇). The Miraflors' box fan was assembled in Chicago, but its electronic guts were imported.

"My father was dead set against(坚决反对某事) it," Krauss said of the move overseas. "I have the same respect for American workers, but I'm going to do what I have to do to survive."

Survival in an age when consumers are hyper-vigilant about prices means shaving expenses again and again. "Nobody wants to be on the shelf with the same item for $1 more," Krauss said.

All the retailers he supplies—including Home Depot Inc. and Target Corp.—drive a hard bargain with manufacturers. But none is as tough as Wal-Mart, Krauss said.

Twice a year, his sales representatives travel to Wal-Mart headquarters to pitch(推销)their products. There, competitors sit side by side, waiting to be ushered into one of 60 glass-sided cubicles—a space some call Vendors' Alley.

Then the haggling(讨价还价)begins. "You give them your price," Krauss said. "If they don't like it, they give you theirs."

The suppliers are at a disadvantage. The Wal-Mart buyer can always go out to the waiting room and find someone who will go lower. "Your price is going to be whittled down like you never thought possible," Krauss said.

After moving much of his manufacturing abroad, Krauss doesn't see any way to push costs lower. "If you're doing things legally, you can't," he said.

He may have to find a way.

At the Serene Avenue store, shopper Sarah Saxon, 17, pulled a $40 Lakewood heater off the shelf. She looked it over, then put it back in favor of an Air Tech model selling for $34.88. She said it looked better than the Lakewood.

"Besides," she said, "it's cheaper."

Wal-Mart's culture of cheap emanates(散发) from Bentonville, a town of 20,000 tucked into the low green hills of northwest Arkansas, where a young Sam Walton opened his first five-and-dime in 1950. Even then, Walton had a vision of a different kind of retail.

Rather than charging a little less than his competitors, Walton wanted to slash prices as much as he could and still make a profit. Other stores would use price breaks (打折) from manufacturers as a way to boost their bottom lines, paying less at wholesale while leaving retail prices untouched.

Walton passed such savings on to his customers as his discount business evolved into Wal-Mart stores in 1962. He figured he would make up the difference in volume. He was right.

By the mid-1980s, Wal-Mart's success had catapulted(弹射) Walton to No. 1 on the Forbes list of richest Americans. Still, he drove an old pickup truck(轻便小货车) to haul around his bird dogs(捕鸟猎犬), refused to fly first class and shared hotel rooms with colleagues on business trips.

Bentonville, like the man who put it on the map, is a combination of Southern charm and Midwestern practicality. The town square is anchored by the original Walton's five-and-dime(now a visitors' center) and dotted with small shops. But the real action is down Business Route 71, where the Wal-Mart Supercenter rises up, big enough to fit three 747s with room to spare.

Across the street is the base of Wal-Mart operations: the Home Office. The world's biggest company occupies an industrial-looking hodgepodge(大杂烩) of windowless work spaces, connected by bunker-like hallways. The drab gray-and-blue walls display the visage and sayings of Sam Walton, who died in 1992:

"Listen to your associates(同事)... They're the best idea generators."

"To succeed, stay out in front of change."

"Swim upstream. Go the other way. Ignore the conventional wisdom."

Lists abound. The best-performing stores. The worst-performing stores. Under a picture of the founder asking, "Who's taking your customers?" is a roster of competing retailers, including Costco Wholesale Corp., Circuit City Stores Inc. and Target, with the name and picture of each company's chief executive.

It's all part of the Wal-Mart culture: a zealous attention to competition, customers and costs.

Wal-Mart employees, unlike their counterparts at other retailers, are forbidden to accept so much as a soda from vendors—or anybody else the company does business with—on the theory that such frills(值得艳羡却并不必需的东西) ultimately are paid for by consumers. The company's meticulous management of the flow of goods, from the factory floor to the store shelf, has shaved shipping and inventory costs to a degree that retailing experts say is unprecedented.

"You could argue that some of what Wal-Mart does to cut costs has been win-win," said Richard S. Tedlow, a professor of business administration at Harvard Business School. "What's being squeezed out is waste."

The company is so ruthlessly efficient that 4% of the growth in the U. S. economy's productivity from 1995 to 1999 was due to Wal-Mart alone, researchers at the McKinsey Global Institute(麦肯锡全球研究院)estimated last year. No other single company had a measurable impact. Wal-Mart also has forced competitors to become more efficient, driving the nation's productivity—output per hour of work—even higher.

Walton, who still is referred to as Mr. Sam throughout the corporation, worked in a ground-floor office barely big enough for a conference table. The current occupant, Chief Executive H. Lee Scott Jr., is the keeper of Mr. Sam's vision. Like all Wal-Mart executives, he empties his own trash and shares budget(廉价的)hotel rooms when travelling. Everyone flies coach(经济舱).

"We do not have limousines," said Scott, who certainly could afford one, having made nearly $18 million last year in salary, bonus and stock, plus options(期权)with an estimated value of $11.3 million. "I drive a Volkswagen Bug(大众甲壳虫汽车)."

Wal-Mart's stinginess reaches from the executive suite to the loading dock.

Some truckers complain that they must unload their own cargo—or pay Wal-Mart to do it. Other big retail chains absorb that cost themselves. "They're awful," said independent driver George Hauschild of Palm Springs. "They don't even let you use the bathroom."

At every one of the 2,966 Wal-Marts in the U. S., thermostats are kept at a steady 73 degrees in summer, 70 degrees(华氏温度,约相当于摄氏 22.78 度和 21.11 度)in winter; raising or lowering the temperature is considered a waste of money.

Such measures seem mild compared with what Wal-Mart has done to cut payroll costs(薪酬开支). In one case, a jury(陪审团)in Oregon last year found that company managers had coerced hundreds of employees to work overtime without pay.

The managers were driven by intense pressure from Bentonville, witnesses said. Managers whose labor costs were considered too high were singled out during the company's weekly in-house satellite broadcasts. In response, managers tampered with electronic time cards(考勤卡机)or bullied employees to work off the clock(不支付薪水的加班), according to trial testimony.

The Oregon jury found last December that Wal-Mart's behavior was illegal and willful. A separate trial to determine damages for the 290 plaintiffs(原告)is set for early next year.

Wal-Mart settled similar overtime suits in Colorado and New Mexico for undisclosed amounts. More than 40 other cases are awaiting trial.

The company says it prohibits off-the-clock work and blames the problems on a small number of rogue managers.

Last month, Wal-Mart ran into trouble because of another cost-cutting practice: using dirt-cheap(不能再便宜的)janitorial services.

A grand jury(大陪审团)is investigating whether Wal-Mart knew that janitors(清洁工;保洁) provided by subcontractors(转包商) were illegal immigrants cheated out of overtime pay. Federal agents raided 61 Wal-Marts across the country and seized boxes of documents from the Bentonville headquarters. Wal-Mart has denied wrongdoing.

Scott, the CEO, lauded(称赞) Wal-Mart's employment record. Even in tight labor markets, he said, the company never has trouble finding workers.

"It is not forced labor," he said. "The truth is, I go to the stores and shake hands with the associates, and they like working at Wal-Mart."

On the Fast Track

Aaron Rios liked working at Wal-Mart so much that he decided to make his career there.

Like two-thirds of Wal-Mart's store managers, Rios started off as an hourly worker—in his case, stocking shoes on the graveyard shift(半夜到早上八点的夜班) at the Wal-Mart in his hometown of Hanford in the San Joaquin Valley.

After two years, Rios was recommended for management training—the company's fast track—leading him to quit community college and pursue a climb through the Wal-Mart ranks.

"There's just something about a Wal-Mart environment," said Rios, who became manager of the Serene Avenue Supercenter in Las Vegas at age 26. "It changed who I am, where I was going and what my career goals were."

Wal-Mart store managers earn about $95,000 annually, including bonuses, according to the company. Supercenter managers earn $130,000.

A management position requires long hours—as many as80 a week—and, often, a willingness to relocate. Rios worked at six California Wal-Mart stores before taking the helm(执掌大权) at Serene Avenue.

"It doesn't come free," said Rios, a divorced father who shares custody of his 2-year-old son.

Still, he said, the benefits outweigh the sacrifices.

"I have an open opportunity. I could go into real estate for Wal-Mart. I could do systems, analysis, accounting. It's endless," Rios said. "If I wanted to go to Germany or Japan or Brazil or any of the markets we have, I believe I could go."

A few weeks later, Rios snared(捕捉) another promotion, moving back to California as a district manager in the Antelope Valley, overseeing seven stores from Barstow to Palmdale.

Larry Allen had his own dreams of climbing the Wal-Mart ladder.

In the fall of 2001, he and his wife, Jacque, left Portland, Ore., where the economy was sputtering, and headed to Las Vegas. He was an executive chef(厨师长) and she worked in catering(餐饮业). They looked forward to a fresh start in unionized casino jobs, making more than $15 an hour, with health insurance and pensions.

But their timing was lousy. Recession and terrorism were hitting the gaming industry hard, and work of any kind was scarce.

Just before their money ran out, the Allens lowered their expectations and took jobs at the Serene Avenue Wal-Mart. Jacque, then 43, worked the counter at the in-store restaurant, Radio Grill. Larry, 46, stocked produce. They each earned $8 an hour.

Despite the letdown(失望), Larry Allen said he attacked the job with enthusiasm. Inspired by tales of well-paid Wal-Mart managers who had started out as hourly employees, such as his manager Aaron Rios, he figured on working his way up. That was Sam's way, he said.

"I've been following Sam Walton since the 1970s," he said. "He's the American dream."

The glow faded quickly. At his 90-day review, Allen said, he received an unenthusiastic write-up(报告) and an hourly raise of 35 cents. His supervisor told him that if he continued working hard, in two years he might make his way up to $10 an hour.

Allen thinks he knows why he received such mediocre marks. For one thing, he was prone to question company policy. Then, Allen committed the ultimate act of disloyalty: He openly promoted unionization.

West Coast Ambitions

For decades, Wal-Mart has tantalized(使……着急) and frustrated union organizers. But the company's move into the grocery business—a labor stronghold—has raised the stakes dramatically.

Union organizers say the high wages and benefits of their members are at risk, as Wal-Mart expands its Supercenters beyond the South and Midwest. The company recently established a beachhead(据点) in Las Vegas, with five centers.

Next stop: California, where Wal-Mart plans to open 40 Supercenters starting early next year. In a sense, it has already arrived. Wal-Mart's low wages are a central factor in the labor dispute between California's three major supermarket chains and the United Food and Commercial Workers(联合食品与商业工人工会).

"They are the third party now that comes to every bargaining situation," said Mike Leonard, director of strategic programs for the UFCW.

Over many years of hard negotiating, the union has won and maintained premier contracts for its 800,000 grocery workers. But with the opening of each new Supercenter, the union's clout(影响力) erodes.

Every one of the giant stores sucks away about 200 UFCW jobs, said retail consultant Burt P. Flickinger III, who runs Strategic Resource Group in New York. That means less power at the bargaining table and less money to hire organizers.

On average, Flickinger says, Wal-Mart's wage-and-benefit package is about $10 an hour less than those offered by unionized supermarkets.

For shoppers, that makes a big difference. A cartful of groceries is 17% to 39% cheaper at a Wal-Mart Supercenter than at a unionized supermarket, according to a survey last year in Las Vegas, Dallas and Tampa, Fla., by investment bank UBS Warburg(瑞银华宝).

Wal-Mart's move into groceries has led 25 regional supermarket chains around the nation to close or file for bankruptcy protection, eliminating 12,000 mostly union jobs, Flickinger said.

With this in mind, Safeway Inc. recently aired a videotaped message to employees, whose contract in Las Vegas expires next fall.

"Wal-Mart wants our customers and your jobs," said Safeway executive Larree Renda. Total wage and benefit costs represent 15% of sales at Safeway, Renda said. At Wal-Mart, they account for 9%.

"If we don't change," Renda said, "you bet we'll lose jobs—and it will be in the thousands."

Staying Unorganized

From their first day on the job, Wal-Mart employees are advised to avoid unions and to report any organizing activities to their supervisors.

"If a union got in here, every benefit we've got could go on the negotiating table, every one of them," says a man identified as Russell, a veteran employee, in a video shown to new hires. "Unions will negotiate just about anything to get the right to have dues deducted out of paychecks. You see, they need big money to pay union bigwigs(大亨) and their lawyers."

Company policy prohibits any union talk in work areas, and organizers say they routinely are asked to leave stores. The retailer sought, and last year received, a court order keeping organizers out of all of its stores in Arkansas. The state Supreme Court nullified(使无效) the order in July.

At the first hint of union activity, Wal-Mart managers are supposed to call a hotline, usually prompting a team visit from Bentonville.

Wal-Mart spokeswoman Mona Williams said the intervention was meant to help store managers respond effectively and legally.

"Our philosophy is that only an unhappy associate would be interested in joining a union," she said, "so that's why Wal-Mart does everything it can to make sure that we are providing our associates what they want and need."

But dozens of times in the last four years, attorneys for the National Labor Relations Board have claimed that the company infringed on the supermarket union's legal right to organize.

Although some of those claims have been thrown out, others have been upheld by administrative law judges, who have ruled that Wal-Mart illegally influenced employees with offers of raises, promotions and improved working conditions just before they were to vote on whether to join a union.

Judges also have found that Wal-Mart illegally implied that workers could lose benefits such as insurance and profit sharing if they unionized.

What's more, managers illegally confiscated(没收) union literature, threatened to close down a store if workers voted to join the union, fired several union supporters and failed to promote others, according to rulings from Minnesota to Florida.

Stymied(阻挠) in their previous attempts to organize Wal-Mart workers, UFCW leaders adopted a new strategy in 2000. They decided to marshal their resources for a concerted organizing effort in one place: Las Vegas.

The union reached out to workers with a Web site and a weekly radio talk show, and posted organizers outside Wal-Mart stores at all hours. When they could, UFCW members would leave union literature inside stores, hoping that workers would see it before managers ordered the material thrown away.

Larry Allen got his first glimpse at a union pamphlet last year as he carried it to the garbage at the Serene Avenue Supercenter. He was hooked, and began advocating for an election to bring in the union.

"Somebody has got to step up and fight for what is right," Allen said.

Ripple Effect(涟漪效应)

Less than a mile away from the Serene Avenue store, another shopping center stands deserted, in desperate need of an anchor.

A year ago, the Raley's grocery store here drew thousands of shoppers who spilled out to neighboring businesses, buying flowers, mailing packages, getting their nails done. Today, the store is gone. The remaining shops are struggling.

"I'm probably down 45%," said Bonnie Neisius, who owns a UPS Store franchise in the center. "I just don't get the foot traffic(人流量) anymore."

A few doors away, Windmill Flowers owner Diana I. Murphy leaned on a table where she would have been arranging bouquets—had there been customers.

"There are a couple of things in play," Murphy said. "The recession, terrorism. And Wal-Mart. It's had a direct effect on me, because they sell flowers, too... They even deliver."

Unlike small towns with boarded-up commercial centers, fast-growing Vegas quickly loses track of its Wal-Mart victims.

Wal-Mart's costs to the community tend to show up in subtler ways.

In an informal survey in the late 1990s of people who used Las Vegas emergency rooms for routine medical care, patients who said they were employed but uninsured were asked where they worked.

"Wal-Mart came up more than any other," said Dr. Raj Chanderraj, a Las Vegas cardiologist(心脏病医生) and chairman of the Clark County Health Care Access Consortium, a group that works to provide medical services to the uninsured.

The reason, say critics: because Wal-Mart pays such low wages, many employees can't afford the health insurance the company offers. And those who do have health coverage through the company often can't afford deductibles(保险中的自付扣除金) that run as high as $3,000 a year.

"Their employees are ending up at the county hospital and become the burden of the county," said Clark County Manager Thom Reilly.

Wal-Mart disputes that. Williams, the company spokeswoman, said that 48% of employees are covered by Wal-Mart's health insurance plan. Among those who aren't, 26% have coverage from another source such as a spouse's employer or Medicare(美国联邦医疗保险计划), Williams said.

The notion that Wal-Mart doesn't provide adequate health coverage is "just rhetoric," she said. "It's simply not true."

According to the Employee Benefit Research Institute in Washington, nearly 44% of workers in the retail sector as a whole have employer-provided health coverage. Among big companies in all industries, the figure is 66%.

Those who accuse Wal-Mart of shortchanging(欺骗) its employees, Williams suggested, don't understand the modern service economy. "Retail and service wages are what they are," she said, "whether you look at a department store, a discount store, the local dry cleaners, the bakery or whatever."

"Wal-Mart is a great match for a lot of people," Williams added. "But if you are the sole provider for your family and do not have the time or the skills to move up the ladder, then maybe it's not the right place for you."

I Still Believe in Wal-Mart

Larry Allen spent about a year advocating for the supermarket union while working at Wal-Mart.

In the parking lot and in the break room(休息室), he passed out fliers and talked up(to talk up: 大声讲; 大胆讲) the benefits of unionizing. But he and his fellow union backers didn't get as far as they hoped. About 42% of workers in the grocery department at Serene Avenue signed UFCW cards—not enough for the union to feel confident about winning an election.

In August, Allen was fired. NLRB attorneys said it was because of his union activities and filed a complaint against Wal-Mart, seeking his reinstatement(复职).

On a recent afternoon outside the Supercenter, dozens of union members rallied to support Allen. "Larry, Larry, Larry," they chanted. Over at the store entrance, the demonstration was a muffled, distant bit of noise. Store managers watched on a screen as surveillance cameras scanned the crowd.

Asked about the commotion(喧哗), a gray-haired Wal-Mart greeter(迎宾员) named Robert just smiled. "They want to make the store union," he said. "But that would make the prices go up for our customers. We can't let that happen."

On some level, even Larry Allen understands. "I still believe in Wal-Mart," said Allen, who now is on the union payroll as an organizer. "I like the idea of it—give a quality product at a low price. It's what the American public wants."

一、作者背景

Columbia University President Lee C. Bollinger (left) presents (from left) Nancy Cleeland, Evelyn Iritani, Abigail Goldman, Tyler Marshall, Rick Wartzman and John Corrigan, *of the Los Angeles Times*, with the 2004 Pulitzer Prize in National Reporting.

爱比盖尔·歌德曼（Abigail Goldman）：1998年成为《洛杉矶时报》商业版记者，此前，她曾在该报和其他报纸杂志实习。

1993年，她毕业于哥伦比亚大学新闻学院，获得新闻硕士学位。其本科学习是在威斯康星大学完成的，专业是历史和政治学。

南希·克莉兰（Nancy Cleeland）：1977年取得亚利桑那大学新闻学学士学位，此后开始了长达30年的记者生涯。在美联社工作一段时间后，她又在《圣迭戈论坛报》（*San Diego Tribune*）等多家报纸供职，在《圣迭戈论坛报》任职期间，她在南美、中美、越南、墨西哥等地做过八年驻外记者。1996年至2007年担任《洛杉矶时报》记者期间，主要报道劳工、移民和国际贸易等问题，并于2007年5月辞职。在她的博客中，她这样解释辞职的原因："洛杉矶地区的贫富差距很大，这里外来务工者①人数众多，他们的工作环境很恶劣，工资很低……但是读者在《洛杉矶时报》却根本看不到这些。这份报纸的编辑政策越来越不支持工会，忽视大量底层民众对经济状况的不满，却大量刊登明星新闻和犯罪新闻。"克莉兰目前供职于总部设在华盛顿的经济政策研究所（Economic Policy Institute），这个智库专门研究经济趋势与政策对美国和全球工人所带来的影响。

---

①主要指非法移民打"黑工"

二、《洛杉矶时报》

Los Angeles Times

Into the abyss of Baghdad

RISE IN BRIBERY TESTS INTEGRITY OF U.S. BORDER

LAPD's flextime dilemma

The battlefield widens for House GOP seats

A legend of base jumping takes leap of faith — his last

In Mexico, young and thin are often job requirements

Front page from October 23，2006

《洛杉矶时报》在加利福尼亚州出版，在美国西部发行，其声望仅次于《纽约时报》和《华盛顿邮报》，被称为美国第三大报。该报历史上属钱德勒家族（Chandler）所有，现为山姆·泽尔（Sam Zell）拥有。

该报几易其主，经历曲折的发展历程。《洛杉矶时报》于 1881 年创刊，但不久就倒闭了。1882 年，哈里森·格雷·欧提斯（Harrison Gray Otis）接管报纸。1917 年，奥迪斯女婿哈里·钱德勒（Harry Chandler）继任。1944 年，诺曼·钱德勒（Norman Chandler）继承事业。1960 —1980 年，第四代业主欧提斯· 钱德勒（Otis Chandler）接手。后来的几任继任者包括马克·威尔斯（Mark Willes）、杰夫·约翰逊（Jeffery Johnson）和戴维·希勒（David Hiller）。2000 年，美国论坛报公司（Tribune Company）收购了《洛杉矶时报》。2008 年，论坛报公司申请破产保护；2012 年底该公司宣布结束破产保护状态，以新的董事会和所有权结构开始重组后的运营。

20 世纪 60 年代以前，该报在全国的影响并不是很大。20 世纪 60 年代以来，它进行了一些改革，主要是扩大报道面，增加国内国际新闻及其他专栏，同时对政府的一些政策持自由主义的批评态度。如 1971 年，它在美国各大报刊中率先提出要美国立即撤出越南。这些旨在改变其以往地方保守主义报纸形象的措施起到了立竿见影的效果。

该报的编辑政策是稳中求变。前 80 年里，《洛杉矶时报》基本上以保守主义思想著称，在钱德勒时期，逐渐转向中间派立场。值得一提的是，从传统上讲，该报在大选中不支持任何派别的总统候选人。1972 年，它因钱德勒家族与尼克松的特殊关系而表示对尼克松支持的做法一度引起员工的哗然，该报从此恪守原则。但是，在 2008 年和 2012 年总统大选期间，《洛杉矶时报》明确支持奥巴马。

截至2013年，《洛杉矶时报》已获得过41次普利策奖。其中，最辉煌的是2004年，《洛杉矶时报》共获得5项普利策奖，成为当年最大的赢家。

三、课文背景

作为全球最大的零售帝国，沃尔玛公司自然会吸引各方关注，大家不仅关心其商业成功的秘密，也越来越重视沃尔玛为我们每个人带来的政治、社会和文化影响。沃尔玛以高度的市场占有率对供货商形成巨大的议价压力，使得其必须以管理和效率为主要利润来源，因而加速了产业效率的提升。但沃尔玛为普通员工提供的工作待遇则非常苛刻，而且禁止员工组织工会。此外，自20世纪九十年代起，沃尔玛加速了其全球化进程，不但四处开店，而且从全球采购商品。这虽然为美国中下层家庭节省了大量生活费用，但是沃尔玛也常常要面对“把美国工作机会输出国外”的指控。在这种背景下，美国不少自由派人士和反全球化人士开始“围剿”沃尔玛，其出售的商品也常常被贴上第三世界“血汗工厂”的标签。本文作者从讲述身边小事入手，引发读者对重大问题的思考。这种以小见大的写法十分值得我们学习与借鉴。

《洛杉矶时报》记者用了几个月的时间在全美各地和中国、孟加拉国、洪都拉斯等地对沃尔玛公司进行了深入采访，撰写出六篇文章，分三天刊登。该系列报道从不同角度介绍了沃尔玛公司，不仅涉及沃尔玛如何引发零售业革命，沃尔玛实现“天天平价”的奥秘，还分析了沃尔玛的迅速扩张给美国经济和世界经济带来的巨大影响。该系列报道的最后一篇文章介绍了沃尔玛如何适应本地文化并影响中国消费者的购买行为，文章标题“*Selling Eel and Chicken Feet—Plus M&Ms and Sony TVs*”（“鳝鱼、凤爪、M&M豆、索尼电视——我们全都卖”）包含了西方人眼里的典型中国元素（一般西方人不吃鳝鱼和凤爪）和典型西方元素，读起来生动俏皮。这些关于失业、劳资关系、全球化等十分严肃的话题在《洛杉矶时报》记者笔下却非常鲜活，读起来毫无枯燥乏味之感，引用普利策奖评选委员会的赞词来说就是“引人入胜”（engrossing）。产生这种效果的主要原因是记者并没有简单堆砌大话、空话，而是讲了很多故事，大量引用被采访者的原话，通过故事主人公的嘴表达记者对“沃尔玛现象”的价值判断。

四、作者主要观点

(1) What is Wal-Mart's image as depicted in this story? Is it a favorable one or not? Why?

(2) While saving big bucks for customers and enabling low-income people to purchase daily necessities, Wal-Mart has in effect revolutionized consumer culture. Why are the reporters so critical of Wal-Mart's rise then? Do you agree with their analysis? Why or why not?

五、写作风格与手法

(1) What has intrigued most about this article in terms of its writing style?

(2) How is comparison and contrast achieved in the story?

(3) Examine the news worthiness of this story. In particular, how are timing, significance, proximity, prominence, and human interest reflected in the story?

(4) What kinds of persons have been interviewed? What other possible sources

might have been consulted?

(5) Does the story seem to be fair or unbiased? Why or why not?

(6) What, if any, is the constructive purpose of the writers?

(7) Are the paragraphs closely connected? Provide specific examples

(8) Comment on the use of the following throughout this story: 1. precise, concise wording; and 2. interesting and varied word choices. Provide specific examples.

(9) When trying to describe how low China's labor cost could go, Western journalists often detail the wage of Chinese laborers. In this story, for instance, the authors compared the hourly wages between workers in Shenzhen and Chicago for doing the same job: 25 cents vs. 13 dollars. What are the implications of such specific numbers? Do you think it is fair to make such comparison? Why or why not?

(10) In what way is it an "engrossing story" as depicted in the citation?

Part Three: Further exploring the text

一、语言点讲解

1. Gray earned $14.68 an hour with a pension and family health insurance. Wal-Mart grocery workers typically make less than $9 an hour.

这两句简单句的结构几乎相同，但前后对比十分强烈。我们发现，在沃尔玛工作，不仅工资低，而且还没有养老金和家庭健康保险。作者就是这样利用事实（facts）不动声色地把自己的好恶表现出来。下面的小标题“Wal-Mart gives. And Wal-Mart takes away.”也是这样强烈对比的例子。你觉得为什么这种简单句反而能带来如此强烈的语言效果？本文中还有不少把沃尔玛与其他公司进行对比的句子，请把它们都找出来仔细研读。

2. U. S. economists say its tightfistedness has not only boosted its own bottom line, but also helped hold down the inflation rate for the entire country.

Tightfisted 与 closefisted、hardfisted，以及后文出现的 penny-pinching 都表示“小气、齐啬”的意思，与中文里“（某人的）手很紧”有异曲同工之妙。Bottom line 在这里指“账本底线”，即财务账目表上最下面的那一行上标明的表示盈或亏的数目（“the final line on a company's accounting statement that shows profit or loss that the company makes at the end of a given period of time after everything has been calculated”）。例如：How will the rise in interest rates affect our bottom line?（利率的提高对我们的利润会产生什么样的影响?）这个短语还常常有以下两个引申义：一是指“底线、要点、最关键的地方”，例如：The bottom line is that we have to increase our sales or take a cut in pay.（我们的底线是必须增加销售额，否则就减工资。）二是指“结果”，例如：The bottom line, however, is that he has escaped.（然而结果他跑掉了。）

3. Fearful of Wal-Mart's ability to undercut them on price, the Ralphs, Vons and

Albertsons chains have sought concessions from their unionized workers in Southern and Central California, leading to a work stoppage now entering its seventh week.

Work stoppage 和 strike 一样，都是泛指（由于抗议低工资、恶劣工作环境等进行的）罢工、停工。更加具体的词语还有 job action（临时性罢工示威，尤其指警察等法律上被禁止罢工的团体进行的罢工）、sit-down strike［（在工厂里）静坐罢工］、go-slow（怠工，故意降低工作效率）、walkout［（工人扔下手中的工具，走出工厂）罢工］、wild-cat strike（未经工会正式同意的罢工，工人自发进行的罢工）等。

4. That's basically the way the Miraflors saw it as they cruised the aisles of the Supercenter—Wal-Mart Store No. 2593—and snapped up deals: Ragu pasta sauce for 89 cents, Aunt Jemima pancake mix for 48 cents, pork shoulder steaks for $1.49 a pound and five cans of Del Monte vegetables for $2.

截至 2009 年 5 月的数据表明，沃尔玛在美国共有 4,260 家商店（其中沃尔玛商店 886 家，沃尔玛购物广场 2,622 家，山姆会员商店 602 家，沃尔玛社区店 150 家），在全球总共有 7,899 家商店。与仅仅提供这些"枯燥"的数字相比，点明"沃尔玛第2,593店"则巧妙地告诉读者沃尔玛的店铺数量多、扩张速度快。在沃尔玛超市，Miraflor 夫妇买了意粉酱、松饼粉、猪肩肉和几个蔬菜罐头，一共才花了 4.86 美元。而且他们买的大多是罐头和低档速食食品，这从一个侧面展示出美国低收入家庭的生存状态。显然，这种写法比"The working-class people simply cannot afford fresh vegetables and fruits."之类的话更生动、更有效。找出本文中其他这类数字，并讨论作者的用意。

5. Glenn Miraflor checked the price and made room for it in their cart.

"To make room for"的意思是"为……腾出空位"，我们可以通过这个字想象到购物车已经装满了商品，要费力挪地方才能把这台鸿运扇塞进去。

6. There, competitors sit side by side, waiting to be ushered into one of 60 glass-sided cubicles—a space some call Vendors' Alley.

这句话展示了供货商与沃尔玛悬殊的力量对比：想要将产品卖给沃尔玛的供货商不得不紧挨着坐在一起（显然并不舒服），"等着被人带进"60 个谈判间中的一个［cubicle 指面积很小的工作间，比"室"（room）的面积小］，而且这些谈判间都由玻璃隔开（里面的一举一动都可能被其他人看到，没有任何私密性，也没有照顾供货商的尊严），难怪这个地方被人称作 alley——只是一条小巷子。想想看，作者是通过什么样的语言手段给我们留下如此深刻的印象呢？

7. Your price is going to be whittled down like you never thought possible.

"Whittle"的本意是从木头上一点一点削下小片，引申为"逐渐削减或减弱"。由于供货商数量众多，沃尔玛在采购时占尽有利条件，可以一分钱一分钱地压价。本文中除了 whittle（the price）down 以外，还使用了很多其他表示压价、削价、降低价格/成本的动词，请把它们都找出来，并比较意思上的细微差别。

二、中西文化比较

论"求异思维"

在本文第三部分，即小标题为"Vendor's Alley"的部分，有几句沃尔玛创始人山姆·沃尔顿的名言，其中一句是："逆流而上。另辟蹊径。抛弃传统智慧。"（Swim upstream. Go the other way. Ignore the conventional wisdom.）。这体现了一种求异思维或逆向思维。从很大程度上说，这是沃尔玛的成功因素之一。

所谓求异思维，是指采用与通常情况下普遍习惯的单向思维完全相反的思路，从对立的、完全相反的角度思考和探索问题的思维。

这种思维没有中西区分，在人类历史上十分普遍。事实上，历史上许多具有创新性和革命性的学说和思想，往往是在逆向思维的基础上建立起来的。比如，哥白尼的日心说相对于地心说；卢梭关于自由、平等和民主的资产阶级政治思想相对于封建专制主义思想；弗洛伊德的精神分析法相对于传统心理学和传统道德规范等等。在中国思想史上，在社会价值观、人生哲学、处事原则等方面，道家所主张的"无为而有为"、"柔弱胜刚强"的"弱者"哲学也是在逆反于儒家的思维模式和习惯心态下而提出来的。

三、语言练习

1. 请用英语解释下列句子。

(1) The prices can't be beat, but the wages can.

(2) For the 26-year-old Ferguson, the draw is simple.

(3) Yet Wal-Mart's astonishing success exacts a heavy price.

(4) With Wal-Mart, the calculus is considerably more complex.

(5) Others insist there is a net benefit whenever consumers can get more for less.

(6) ...big enough to fit three 747s with room to spare.

(7) "I've been following Sam Walton since the 1970s," he said. "He's the American dream."

(8) But the company's move into the grocery business—a labor stronghold—has raised the stakes dramatically.

(9) ...the Raley's grocery store here drew thousands of shoppers who spilled out to neighboring businesses...

(10) Unlike small towns with boarded-up commercial centers, fast-growing Vegas quickly loses track of its Wal-Mart victims.

2. 请将下列短语翻译成英文，并比较中英文表达方式的异同。

(1) 总部设在加州的企业

(2) 财政年度

(3) 消费品

(4) 主权国家

(5)（超市的）结账通道

(6) 引起混乱/恐慌

(7) 不管情况或结果是好是坏

(8) 世界羡慕的对象

(9) 在超市走道穿行（以浏览商品）

（10）抢购特价商品
（11）风扇的内部电子元件
（12）对价格超级敏感
（13）业绩最佳/最差店面
（14）传统思想
（15）加班却拿不到加班费
（16）与（已离婚的配偶）共同享有子女抚养权
（17）以极大的热情和干劲投入工作
（18）靠自己的努力步步高升
（19）申请破产保护
（20）侵犯……（做某事）的合法权利

3. 请将下面的句子或段落翻成中文，并比较中英文表达方式的异同。

By squeezing suppliers to cut wholesale costs, the company has hastened the flight of U. S. manufacturing jobs overseas. By scouring the globe for the cheapest goods, it has driven factory jobs from one poor nation to another.

By the company's own admission, a full-time worker might not be able to support a family on a Wal-Mart paycheck.

When a Supercenter moves into town, competitors often are wiped out, taking high-paying union jobs with them.

But when the family's credit card debt topped $10,000, Wal-Mart's deals suddenly looked irresistible.

"We have split brains... Most of the time, the half of our brain that wants the best deal prevails."

Wal-Mart's culture of cheap emanates from Bentonville, a town of 20,000 tucked into the low green hills of northwest Arkansas, where a young Sam Walton opened his first five-and-dime in 1950. Even then, Walton had a vision of a different kind of retail.

Bentonville, like the man who put it on the map, is a combination of Southern charm and Midwestern practicality.

The world's biggest company occupies an industrial-looking hodgepodge of windowless work spaces, connected by bunker-like hallways. The drab gray-and-blue walls display the visage and sayings of Sam Walton, who died in 1992.

After two years, Rios was recommended for management training—the company's fast track—leading him to quit community college and pursue a climb through the Wal-Mart ranks.

They decided to marshal their resources for a concerted organizing effort in one place: Las Vegas.

Part Four: Exploring beyond the text

一、自我反思

1. 我学到了什么？我要如何改进？

2. 一篇高质量的国内新闻报道的基本标准是什么？我能清楚地告诉别人吗？该篇报道的记者爱比盖尔·歌德曼和南希·克莉兰是如何达到这些标准的？我能向别人解释清楚吗？

二、知识扩展

1. 请访问沃尔玛的网站 http://www.walmart.com/（美国网站）、http://www.walmartchina.com/（中国网站），进一步了解沃尔玛的企业历史、企业文化以及企业理念。

2. 收集世界各地反对沃尔玛行动的资料，人们为什么要反对沃尔玛？这些理由有道理吗？

3. 进一步了解经济全球化及其影响，在收集尽可能多的观点的前提下做出自己的判断。

三、能力扩展

1. 就此篇报道撰写一篇 500 字左右的评论。

2. 采访沃尔玛、麦当劳、肯德基或其他国际连锁企业的几名导购员或收银员，了解他们对自己工作环境和待遇的看法，并撰写一篇 1000 字左右的新闻稿。

3. 本文引用了沃尔玛创始人 Sam Walton 的一些话，比如"Listen to your associates ... They're the best idea generators."；"To succeed, stay out in front of change."；"Swim upstream. Go the other way. Ignore the conventional wisdom." 等。你是否同意这些观点？请就其中的一句话进行评论，撰写一篇 500 字左右的文章。

Text B Scouring the globe to give shoppers an $8.63 polo shirt

Wal-Mart, once a believer in buying American, extracts ever lower prices from 10,000 suppliers worldwide. Workers struggle to keep pace.

BY Nancy Cleeland, Evelyn Iritani and Tyler Marshall

Times

November 24, 2003

导读：课文 B 的重点从美国国内转向世界：沃尔玛的规模如此之大，其千方百计追求低成本的做法对全球政治、经济产生了影响。沃尔玛所做的决定可以影响其供货商支付的工资、工作环境、生产规范，甚至当地政府的政策。这篇报道还用了大量笔墨为读者介绍沃尔玛供货商在价格压力下采取的各种不合规做法，讨论了沃尔玛引发的社会和道德问题。

SAN PEDRO SULA, HONDURAS—When Wal-Mart Stores Inc. demands a lower price for the shirts and shorts it sells by the millions, the consequences are felt in a remote Chinese industrial town, at a port in Bangladesh and here in Honduras, under the corrugated(波纹铁皮的)metal roof of the Cosmos clothing factory.

Isabel Reyes, who has worked at the plant for 11 years, pushes fabric through her sewing machine 10 hours a day, struggling to meet the latest quota scrawled(潦草地写) on a blackboard.

She now sews sleeves onto shirts at the rate of 1,200 garments a day. That's two shirts a minute, one sleeve every 15 seconds.

"There is always an acceleration," said Reyes, 37, who can't lift a cooking pot or hold her infant daughter without the anti-inflammatory(消炎的) pills she gulps down every few hours. "The goals are always increasing, but the pay stays the same."

Reyes, who earns the equivalent of $35 a week, says her bosses blame the long hours and low wages on big U. S. companies and their demands for ever-cheaper merchandise. Wal-Mart, the biggest company of them all, is the Cosmos factory's main customer.

Reyes is skeptical. Why, she asked, would a company in the richest country in the world care about a few pennies on a pair of shorts?

The answer: Wal-Mart built its empire on bargains.

The company's size and obsession with shaving costs have made it a global economic force. Its decisions affect wages, working conditions and manufacturing practices—even the price of a yard of denim—around the world.

From its headquarters in Bentonville, Ark., the company has established a network of 10,000 suppliers and constantly pressures them to lower their prices. At the same time, Wal-Mart buyers continually search the globe for still-cheaper sources of supply. The competition pits vendor against vendor, country against country.

"They control so much of retail that they can put someone into business or take someone out of business if they choose to," said Pat Danahy, a former chief executive at Cone Mills Corp. in Greensboro, N. C., one of the few surviving U. S. textile producers.

In Honduras, the pressure keeps factory managers on edge, always looking for ways to cut expenses without running afoul(与……冲突) of labor laws or Wal-Mart's own contractor rules, which call for "reasonable employee work hours."

"I think we have reached the limit," said Shin Woo Kang, manager of the enormous Han Soll Textile Ltd. sewing plant on the outskirts of San Pedro Sula. The plant employs 1,600 workers, mostly young women. Wal-Mart is its biggest customer.

The brightly lighted factory is filled with humming machines, mounds of clothing parts and fast-moving hands. Down one production line, pieces of navy blue fabric take shape as Bobbie Brooks polo shirts, each bearing a Wal-Mart price tag of $8.63.

Kang said Wal-Mart was paying Han Soll about $3 a shirt—a few cents less than last year.

Asked what he would do if the retailer pressed for an even lower price, Kang grew quiet. "We would have to find something," he said finally. "Honestly speaking, I don't know what it is."

To cut costs, Honduran factories have reduced payrolls and become more efficient. The country produces the same amount of clothing as it did three years ago, but with 20% fewer workers, said Henry Fransen, director of the Honduran Apparel Manufacturers Assn. which represents nearly 200 export factories.

"We're earning less and producing more," he said with a laugh, "following the Wal-Mart philosophy."

That's harsh medicine for a developing country. The clothing industry is one of the few sources of decent jobs for unskilled workers in this nation of 6 million. Many of those jobs depend on Wal-Mart.

"You could be looking at a government meltdown if something were to happen to this industry," said Raja Rajan, a factory manager active in the apparel association.

In Rajan's view, Wal-Mart is so important to the stability of Honduras that leaders should cultivate stronger ties with the company, almost as they would a foreign country. He has lobbied the government to send high-level envoys to Wal-Mart's Arkansas headquarters, something Bangladesh and other countries already do.

Even with such efforts, Rajan fears that the migration of sewing jobs to China and other lower-cost countries can't be stopped, only slowed.

Chuck Wilburn figures that his 1,300 employees will be among the casualties. He manages a factory on the outskirts of San Pedro Sula that cranks out(crank out:制成;制造)clothing for Wal-Mart, Target Corp. and other retailers.

Wilburn's employer, Oxford Industries of Atlanta, once owned 44 factories in the American South. It shuttered them all in the last 15 years and moved the work to cheaper locales. That's how Wilburn found himself in Honduras.

He is proud of his clean, modern factory. "It's nicer than the one I ran in South Carolina," Wilburn said.

Still, he has had trouble turning a profit. He laid off 500 employees two years ago. Even here, it's hard to meet Wal-Mart's prices. Wilburn expects that Oxford will close his factory in the next few years and move on to another country where basic cotton clothes, such as Wal-Mart's Old Glory khaki pants, can be produced for less.

"Our business is a lot of twill(斜纹布)stuff," he said. "That will be gone."

Waving the Flag

It wasn't long ago that Wal-Mart was fighting to keep manufacturing jobs on U.S. soil.

In 1985, founder Sam Walton launched his "Bring It Home to the USA" program. "Wal-Mart believes American workers can make a difference," he told his suppliers, offering to pay as much as 5% more for U.S.-made products.

In his 1992 memoir, "Made in America," Walton claimed that the program had saved or created nearly 100,000 jobs by using "the power of this enormous enterprise as a force for change."

But the late Walton's much-trumpeted effort soon was overtaken by the rise of the global economy. The spread of the Internet and other technology, along with U.S.-led efforts to tear down trade barriers, made it easier to move goods and capital across borders.

To maintain its edge on pricing, Wal-Mart quietly joined other retailers in a worldwide search for the cheapest sources of production.

In apparel, the process begins with Celia Clancy. From a renovated warehouse near the company's headquarters, the Wal-Mart executive vice president oversees the world's largest clothing budget, estimated at $35 billion in 2000.

Clancy gives her buyers a "Plus One" mandate every year: For each item they handle, they must either lower the cost or raise the quality.

To demonstrate, she pulled a pair of girls' shorts off the wall of her cramped(狭促的)office and gave them a tug.

"This was a dumb little knit pull-on short," Clancy said. "We improved the fabric, put some more fashion in it and are selling it for the same price as last year—$5.19."

Keeping prices low like this means squeezing costs at every step. Clancy and her buyers have trimmed back the number of brands, styles and color schemes. That allows Wal-Mart to consolidate its purchases of fabric, accessories and thread and to wrangle steep discounts from suppliers.

Clancy's buyers used to rely on a Hong Kong company and other intermediaries to find bargains overseas. This year, Wal-Mart established its own global procurement(采购)division to hunt for the cheapest raw materials, manufacturers and shipping routes. Last year, for instance, the company rerouted cargo from a port in Hong Kong to the southern Chinese province of Guangdong, where shipping rates were lower. The savings: $650,000.

In purchasing fabrics such as denim and khaki, Wal-Mart plans to approach three to five mills around the world and pit them against each other. "We'll be putting our global muscle on them," said Ken Eaton, head of the global procurement division, which has 21 offices in 18 countries.

Eaton believes he can reduce costs at least 20% by cutting out the middleman and buying directly from foreign factories. He feels a sense of urgency about his mission, in part because he believes the company's "Buy American" focus left it playing catch up.

"Honestly, we're kind of late to the party," he said. "There are a lot of companies out there that have been direct-importing and understanding the global aspect of sourcing for a long, long time."

As late as 1995, Wal-Mart said imports accounted for no more than 6% of its products. Today, consulting firm Retail Forward estimates that 50% to 60% of the merchandise in the company's U.S. stores is imported.

Wal-Mart Chief Executive H. Lee Scott Jr. said in an interview that the trend reflected an inescapable reality: U. S. consumers aren't willing to pay even a little extra for a "Made in America" label.

"The customer ultimately drives that," he said.

Big in Bangladesh

Wal-Mart is the most powerful corporate citizen in Bangladesh, even though it doesn't operate a single store in the country.

When the company complained to Bangladesh's Export Promotion Bureau this spring about delays in moving cargo, the response was swift.

Officials in the southern port of Chittagong are speeding up efforts to reduce paperwork and modernize facilities. Over the objections of labor leaders, port officials also are building a five-berth(五泊位码头)container terminal that will be privately managed. Already, giant cranes have helped shorten a ship's turnaround time from six days to fewer than four.

It's no wonder Wal-Mart wields such clout in this country, where nearly half the population lives in poverty. The company bought 14% of the $1.9 billion in apparel that Bangladesh shipped to the U. S. last year.

"Wal-Mart is our biggest customer and it's important to me," said Commerce Minister Amir Khasru Mahmud Chowdhury. But, he added, Wal-Mart's prices "are coming down all the time—that's the biggest threat to us."

Bangladeshi factory owners say Wal-Mart and other retailers have asked them to cut their prices by as much as 50% in recent years.

One apparel manufacturer described a visit from a Wal-Mart buyer who showed him a European-made garment that retailed for $100 to $130. The buyer asked the Bangladeshi to produce a knockoff for $10 a dozen. He declined.

"They say to come down in price, but we have to make a profit," complained another clothing maker. Hoping to land a Wal-Mart order for 600,000 fleece jackets(抓绒衣)this year, he bargained down his suppliers of fabric, thread and fastenings, and managed to cut his price by 20%.

It wasn't good enough for Wal-Mart. "They said they will place the order in Vietnam or China," he recalled.

Syed Naved Husain had hoped to avoid this sort of nickel-and-diming by going upscale.

As head of the apparel division for Beximco, Bangladesh's largest private company, Husain spent $300 million in 1995 to build a computerized textile and apparel manufacturing center in a rice paddy outside Dhaka. He hired hot designers from Asia and Europe.

Within a few years, he was manufacturing clothes for European retailers Diesel and Zara, and his lushly landscaped "manufacturing oasis" had become an industry showpiece.

But the market has started to change. Wal-Mart is selling more-fashionable clothes, and Husain's high-end customers are nervous. They are pushing him like never before to cut costs.

"Unfortunately," Husain said of Wal-Mart, "they've created a model that has taken the world by storm."

U. S. retailers began making their way to Bangladesh in the 1980s. They found a large population of poor, young women willing to work from dawn to dusk for a few pennies an hour.

Many factories lacked ventilation and fire escapes. Labor activists estimated in the mid-1990s that as many as 50,000 Bangladeshi children were sewing apparel for companies such as Wal-Mart and Kmart Corp.

The resulting outcry prompted a government crackdown on the use of child labor and led companies such as Wal-Mart to require suppliers to adhere to labor laws and safety standards.

Sheikh Nazma, a former child laborer, has seen the way Wal-Mart can help clean things up.

She worked at a Dhaka garment factory that had no clean drinking water and only a few filthy toilets for hundreds of employees. After the owner refused to pay their wages for three months, the employees complained to Wal-Mart, the factory's main customer.

"Wal-Mart interfered, and the owner paid our salaries and overtime and even paid bonuses to each worker," recalled Nazma, who later helped launch the Bangladesh Independent Garment Workers Union Federation.

But Nazma and others say Wal-Mart undermines its good efforts with its incessant push for lower prices. To fill orders on short schedules, factories often force their employees to work overtime or stay on the job for weeks without a day off, according to Sayeeda Roxana Khan, a former factory manager in Dhaka. To conceal such practices, auditors say, some factories keep two sets of books(账本).

"It's the workers who suffer when entrepreneurs have to survive by cutting corners," said Khan, who now works for Verite, a firm that conducts factory audits for Tommy Hilfiger, Levi Strauss and other U. S. companies.

Khadija Akhter can attest to that. For about $21 a month, nearly three times what a maid or cook would make, the 22-year-old worked in a Dhaka factory, performing final checks on men's shirts and trousers.

Employees, she said, often worked from 8 a. m. to 3 a. m. for 10 to 15 days at a stretch to fill big orders from Wal-Mart. Exhausted, she quit after a year and took a lower-paying but less grueling job.

All the speeding up by Bangladeshi factories may not be enough to satisfy Wal-Mart.

A. Hasnat, Wal-Mart's general manager in Bangladesh, said the country's factories need to become more efficient still. From his vantage, many are poorly managed, have outdated equipment and run too slowly.

"I think they need to improve," he said. "When I entered a factory in China, it seemed they are very fast."

3,000 Factories in China

Eyes down, hunched forward, 20-year-old Ping Qiuxia steered a pair of green women's briefs through a sewing machine. Then her fingers whipped the briefs 180 degrees and moved them back toward her, this time with elastic bands stitched neatly around the edges. Within seconds, she was at work on the next pair.

The garment was part of a 6,000-piece order scheduled for shipment to Wal-Mart stores in Germany. For nine hours a day, sometimes six days a week, Ping and other employees of the Gladpeer Garment Factory in the southern Chinese city of Dongguan churn out undergarments, sleepwear and children's clothing.

In southern China, Wal-Mart has found all the ingredients it needs to keep its "every day low prices" among the lowest in the world.

Although labor costs more here than it does in Bangladesh, China offers other advantages: low-cost raw materials; modern factories, highways and ports; and helpful government officials.

Wal-Mart has been instrumental in making this corner of China the world's fastest-growing manufacturing zone. Last year, the company shipped \$12 billion in products out of China, 20% more than in 2001.

The marriage between the world's largest and most efficient retailer and China's low-cost factories is setting a new global "cost standard" for manufactured products, according to consulting firm Deloitte Touche Tohmatsu(德勤全球国际会计公司).

The phenomenon is rattling competitors worldwide and worrying international labor activists. They cite the Chinese government's hostility toward organized labor and its lack of worker protections.

"Wal-Mart has really been at the forefront in driving down wages and working conditions," said Kent Wong, director of the UCLA Labor Center, who has made two trips to China in the last year. "They're not only exporting the Wal-Mart name and the corporation and the identity. They're also exporting that way of doing business."

Wal-Mart has more than 3,000 supplier factories in China, and the number is expected to rise. But that doesn't mean workers in China are secure.

Gladpeer used to make clothes in Hong Kong. It moved production to China in the 1980s because costs were much lower, said Simon Lee, a managing director of the family-owned firm.

Gladpeer's 1,200 workers—mostly young women—are paid about \$55 a month and live in clean but cramped dormitories, eight to a room.

But Lee is likely to reduce his employment in Dongguan soon. He is planning to open a new factory in Guangxi province, a remote region of western China where labor, electricity, housing and taxes are cheaper. "Competition is intense, and our biggest single issue is cost," Lee said. "Many customers look at cost first, then they look at the workmanship. That's why we're going to Guangxi."

Cleeland reported from Honduras, Iritani from Bangladesh and Marshall from China. Times staff writer Abigail Goldman and Hong Kong bureau researcher Tammy Wong contributed to this report.

Unit Three　Beat Reporting

专题报道

单元导航

本单元我们将讨论专题报道。本单元共两篇文章，皆讲述了鲜为人知的癌症患者的生活状态。课文A讲述了癌症患者Elizabeth与病魔抗争的曲折经历，包括与丈夫的紧张关系。课文B讲的是一位八岁的白血病患者与其父母面对困难挫折和磨难的态度。

Part One：Preparing to explore

一、专题报道

1. 定义

“Beat”是一个新闻术语，意思是“负责采访的区域或领域”（a reporter's regular, assigned territory, either geographically or topically）。

“Beat reporting”指对某一话题或某一领域或组织机构等进行的全面系统的报道。“Beat reporter”往往对其报道对象进行长期关注和研究，具有全面深刻的了解，从而不仅仅提供新闻事实，而是撰写出包含深度分析和评论的新闻作品（sustained and knowledgeable coverage of a particular subject or an activity）。

因此，“Beat reporting”相当于我们常说的新闻“跑口制度”，即媒体按照不同领域对记者作分线采访的安排。“Beat reporter”也大致相当于“跑口记者”，如财经口记者、时政口记者、教育口记者等。但是，作为一种新闻类别，“Beat reporting”译成“专题报道”更好一些。

2. 普利策专题报道获奖作品

普利策专题报道奖于1985年设立。1985年至1990年，奖项名为“Pulitzer Prize for Specialized Reporting”（特别报道奖），1991年至2006年改名为“Pulitzer Prize for Beat Reporting”（专题报道奖），2007年后这一奖项被取消。普利策奖评审委员会在作出这个改动时专门强调，跑口记者发表的新闻作品可以归类到国内报道、调查报道、解释性报道及新设立的地方报道这些新闻奖项中。

从 1985 年至 2006 年的获奖作品来看，专题报道的选题都是些较为复杂的问题，如医学问题、科学话题、灵长类动物研究的道德问题、高校学术造假、大学招生黑幕、公司管理混乱问题、华尔街金融问题、教区及教区居民话题、航空工业问题（飞机质量控制）、税法上的漏洞和不平等、美国反恐运动中的争议等问题。

3. 基本写作特征

从普利策评奖审委员会给予专题报道获奖作品的赞词来看，优秀专题报道作品具有以下基本特征：

（1）专业性（expertise）。需对报道主题进行详尽的考察，全面透彻掌握实情。

（2）创新性（originality）。在报道理念、思路和方法等多方面进行创新。

（3）深刻性（poignant/trenchant/incisive story）。分析问题尖锐深刻。

（4）故事构思的巧妙性（masterful story）。在写作手法上，具有精湛的艺术，引人入胜。

二、课前讨论

1. According to the Centers for Disease Control and Prevention(CDC), cancer is the No. 2 killer of Americans, after heart disease. Why do you think cancer is one of the leading causes of death in such developed countries like the US?

2. If you were assigned to write a feature story about cancer patients, what perspective(s) would you adopt?

Part Two: Exploring the text

Text A SICKNESS AND HEALTH

A wife's struggle with cancer takes an unexpected toll

As Lizzie O'Donnell recovered, tensions rose in marriage; angry words in the ICU(intensive care unit 的缩写：重症监护室，加护病房), a truce over twin beds.

BY Amy Dockser Marcus

The Wall Street Journal

September 8, 2004

In their more than three decades together, one issue has posed the biggest threat to James and Elizabeth O'Donnell's marriage: cancer.

Nearly 10 years ago, Mrs. O'Donnell found a lump(肿块) in her breast. At first, she wasn't worried. A routine mammogram(乳腺 X 光造影) a month earlier showed no signs of a tumor(肿瘤). But the lump grew so quickly during a two-week vacation in Hawaii that Mrs. O'Donnell went to see her doctor days after returning home to Indiana. The doctor ordered an immediate biopsy(活组织切片检查). The 42-year-old mother of three boys was diagnosed with advanced(晚期的)breast cancer and told she had only a 5% chance of surviving the next year.

She proved the doctors wrong. Mrs. O'Donnell began chemotherapy(化学疗法)treatments in February 1995, underwent two surgeries, including a mastectomy(乳房切除), and finished her chemotherapy in August 1995. She is now considered cancer-free. She and her husband call that a miracle and say they know how lucky they are. "We had the same goal," Mrs. O'Donnell says, "to keep our family together."

Her survival came at a price. Mrs. O'Donnell, now 51, has chronic health problems arising from her cancer treatment. Just six weeks after her last chemotherapy session, her heart failed—a side effect of the drugs used to eradicate the cancer. She underwent a heart transplant(心脏移植)in June 1996. That, in turn, caused other problems.

The medications she must take every day to ensure her body doesn't reject the heart have weakened her bones, causing spinal deterioration and making her walk with a slight limp. In the past 18 months alone, she has endured shingles(带状疱疹), double pneumonia(双侧肺炎), kidney disease, and two incidents when clots blocked her pulmonary arteries(肺动脉), causing her to be hospitalized. She never stops wondering if the cancer will return someday.

The cancer and related health problems have put the O'Donnells' marriage under siege. "I ponder sometimes how much has been lost... as a consequence of sweet Lizzie's illnesses," Mr. O'Donnell wrote in1999 in a journal he keeps. "Her breathtaking good looks; her shapeliness; her breasts; her lovemaking; her lovely tummy; her walks with me; her ability to be counted on for X or Y; her hair on her head; her not needing to shave; her constant need of medical care; her silence when sleeping."

These "all have been 'little deaths,' "Mr. O'Donnell added, "that have powerfully tugged me to despair and grief."

Thanks to advances in medicine, more people are surviving cancer these days, creating new kinds of personal challenges. Even as attention is starting to focus on the many physical and emotional issues cancer survivors face, marriage remains a topic that makes many uncomfortable. "We tell patients that if they had a strong marriage before cancer, they will have a strong marriage after cancer," says a spokeswoman for Living Beyond Breast Cancer, a support group. (Good angle often neglected in medical-related stories. Beyond the technical stuff...)

Michael Glantz, an oncologist(肿瘤科医生) who treats brain-cancer patients at the University of Massachusetts Medical Center in Worcester, recently conducted a study looking at whether couples divorced or separated more frequently after a cancer diagnosis. Among 214 couples in which one of the partners had a malignant(恶性的)brain tumor, the rate of divorce was six times as high as the control group(对照组). The vast majority of divorces were in cases where the wife was sick, not the husband. This led Dr. Glantz to conclude that "being a female diagnosed with cancer is a risk factor for divorce," and to call for more study.

The question of whether cancer is a factor in divorce is controversial, because the overall divorce rate is high and this is still a new area of research. Some centers, including Dana-Farber Cancer Institute in Boston and the University of California San Diego Cancer Center, are experimenting with ways to help couples. New programs mark a shift from focusing on the individual patient to looking at "how the couple is faring as a couple with cancer," says Karen Kayser, a professor at Boston College Graduate School of Social Work in Chestnut Hill, Mass.

Summer Getaway

Despite the steady decline in Mrs. O'Donnell's health, every summer the couple spends several weeks in the Catskills. They come to the home in Elka Park, N. Y., owned by Mrs. O'Donnell's family, where she spent summers as a girl. Staying in the house, filled with the same furniture and paintings that have always been there, allows them to remember a time before cancer transformed their relationship.

This is where they met in 1967. Mrs. O'Donnell, then 14, was painting sets at the local theater where she met Mr. O'Donnell, who had the lead(主角) in a summer-stock production(夏季轮演剧目) called "Fancy Meeting You Again." He was a 19-year-old college student working as a tennis instructor. They had their first kiss in her parents' kitchen after he brought her home from a dance. They married four years later, in a church down the road, when she was 18.

After more than two decades of marriage came Mrs. O'Donnell's cancer diagnosis. The couple had just moved to Huntington, Ind., from an affluent Boston suburb. Mr. O'Donnell had given up a banking job to teach economics at Huntington College, a 1,000-student Christian school. The Victorian house they bought near the main campus had a tarp(防水布) on the skylight(天窗) and no running water in the kitchen when they moved in.

At first, they tried not to let cancer overwhelm their relationship. When one of them felt frightened by Mrs. O'Donnell's treatments, they asked the other for a "cancer free" period. It could last an hour or a day, but during this time, they agreed not to talk about anything related to her health crisis.

On the two-hour drive to Indianapolis for chemotherapy treatments, Mrs. O'Donnell, an avid gardener, drew sketches, designing an arbor(藤架) she asked her husband to build for climbing plants. A stay-at-home mother, she tried to ensure her sons' lives continued as normally as possible. She arranged for neighbors to take the boys to school and sports practices. Her mother moved in for a while to take over cooking and cleaning.

The couple soon discovered they had extremely different coping styles, and this became an area of contention. Whenever someone asked Mrs. O'Donnell how she was doing with the chemotherapy, she gave a relentlessly positive answer—even if that someone was her husband...

In September 1995, about a month after Mrs. O'Donnell had finished her last chemotherapy treatment, Mr. O'Donnell brought her to the emergency room. She had a cold and felt weak; they wanted to make sure nothing was wrong.

The doctors admitted her for tests and that Sunday, when her husband came to visit, he found her lying in an intensive-care unit, hooked to a heart-monitor machine. Mrs. O'Donnell handed her husband some documents explaining the condition doctors had diagnosed. The drugs that killed her cancer tumor had also severely weakened her heart muscles. Without a heart transplant, she would die.

Mr. O'Donnell read the information in a panic, his eyes welling up with tears. But when he looked up, he was shocked to find that his wife had a smile on her face. "Jimmy," she said, her voice upbeat. "I don't have cancer."

The pity and sadness he felt seeing her lying in the hospital bed quickly gave way to another emotion: anger. "Why are you smiling?" he recalls demanding, his voice rising to a yell. "You have heart failure. You could die."

Looking back on it now, Mr. O'Donnell, 56, says his outburst occurred because "I felt managed by Lizzie, when what I wanted most of all was her honesty about her fears."

Mrs. O'Donnell remembers that moment differently. She says her greatest fear had been a recurrence of cancer, and she felt relieved to learn that she had heart problems instead. "I had grown to respect and fear cancer as a pernicious(致命的) and sneaky enemy," she says. "I felt the doctors knew a lot more about how to treat heart failure."

They realized their journey as a couple had suddenly diverged. They lived through the same events but experienced them in completely different ways. "We had always said we were in this together," says Mrs. O'Donnell. "But we weren't moving through it the same way."

If Mrs. O'Donnell was a half-hour late from a shopping trip, her husband feared the worst and lost his temper when she returned. He kept asking doctors questions at appointments, long after Mrs. O'Donnell felt there was a need. By April 1996, when Mrs. O'Donnell was admitted to the hospital to await her heart transplant, she no longer told him when the doctors would be coming to see her. She gave him only the broadest outlines of what the doctors said.

Once, Mr. O'Donnell learned that his wife had seen a gastrointestinal(胃肠的) specialist only after he saw an unfamiliar name on a bill. When he asked her about it, she told him that one of the consequences of her weakened heart was that other organs were starting to shut down. "I picked and chose what to tell him based on what I thought the toll would be to him," she says. "In preserving Jimmy, I was also preserving myself."

Holding Back(隐瞒)

Mr. O'Donnell constantly wanted to talk about what was happening. But his wife held back, because she started to feel that talking about it was a waste of time and too depressing. "Jimmy was always aware and ready to discuss what everything was like," she says. But how could she explain how it felt to have their youngest son, Jonny, then 7, visit her at the hospital, and her pain at having to say goodbye, unsure if she would ever see him again? "I don't think he could understand what that was like, leaving the children," she says. "I thought even if I talked and talked, there was no way he could ever know what that was really like."

Mr. O'Donnell says he was overwhelmed. "I wish for relief," he wrote in his journal in 1996 while his wife stayed at the hospital awaiting the transplant, "but it doesn't come." A born-again Christian like his wife, Mr. O'Donnell continued to go to church and keep up with a Bible-study group they had joined. But he found that his faith—not only religious faith but also in his marriage's ability to withstand such chronic stress—were being tested.

"There was never an issue that I would be unfaithful to Lizzie in finding someone else," he says. "It was an issue of being unfaithful by not being loving."

At the time of her mastectomy in 1995, Mrs. O'Donnell worried that the loss of her breast would affect their relationship. "I knew the adjustment would be hard," she says. But Mr. O'Donnell had an even more difficult time accepting the dramatic body changes that took place following Mrs. O'Donnell's heart transplant in June 1996.

Within weeks after the heart transplant, she gained more than 60 pounds. The high doses of steroids(类固醇) she was given to prevent her body from rejecting the new heart caused hair to grow all over her body. She says she had "so much hair on my arms that I could braid it, and rolls of fat on my back." The sudden transformation, she says, "was horrifying to me."

Mr. O'Donnell says he often watched their son Jonny play with his mother, oblivious to the fact that she looked completely different. "It didn't matter to him how his mother looked, that her face had grown round like a moon because of the steroids," he says. "He loved her and was blind to those changes and I was not. It is not something that I am proud of."

Since Mrs. O'Donnell's cancer treatment, Mr. O'Donnell's own health had started to deteriorate. He couldn't sleep at night. During the day, he felt his heart racing. He was anxious all the time. In 1997, he fell asleep at the wheel, drove off the road and ended up in a swamp. He emerged without a scratch.

The couple could no longer do the things they had always enjoyed—walks around the neighborhood after dinner, trips abroad to explore gardens, spontaneously deciding to go out for the evening. Mr. O'Donnell started taking on household chores his wife no longer had energy to do: making beds, washing dishes, laundry, vacuuming and grocery shopping. He dropped Jonny off at the bus in the morning and was there to pick him up in the afternoon. Sometimes Mrs. O'Donnell would feel better and be able to return to some of her old routines, but "it was always unpredictable," says Mr. O'Donnell.

He felt guilt, he says, about his inability to cope with all the changes. He even wondered if stresses he had put on her had somehow contributed to her cancer. But what he felt most, he says, was fear, that his wife would die and he wouldn't know how to carry on. When he pressed her to write letters about her wishes for her children that he could give to the boys if she died, she refused. She says she felt that doing so would have been admitting she was giving up. "You're going to slip away and I won't know key things," Mr. O'Donnell told her.

Four-Page Letter

Over the years, he kept pressing his wife to talk more. In March 1999, he wrote her a four-page letter outlining how overwhelmed he felt by taking over household chores, while continuing to work. He felt they needed to talk more about how their lives had changed, and that knowing how she felt might help him deal with his own fears. She thanked him for the letter and said they would discuss it. But when two weeks passed without her raising the issue again, he took matters into his own hands.

The couple had been attending Bible-study sessions every other Sunday night with male professors from the college and their wives. The couples met to discuss a particular passage and share events in their lives. At an April 12, 1999, session, Mr. O'Donnell brought up his communication problems with his wife. He asked the group members to pray either for the couple to communicate better or for Mr. O'Donnell to accept their level of communication as it was.

Mrs. O'Donnell was shocked by the unexpected public airing of their difficulties, even among people she considered friends. She ran from the room crying. When they got home, she spent the night in the bedroom downstairs and refused to discuss the incident. "I felt at that point that there had been enough talking," she says. "Things are a mess," Mr. O'Donnell wrote in his journal that night.

From time to time during Mrs. O'Donnell's illnesses, she slept alone downstairs. Sometimes she stayed there when side effects from her chemotherapy treatments kept her in the bathroom all night long. Before the heart transplant, she was simply too weak to climb the stairs to their bedroom on the third floor. But even after the transplant, she began sleeping downstairs more often.

Talking about the physical changes in Mrs. O'Donnell's body didn't seem to alter the tension. "I remember telling Jim, 'I can't help what's happening,' "she says. "It didn't make any difference to Jim. I could see the look in his eyes." Yet, there were times, she says, when she understood her husband's difficulty adjusting. When she looked in the mirror, she didn't recognize herself. "It struck me over and over afresh every morning, just like it did Jim," she says. "I was not blind to what was happening to my body. Neither of us liked it."

When Mr. O'Donnell was invited to a function at the college, she would spend considerable time dressing up and fixing her hair. "I did absolutely the best I could, and there was no comment, no 'you look nice tonight,' "she says. "There was nothing. It was a great sorrow that I carried." Mr. O'Donnell doesn't dispute the hurt he inflicted. "I was a monster," he says.

Each evening, Mrs. O'Donnell would suggest that she sleep downstairs so she wouldn't disturb her husband. Sometimes he would protest, but in the summer of 1999, he stopped. Mrs. O'Donnell snored at night, most likely due to physical changes from the medications she was taking. The medications also resulted in her having uncontrollable leg spasms(痉挛) at night, causing her to kick him. For three months, they didn't sleep in the same room. "I was giving up," he says about that period in their marriage.

But Mrs. O'Donnell insisted they find a way to be together. She suggested giving up their queen-size bed and buying two twin beds. Mr. O'Donnell resisted, saying they had to sleep in the same bed or in different rooms. Hoping to save their marriage, he eventually agreed to the change, and they started sharing the same room again. He bought ear plugs and a sound machine to deal with the snoring.

He also spoke with a doctor about his constant fears, and was taking medication that helped lift his depression. Mr. O'Donnell says he began to accept the idea that "there is to be no closure."

In some ways, he says, his prayers at the Bible-study session that caused his wife to cry had been answered. Mrs. O'Donnell tried to talk more about her feelings. And he began to realize that her refusal to endlessly discuss her fears was one of the ways she kept going. "I started to wonder if by pushing her to cope in a different way, I might be hurting her, maybe even shortening her life," he says.

While their communication has improved since then, the issue still comes up. A few weeks ago, Mr. O'Donnell wanted to talk again about all they had endured. Mrs. O'Donnell demurred(反对). "These are the good times," she told him. "Everything is fine."

Both of them have spoken about their experiences in efforts to help others in similar situations. Earlier this year, a collection of Mr. O'Donnell's letters about his wife's cancer diagnosis and heart transplant, called "Letters for Lizzie," was published by a Christian publishing house. The letters chronicle the vicissitudes(变化，波动) of Mrs. O'Donnell's illnesses and some of the difficulties they faced in their marriage.

At the back of the book there is a picture of a much younger Mrs. O'Donnell, holding Jonny as a baby. Her dark hair is cut in a fashionable style, and there's a wide smile on her face. It bothers her, she says, to hear her husband talk at book readings about the toll her illnesses have taken on the way she looks. She says it makes her feel he's implying, "I was once so beautiful and then poof." He says he doesn't feel that way.

When she is feeling well, Mrs. O'Donnell now volunteers 20 hours a week at a hospice(临终关怀医院) where she was once a patient. Mr. O'Donnell says he is moved by her commitment. He recently nominated her for an award recognizing exceptional volunteers who work under challenging circumstances. Mrs. O'Donnell won the award this year for Indiana. Sometimes, Mr. O'Donnell says, he wonders "if she tells the patients things about her sickness that she won't tell me." Mrs. O'Donnell says that isn't the case.

As the years have gone by, they have increasingly found themselves alone. Their older sons, Nick and Andrew, have finished college. Nick is married. Jonny is now 16 and has his first girlfriend. He didn't want to come to Elka Park this summer with his parents. They realize this may have been the last summer he'll spend with them.

In the past few months, there have been what the couple calls "moments of grace." Mrs. O'Donnell has felt better and had more stamina(精力). She is taking fewer steroids these days, so the side effects are less severe. Earlier this year, she suddenly started losing weight. At first, she thought the cancer was back and had her doctor run full body scans. All the tests were negative. Doctors don't have an explanation for the weight loss but it has marked a change in their relationship.

"I don't feel beautiful to myself," she says, "but I recognize myself again. I look more like the way I imagined I would look at the age of 51." Mr. O'Donnell has been more relaxed and affectionate, she says. Mr. O'Donnell acknowledges the weight loss has made a difference. "I regret feeling put off(使厌恶) by her. I knew it wasn't right," he said. "I look at what is happening now as a gift."

Last month, Mrs. O'Donnell's sisters came to visit. They sat on the porch with the couple and recalled the two years when Mrs. O'Donnell had cancer and then a heart transplant as a nightmare that had thankfully ended. But for Mr. and Mrs. O'Donnell, it is never over.

Mrs. O'Donnell says she is always aware that the average transplanted heart lasts 10 years and that she has already had hers for eight years. If the medication she is taking to help her kidneys work loses effectiveness, she faces the prospect of dialysis(血液透析) or a kidney transplant. They don't make long-term plans. "I never think about what we'll do together when Jim retires," says Mrs. O'Donnell. She says the furthest out she has planned is this Christmas, when her son and daughter-in-law will visit.

They also try to see themselves as any middle-age married couple. On a recent day, Mr. O'Donnell, dressed in khakis and a blue polo shirt, brings out lemonade and they sit next to one another on wood chairs painted the same lime green as the porch, their feet touching under the table. Last month, they celebrated their 33rd wedding anniversary. They still like to take long drives together, explore old homes and find a new restaurant to try.

Last summer, Mrs. O'Donnell was too weak to walk in the hills surrounding the house in Elka Park. Her husband, sons and daughter-in-law hiked to a monument erected in 1868 by a grieving husband whose wife died in childbirth. Mr. O'Donnell wanted to take a group picture at the top for the family's Christmas card, and Mrs. O'Donnell was upset she couldn't go. This year, she and her husband walked there together. She climbed to the top, looking out at the trees and mountains, "and saw a view I thought I'd never see again," she says. The next day, she was so weak she spent the entire day in bed. But she believes, "If Jim and I didn't have these tiny moments together, we wouldn't make it."

A few weeks ago, Mrs. O'Donnell was in the kitchen of their Elka Park home when

Jonny suddenly asked her, "Mom, do you think that someday I will be happily married?"

The question caught her off-guard(让某人措手不及). She thinks the issue was on his mind not only because he has a girlfriend but also because of what he has seen his parents endure during the past 10 years. She says she didn't hesitate with her reply. "Yes, Jonny," she told him, "I think you will be happily married."

Does she consider herself happily married? "Yes," she said. "I do."

Mr. O'Donnell's reply was more cautious. "In an imperfect world, I am as happily married as I think anybody can be," he said.

A look of surprise seemed to flicker across Mrs. O'Donnell's face. The plate of pasta she cooked and was about to serve remained suspended in her hands as she considered what to say next. "That sounds like a qualifier to me," she said, her voice calm and soft. "But I think I know what you mean." Then another meal together got under way.

一、作者背景

Columbia University President Lee C. Bollinger presents Amy Dockser Marcus with the 2005 Pulitzer Prize in Beat Reporting.

埃米·岛克瑟·马库斯（Amy Dockser Marcus）：1987 年以优异成绩毕业于哈佛大学。毕业后她先供职于《美国律师杂志》（*American Lawyer*），次年加入《华尔街日报》，先是报道法律新闻，后又远赴中东担任驻外记者。2000 年至 2002 年她离开《华尔街日报》，成为《钱经》（*Money*）杂志的记者，后来又返回《华尔街日报》。马库斯撰写的报道曾多次获奖，她还出版过几本关于阿以冲突和中东历史的书籍。马库斯在 2004 年和 2005 年分别获得哈佛大学医学院和匹兹堡大学癌症中心的媒体奖学金，潜心研究癌症报道方法。

马库斯因于 2004 年 3 月至 12 月期间在《华尔街日报》发表系列文章而获得 2005 年普利策专题报道奖，获奖文章共有 9 篇，全部是有关癌症病患的报道，涉及病患与家人的生活、癌症治疗新手段、对癌症的研究、新药品试验、如何与病魔做斗争、早期发现癌症的新方法等一系列话题。文章有对当事人生活的白描，有对科学知识的普及，也有为读者提供的健康资讯。作者在哈佛大学医学院和匹兹堡大学癌症中心的经历显然为她的写作打下了坚实的基础。除了对医学知识进行深入浅出的解释外，她的作品通过对生活琐事入微的刻画展示了癌症病患者家庭种种不为人知的痛苦与坚强。她的文字不仅细腻贴切，而且有很强烈的画面感。正如普利策奖评选委员会在赞词中说的那样，马库斯讲述故事的手法非常精湛（masterful）。

二、《华尔街日报》

THE WALL STREET JOURNAL.

What's News—

Oil Find Will Spur Industry Change

Wal-Mart Stores Drop Cookie-Cutter Approach

The January 2nd，2007 front page of *the Wall Street Journal*

《华尔街日报》是道琼斯公司的旗舰报纸，是全球最具影响的国际性财经报纸之一，除美国本土版以外，还有欧洲版和亚洲版。道琼斯公司于 1882 年由三位年轻的美国记者查尔斯·道（Charles Dow）、爱德华·琼斯（Edward Jones）和查尔斯·博格斯特莱斯（Charles Bergstresser）创立。《华尔街日报》在这三人的努力下于 1889 年 7 月 8 日问世。1902 年，已在道琼斯工作多年的记者克莱伦斯·巴伦（Clarence Barron）买下了公司的控制权。这四个人共同创立了《华尔街日报》的独立、大无畏的财经报道风格。巴伦去世后，《华尔街日报》一直由其后人班克罗夫特家族（the Bancroft family）控制。2007 年，默多克的新闻集团收购了道琼斯公司，《华尔街日报》也因此再易其主。

伯纳德·基尔格（Bernard Kilgore）是《华尔街日报》历史上的一位重要人物。他 1941 年成为《华尔街日报》执行总编，并于 1945—1967 年担任道琼斯公司首席执行官。基尔格奠定了今天《华尔街日报》的版面设计风格，并将报纸涵盖的内容扩展到商业、经济以及消费者等与商业息息相关的各个生活领域。20 世纪 60 年代，《华尔街日报》又增加了社会问题、科技、教育、外交等方面的内容。

长期以来，《华尔街日报》一直是美国发行量最大的报纸。就财经报道而言，《华尔街日报》的主要竞争对手是英国的《金融日报》(*Financial Times*)。

《华尔街日报》言论版的政治立场比较保守，但是，有学者研究发现，《华尔街日报》刊登的新闻是偏向自由派观点的。其哲学是支持“自由人民和自由市场”。

截至 2013 年，《华尔街日报》已先后获得 37 次普利策奖。

三、课文背景

人们往往把癌症和死亡画上等号，尤其是晚期癌症患者更会受到极大的心理冲击，感到极度恐惧和绝望，这些都是我们可以想象到的。随着科技的进步，临床诊断与治疗技术的日益完善，癌症病人的存活率、治愈率也在显著增加。但“治愈”了的癌症患者会面临哪些身体上、精神上和情感上的困难呢？本文的作者“另辟蹊径”，将这些平时我们无法在媒体上接触到的故事用平实的语言展现出来，为读者带来别样的感触。其精湛的写作手法尤其值得我们学习。

四、作者主要观点

(1)Do you think the reporter is describing the ordeal of the O'Dennells merely for the sake of story-telling? What might be some of her other purposes in writing this story?

(2)How would you describe the socio-economic class of the O'Donnells? What clues can you find in the story? Do you think this factor plays a role in the cancer-fighting endeavor?

五、写作风格与手法

(1)What has intrigued you most about this article in terms of its writing style?

(2)What, for the average reader, is the source of interest in the news contained in the story?

(3)Is the description detailed or suggestive? Is it effective? Why?

(4)What information is played up as the feature in the first few paragraphs?

(5)Are the parts of sentences combined in firm, closely knit construction? Provide specific examples.

(6)Are the paragraphs closely connected? Provide specific examples.

(7)Is the style concise or wordy? Provide specific examples.

(8)In what way is it a “masterful story” as described in the citation?

(9)How are different perspectives on the same issue presented? Are they presented in an effective way? Why or why not?

(10)What's your overall impression on Mr. and Mrs. O'Donnell? Are they presented as “role models” for others to emulate?

(11)Is there any important information on the O'Donnells that the reporter fails to provide in this story?

Part Three: Further exploring the text

一、语言点讲解

1. 标题中的“sickness and health”直译为“疾病与健康”，这是基督教婚礼上牧师要求夫妇双方重复的结婚誓言（wedding vows）的重要组成部分，期待夫妻双方同风雨、共患难，不弃不离。下面是一段比较有代表性的誓言：“I,(Bride/Groom),take you(Groom/Bride),to be my lawfully wedded(wife/husband),to have and to hold from this day forward,for better or for worse,for richer,for poorer,in sickness and in health, to love and to cherish;from this day forward until death do us part.”另外，本文标题写得也很有技巧，短短30个字就把整篇文章的主要矛盾与核心内容都概括出来了，尤其是标题中的unexpected，tensions，angry和truce马上能抓住读者的眼球。

2. 在讲故事时，衔接是十分重要的。我们看看这篇文章的前七段。文章导语在交代故事主人公的最核心信息后用一个字“cancer”结尾，为整篇文章定下基调，给读者留下深刻印象。第二段马上介绍女主人公O'Donnell太太罹患癌症的过程，结尾引用医生的诊断，即她患上了乳腺癌，已经到了晚期，只有5%的存活率。第三段用了一个简单句“She proved the doctors wrong.”让读者的心情为之一振。读者在感到欣慰的同时也通过该段最后一句O'Donnell太太的原话感受到了她的坚强。但第四段的开头却给读者的心头泼了一瓢凉水：“Her survival came at a price.”保住了性命的O'Donnell太太需要付出什么代价呢？除了治疗癌症所带来的新的健康问题（在第四段和第五段有详细交代），癌症还影响了原本温馨和睦的夫妻关系（第六段第一句点明了这一点），这恐怕是一般读者无法体会的。记者这时大段引用O'Donnell先生的日记和评论，试图让读者亲历其境，了解主人公的痛苦。在讲完这个故事后，记者很自然地过渡到这篇新闻的主旨，即关注癌症存活者生活质量这一不太被大众关注的问题。我们看到，记者的讲故事技巧很高超，环环相扣，毫不拖沓，读者在不知不觉中就会被吸引，进而有兴趣把文章读下去。你能在文章的其他部分找到类似的例子吗？

3. “Why are you smiling?” he recalls demanding,his voice rising to a yell.

“Demand”一词的语气非常强硬，几乎是命令的口吻，用英文解释就是“to ask for urgently or forcefully”。这个字与后面的yell让读者马上嗅到了病房里极度紧张的空气。

4. A born-again Christian like his wife, Mr. O'Donnell continued to go to church and keep up with a Bible-study group they had joined.

这里的“born-again Christian”指“重生的基督徒”，这是福音教派基督徒及原教旨基督徒称呼自己宗教信仰的俗称。“福音教派基督徒”（Evangelical Christian）在美国通常用以指那些强调个人“属灵经验”重要性的新教基督徒，属于基督徒中较为保守的人群。而“原教旨基督徒”（Fundamentalist Christian）则通常是“福音教派基督徒”中立场最为激进的一群。“重生”是指基督徒自己经历过某种属灵的经验，“接受基督成为生命中的救主”，从而觉得以前都白活了，真正的生命现在才开始。

5. On a recent day, Mr. O'Donnell, dressed in khakis and a blue polo shirt, brings out lemonade and they sit next to one another on wood chairs painted the same lime green as the porch, their feet touching under the table.

记者寥寥几笔就为我们生动地勾画出当时的场景。一方面，我们看到了“画面”中的几种颜色：卡其色（的裤子）、蓝色（的 T 恤衫）、透明色（的柠檬水）和橙绿色（的木椅子和门廊）。另一方面，我们还能通过对 O'Donnell 动作细节的描写（两人紧挨着坐下，两双脚在桌底轻轻触碰）体会主人公的心理活动。这看似简单的描写其实体现了作者敏锐的观察力和细腻的语言感受力。

二、中西文化比较

论“互助”

在本文中，作者提到 O'Donnell 夫妇每隔一周参加一次“读经会” (bible-study sessions)。有一次，O'Donnell 先生谈到他与妻子之间有些感情隔阂而产生了沟通上的问题，希望大家能够帮他出出主意，改善他们的关系。在读经会上，大家除了互相帮助和安慰外，还一起祈祷，分享喜悦。这种小组形式的宗教活动在美国基督教社区较为普遍，是美国宗教文化的一个重要部分。

“互助”和“互相疗伤”是《圣经》中的教义。《圣经》上说：“你们不可停止聚会，好像那些停止惯了的人，倒要彼此劝勉。既知道那日子临近，就更当如此。”(Let us not give up meeting together, as some are in the habit of doing, but let us encourage one another—and all the more as you see the Day.)（希伯来书 10：25，《新国际版圣经》）。可以说，宗教为美国社会提供了一种组织社会的形式，一套调适和整合、凝聚社会的机制和体系。

在我国，在一些基督教团体中，也会有类似的做法，但多数人依靠其他社会组织和团体，或者更确切地说靠家人或朋友。当你的生活出现麻烦或苦恼时，可能第一个向家人或朋友寻求帮助。家人的重要性不必说了，朋友的重要性再说几句。《论语》中写到“有朋自远方来，不亦说乎！”季羡林先生在《论朋友》中写到，在中国几千年的历史上，重视友谊的故事不可胜数。最著名的是管鲍之交、钟子期和伯牙的故事等等。刘、关、张三结义更是有口皆碑。一直到今天，我们还讲究“哥儿们义气”，发展到最高程度，就是“为朋友两肋插刀”。另外，我们还常听到一句话就是“出门在外靠朋友”，以及周华健唱的“朋友一生一起走”。

在中国，“朋友圈”似乎也是社会的一种组织形式，是凝聚社会的一个重要机制。希望朋友们多聚会，多互助，多关心。

无论是通过读经会提供的互助，还是通过家庭和朋友的互助，形式并不重要，重要的是互助精神是社会的基本精神，体现了对生命和尊严的尊重、维护和关切。

三、语言练习

1. 请用英语解释下列句子。

(1)... they tried not to let cancer overwhelm their relationship.

(2)“I felt managed by Lizzie, when what I wanted most of all was her honesty about her fears."

(3)"In preserving Jimmy, I was also preserving myself."

(4)But when two weeks passed without her raising the issue again, he took matters into his own hands.

(5)Mr. O'Donnell says he began to accept the idea that "there is to be no closure."

(6)"I was once so beautiful and then poof."

2. 请将下列短语翻译成英文，并比较中英文表达方式的异同。

(1)……要付出代价

(2)慢性健康问题

(3)心力衰竭

(4)让他们的婚姻亮起了红灯

(5)藤蔓植物/攀爬植物

(6)全职母亲

(7)应对困难/解决问题的方式

(8)泪如泉涌

(9)癌症复发

(10)对种种变化视而不见

(11)在开车时睡着了

(12)(司机)冲出路面

(13)默默离开

(14)化疗副作用

3. 请将下面的句子或段落翻译成中文，并比较中英文表达方式的异同。

(1) These "all have been 'little deaths,'" Mr. O'Donnell added, "that have powerfully tugged me to despair and grief."

(2) Staying in the house, filled with the same furniture and paintings that have always been there, allows them to remember a time before cancer transformed their relationship.

(3)On the two-hour drive to Indianapolis for chemotherapy treatments, Mrs. O'Donnell, an avid gardener, drew sketches, designing an arbor she asked her husband to build for climbing plants.

(4) Whenever someone asked Mrs. O'Donnell how she was doing with the chemotherapy, she gave a relentlessly positive answer—even if that someone was her husband.

(5)The doctors admitted her for tests and that Sunday, when her husband came to visit, he found her lying in an intensive-care unit, hooked to a heart-monitor machine.

(6)She says she had "so much hair on my arms that I could braid it, and rolls of fat on my back."

(7)When she looked in the mirror, she didn't recognize herself. "It struck me over and over afresh every morning, just like it did Jim," she says.

(8)"In an imperfect world, I am as happily married as I think anybody can be."

Part Four: Exploring beyond the text

一、自我反思

1. 我学到了什么？我要如何改进？

2. 一篇高质量的专题新闻报道的基本标准是什么？我能清楚地告诉别人吗？该篇报道的记者埃米·岛克瑟·马库斯是如何达到这些标准的？我能向别人解释清楚吗？

二、知识扩展

1. 从广义上说，本单元的两篇新闻都可以算作"健康传播"（health communication）的具体例子。在西方，对健康传播的研究已日趋成熟。请查找资料，了解这个领域的定义、研究目的、研究方法、研究案例等，并讨论在中国背景下从事健康传播的可能性与意义。

2. 收集有临终关怀医院（hospice）的资料和报道。

三、能力扩展

1. 就此篇报道写一篇 500 字左右的评论。

2. 就你最关注的一个高等教育问题采访身边的老师和同学，用中文写一篇 1000 字以内的教育类专题报道。注意学习本单元作者转承启合的技巧。

3. 仔细观察几名室友在宿舍的一次聊天，尤其是大家的表情、神态、动作和语言，并写一篇 500 字左右的文章。

Text B The challenge of kickball[(按棒球规则进行的)儿童足球游戏]

After leukemia(白血病), family struggles to define "normal". Jack Streeter, 8, joins ranks of cancer survivors coping after treatment.

BY Amy Dockser Marcus

Wall Street Journal

June 9, 2004

导读： 这篇课文的主人公是 8 岁的 Jack Streeter，他 3 岁时就罹患白血病。长期的放疗和化疗虽然保住了他的性命，但却给他带来了一系列副作用，不啻为一枚枚定时炸弹。除了各种健康隐忧以外，Jack 和父母发现很难重新返回原来的生活状态。随着癌症治疗水平的提高，病人的愈后精神状态和生活质量问题变得越来越重要。实际上，在癌症治疗结束后，病人及其亲属面临的各种压力反倒更大，而这一点往往不为人知。记者讲述这个故事的用意之一大概也是要教育读者吧。

NATICK, Mass. —This month, Jack Streeter will finish the second grade, his first full year at school since being diagnosed with leukemia. By any measure, it will be a celebratory moment.

Two years ago, his parents thought he was going to die. Now the 8-year-old boy is back at school, and thriving. He sits in the top reading group in his class. He just earned a purple belt(紫带,高级别空手道练习者)in karate(空手道)and hit a single (一垒打,击球手安全到达一垒的一击)at a recent baseball game. This summer, he plans to go to camp.

Still, this year has been anything but ordinary for the family. After years of focusing on saving Jack's life, they are now facing a new challenge: trying to get back to normal.

"There are so many things we have to worry about for the rest of his life," says Jack's mother, Debby. "But how can I say that without sounding ungrateful, when I am so happy he is alive?"

Reminders are frequent that Jack's treatment will continue to cause him health problems. In the past two years, he had 13 cavities(cavity:蛀洞)filled and two teeth pulled. His years of chemotherapy and radiation(放射疗法)put him at increased risk for a range of dental problems. He underwent two surgeries to remove cataracts(白内障)in his eyes, another side effect of the drugs. His mother insists he wear sunscreen whenever he's outside because the full-body radiation makes him more susceptible to melanoma(黑素瘤). He is tested regularly for potential cognitive(认知的)and learning issues.

There have been less-anticipated problems too. Mrs. Streeter, 43, who stopped working two years ago to take care of Jack full time, says she feels adrift now, unsure whether he is well enough for her to return to work. For her husband, Larry, 48, Jack's recovery is bringing back uncomfortable echoes of an ordeal in his own life. The couple say they find it difficult to engage in small talk with other parents in this affluent suburb, 25 miles from Boston. Their relationship with many neighbors, people who rallied around the family after Jack got sick, has become strained now that he is better.

"For many people," says Scott Armstrong, Jack's oncologist at the Dana-Farber Cancer Institute in Boston, "one of the most stressful parts of cancer comes when the treatment stops."

For decades, cancer treatment has focused on trying to save a person's life, not on how it was lived afterward. But in recent years, new therapies have helped increase the number of people surviving five years or more after diagnosis. With this growing success has come the recognition that cancer survivors have special physical and emotional needs. Many will finish treatment and go back to their old lives, only to find that their lives aren't the same.

The President's Cancer Panel, an advisory board established by Congress, released a report on Friday calling for more services to deal with problems people face after treatment is over. The report concludes that some survivors suffer depression and other psychological issues for years.

"We have always focused on how patients physically survive the toxicity(毒性)of treatment," says Mary Morris, survivorship-research coordinator at the University of Nebraska Medical Center in Omaha, one of several hospitals that have launched studies tracking the long-term health, social and emotional issues of cancer survivors. "But we need to learn more about how they emotionally survive and get on with their lives." Children with cancer pose special challenges of survival, since their experience also transforms the lives of their parents, and often their wider community.

Jack was diagnosed with cancer when he was just 3 years old. His mother noticed he was unusually fatigued, and while giving him a bath, saw bruises all over his body. He spent the next two years undergoing chemotherapy. He seemed to respond, and doctors were optimistic he would be among the 80% of children who are disease-free after two years of treatment.

But in 2001, just a few weeks after starting kindergarten, Jack relapsed(复发). When doctors told his father the leukemia had returned, "I feared this was it," Mr. Streeter recalls. His best option, doctors said, was a bone-marrow transplant(造血干细胞移植).

After the transplant, Jack stayed home for eight months, because he had no resistance to disease. He had a tutor until he got stronger. When he was finally well enough to go back to school in April 2003, his parents were overjoyed—and conflicted.

"We can't begin to tell everyone how long we've waited for this day!" Mr. Streeter wrote in an online journal entry. "On the one hand, we were so happy to see Jack return to school with his friends," he wrote. But they were also nervous, he said, knowing Jack's exposure to bacteria and viruses was going to increase.

Following Rules

This year, Nell Getz, Jack's second-grade teacher at Natick Memorial Elementary School, says she has focused on getting him used to following rules. Some things he needed to learn are common issues for children who haven't spent much time in a classroom. When Jack knew the answer to a question, he shouted it out without raising his hand. He had a hard time standing quietly in line.

In order to support Jack's transition back to school, four children from his neighborhood were placed in class with him. Mrs. Getz says his two closest friends were always trying to take care of him, bringing him paper or books. She put a stop to that, insisting Jack fend for himself (照料自己). "More than the other children here, Jack doesn't want to be different," she says. "He doesn't want to be the sick kid anymore."

Earlier in the year, Mrs. Getz tried to get Jack to talk about his cancer experiences in class but he repeatedly refused, she says. She stopped asking. When she asked the children to write about something they did that was courageous, Jack wrote about breaking a board with his hands at karate class. One morning, in a group discussion, a girl mentioned Jack had been in the hospital. Mrs. Getz asked him if he wanted to say something about that. Jack declined, she says, looking down at his sneakers.

Where Jack struggles in school is mainly at recess, Mrs. Getz says, when his closest friends go off to play kickball. Self-conscious about being less athletic, Jack, who has close-cropped blond hair and glasses, stands on the sidelines. When he first returned to school, he didn't know the rules of baseball, basketball or other games the kids played in gym. He had spent a lot of time in bed and playing video games. His face was puffy from the steroids he took, and he had very little stamina.

The Streeter Family: Jack, Larry, Annika and Debby

A few months ago, one of his friends was reaching to pick up a mitten that fell on the floor and elbowed Jack in the stomach as he got up. Jack hit the boy in the jaw, knocking him to the ground, and got sent to the principal's office.

Jack still won't talk about the incident. His mother thinks it came out of his growing frustration at always being the smallest, at having to try so hard to keep up physically with his friends. "When he first went back to school, he got a pass," says Mrs. Streeter. "He was the kid who had cancer. Now, he's treated like everyone else. I think he was tired of people pushing him."

For Mr. Streeter, Jack's struggles remind him of his own. Twenty years ago, at the age of 28, doctors found a large mass in Mr. Streeter's chest. At first, they thought it was benign(良性的). But during surgery, after they broke his ribs to get to it, they saw it had grown close to his heart and couldn't be removed. More tests indicated it was malignant(恶性的), and the cancer had spread to lymph nodes(淋巴结) in his abdomen. Mr. Streeter, who was married to his first wife and had a 1-year-old child at the time, underwent a year of treatment, including chemotherapy and radiation. He lost all his hair and, at 5-feet-8, dropped to 106 pounds.

He pushed himself to go back to his job as an information-technology specialist as soon as he could. Friends would stop by his desk, he says, tell him he looked terrible, and wonder why he wasn't home resting. Instead, he started working out everyday. "I wanted to prove to everyone that I was healthy, that I had beaten it," says Mr. Streeter, who keeps in shape by training for an annual 160-mile bike ride to raise money for cancer research.

Mr. Streeter says he and his first wife grew apart(合不到一起). Two years after being diagnosed with cancer, he moved out of the house. The couple, who had two children together, later divorced.

He knew Debby from work and they started dating. They married, and had Jack and his younger sister, Annika, now 5. "I have been reliving everything since Jack got diagnosed," Mr. Streeter says. "Not just the being sick part, but also the difficulties in going back to your regular life."

New Focus

In April, Mrs. Streeter was in the gym at Jack's school, which was holding its annual "jumpathon"(跳绳筹款) for charity. The gym was packed with children and parents watching third-and fourth-graders jumping rope. Music blared, children shouted. The students were raising funds for the American Heart Association.

For the previous two years, the event raised money for cancer research. The first year it was called "Jump for Jack," and children wore T-shirts with Jack's name on them. Last year, when Jack was able to attend class for the final months of first grade, they called it the "Jack is Back" jumpathon. The children raised a total of more than $30,000 in those two years.

Todd Kiley, the physical-education instructor who spearheaded the drive, says now that Jack is at school full time, he thought it was time to focus on another cause. Next year, Jack will be jumping rope with others in the third grade. "I didn't want to put that kind of pressure on him," says Mr. Kiley, "having him jump rope for something associated with himself. I don't want to single him out."

Mrs. Streeter looked around at the gym, decorated with banners. Jack's name was nowhere to be found. "It's strange to be here just as another parent coming to a school event," she says. "Strange but good." Yet this year, when children knocked on her door asking for a pledge(捐款), she says she was reminded how hard it is to put everything behind them. Confused, the children forgot the name of the charity and said they were collecting money for "jumping for Jack."

It hasn't been easy for the Streeters' neighbors to move on either. In many ways, Jack's health dominated the life of the neighborhood for years, and the family acknowledges an outpouring of support. But now that Jack's treatment is over, "our relationship with the Streeters is not the same as it once was," says Rick Savoia, one of the neighbors. "We miss the closeness."

When Jack was diagnosed in 1999, Mr. Savoia's wife, Tina, was the first person Mrs. Streeter called. Mrs. Savoia later organized the neighbors so that someone cooked food for the Streeters every night. The couple frequently babysat Annika so the Streeters could stay with Jack in the hospital.

One day, after visiting Jack, Mr. Savoia says it hit him that it could have been his son, Nick—who is one of Jack's friends—lying in that hospital bed. Mr. Savoia, who had never been a runner, started training for the Boston Marathon as part of a Dana-Farber program to raise money for cancer research. Mr. Savoia has raised more than $13,000 every year for the past four years running the Marathon in honor of Jack.

Mr. Savoia's eyes welled up as he described how, every year before the Marathon started, he wrote the words, "For Jack," on the front of his shirt. Whenever Mr. Savoia started to falter and wasn't sure he would finish, he says there was always someone on the sidelines that called out, "Keep going for Jack!" That still inspires him, he says.

In February, Mr. Savoia and Mr. Streeter went out for beer. Mr. Savoia says he confronted Mr. Streeter, asking him why he stands apart(远离)when the families watch their kids playing baseball, and why he no longer goes to as many neighborhood functions. For both men, the conversation was the first time they'd talked openly about what had been simmering beneath the surface. It also revealed how the end of Jack's treatment has widened, not closed, the gap between their lives.

Mr. Streeter told his friend that he finds it tough to join in the light-hearted banter (轻松幽默的谈话) of his neighbors. It's hard for others to appreciate that Jack's immunizations were totally wiped out by chemotherapy and he remains more vulnerable to infection than other children. He also articulated aloud for the first time his deepest fear: that even now, more than two years after Jack's bone-marrow transplant, Jack might die from his disease—that he could relapse or get another cancer. Mr. Savoia says his feelings were hurt, though, when Mr. Streeter added, "You don't get it."

"Maybe we don't get it totally because it's not happening to our child," Mr. Savoia said in a later interview. "But we've tried as hard as we can to get it. If we slip up(出差错)sometimes, if we make a mistake or miss something, I think it should be forgiven." He says he knows the Streeters are still struggling with how to return to normal life. He wants that life to include his family but concedes he isn't sure it will. "I don't know what their definition of normal is anymore," he says.

Mr. and Mrs. Streeter say they aren't sure either. In March, the couple spent a weekend at a retreat sponsored by a camp for children with chronic or life-threatening illnesses. As they sat in a room with 20 other couples who had shared similar experiences, Mr. Streeter said, "This is where I feel I belong." At one point, a priest spoke to the group, telling them it's their responsibility to learn how to live in a world of smaller hurts and more easily corrected grievances. "We've expected others to understand our world and they can't," Mr. Streeter says. "But can we go back to their lives? I don't think it's possible."

Jack's health will need to be closely monitored for the rest of his life. Mrs. Streeter says she recently looked up the medications that Jack used to take on a Web site run by the Children's Oncology Group, a consortium of hospitals that treat pediatric(小儿科的) cancer patients. One of his chemotherapy drugs, methotrexate, puts him at a higher risk for learning and memory problems, according to the group. It said ifosfamide, which Jack received after his relapse, increases his risk of getting a second cancer.

For children who have had the kind of radiation treatment that Jack had, there is a 95% or higher chance that they will be sterile(无生育能力), according to Charles Sklar, director of long-term follow-up at Memorial Sloan-Kettering Cancer Center in New York. Radiation to the brain, which Jack underwent twice, can also stunt(阻碍……发育) growth. Worried because Jack is physically smaller than his peers, his parents recently took him to an endocrinologist(内分泌科医生)to discuss the possibility of taking growth hormones.

At Memorial Sloan-Kettering, child-cancer survivors are tested for cognitive problems every year to two years, even through college. Jack gets similar exams on a regular basis. "Problems can emerge for the first time 10 to 15 years down the line," says Dr. Sklar. "Radiation involves a progressive insult to the brain."

Now that Jack has passed the two-year mark since his bone-marrow transplant, the danger of relapse is receding, says Dr. Armstrong, his oncologist. But then, the doctor leaned over and knocked on a wood panel on the wall(在英语国家，人们认为用手指敲击墙上的木板可以确保好运). After Jack completed the standard treatment of two years of chemotherapy, his parents threw a big party to celebrate in June 2001. Dr. Armstrong attended. At the time, it seemed Jack had responded successfully to the treatment.

When Jack relapsed a few months later, Dr. Armstrong was devastated. "I will never go to another patient's party again," he says.

Jack's unwillingness to talk about his experiences is another source of worry for his parents. According to the President's Cancer Panel report, 20% of childhood-cancer survivors experience posttraumatic stress disorder(创伤后压力心理障碍症), sometimes years after treatment ends. On the advice of a social worker at Dana-Farber, Mrs. Streeter started keeping a scrapbook of Jack's cancer journey. Someday, she believes, he may want to discuss what happened to him.

For now, Jack prefers to put cancer behind him. On a recent morning, he was playing in the backyard with his sister. Dressed in his uniform for baseball practice, he spread a deck of trading cards(印有棒球明星等的卡片) on the table on the porch. "I wasn't into sports at first," Jack said. "Now I want to do what my friends do."

He said his friends don't ask him anymore about what it was like to have cancer. "I don't really like to talk about it," Jack said. "We like to talk about sports." When asked what he missed most when he was sick and couldn't go to school, he looked up from the cards for the first time. "Everything," he said. "I missed everything."

Mrs. Streeter says that, in some ways, Jack has been more successful than his parents in finding his way back to the routines and rituals of everyday life. "For me, I never feel I belong in the same world as my neighbors," she says.

Annika needed to get ready for a birthday party and couldn't find her friend's present. She wanted her hair to be brushed and braided. Jack asked to hit some baseballs before practice started. He debated whether he should wear cleats(防滑鞋) instead of his sneakers. "People are scared about what happened to us, what happened to Jack," said Mrs. Streeter, as she listened to her children's chatter. "They want us to go back to normal quickly because the sooner we do, they can put away their fears and go back to normal too."

She's realized that surviving cancer involves more than physical recovery, she said. "I keep waiting to go back to the way things were," Mrs. Streeter said. "But then I think: What if that doesn't happen? What if this is normal?"

Unit Four International Reporting
国际报道

单元导航

本单元将讨论国际新闻。本单元共有两篇文章，皆以俄罗斯与车臣民族之间的矛盾为话题。课文 A 描述了由车臣分裂分子的寡妇、妻子或姐妹组成的人称“黑寡妇”的自杀式爆炸组织者的生存状况。课文 B 讲的是车臣分裂主义武装分子在俄罗斯南部北奥塞梯共和国别斯兰市第一中学制造的劫持人质事件。

Part One：Preparing to explore

一、国际报道

1. 定义与意义

国际报道是与国内报道相对指称的新闻报道。凡其他国家和地区内发生的新闻事件及新闻人物均可列入国际报道范围。它涉及各国的政治、外交、经济、军事、科技、文化、体育、卫生、教育等各领域新闻信息的传播，一直是新闻报道的主要内容之一。国际报道常常受到本国外交政策，意识形态，新闻价值和国家利益等因素的影响。

随着全球政治、经济、文化往来和交流的发展及信息传播技术的提高，人们对国外新闻事件的关注度也在日益提升。国际报道越来越重要，并成为帮助本国受众了解世界局势、掌握国外各方面动态以及交流各种信息的重要渠道。

2. 普利策国际报道奖

普利策国际报道奖于 1948 年设立。从往届获奖作品的内容来看，涉及的区域覆盖面并不广泛，基本集中在美国比较关注的几个世界热点国家或地区，主题也相对狭窄，关注的多是暴力、战争、屠杀、疾病和金融危机等问题，而且有很强的意识形态因素。

概括起来，20 世纪五六十年代，普利策国际报道获奖作品的选题多集中在苏联、古巴、波兰及亚洲等国家的政治局势，其中提及最多是苏联，与苏联局势相关的作品曾七次获奖。另外，就是朝鲜战争和越南战争，其中越南战争更多一些，关于越战的报道曾四次获奖。20 世纪七八十年代，国际报道范围有所拓展，其重点转向非洲、拉美、亚洲及中东地区，如南非、中美洲、印度、柬埔寨、菲律宾、中国、以色列等国家的政治经济局势，其中有关中东和非洲问题的报道得奖机会较多。20世纪90年代，国际报道获奖作品的主题是伊拉克战争、海湾战争、阿富汗和波黑政局以及苏联金融危机等。进入21世纪，美国国际报道一方面关注拉美和非洲事务，如墨西哥的毒品问题、刚果等国家的政治斗争和乌干达等国家的艾滋病等，另一方面继续关注伊拉克和阿富汗局势，尤其是美军自身的状况和战乱地区的人民生活状况。更重要的是，这段期间，有关中国问题的报道突显出来，2006年、2007年和2013年的国际报道奖都颁给了关于中国问题的系列报道，分别是关于中国的法制弊病，关于中国经济的快速发展带来的诸如社会不平等和污染方面的问题，以及关于中国政府高官腐败的问题。

3. 基本写作特征

从普利策奖评审委员会给予国际报道获奖作品的赞词来看，优秀国际报道作品具有以下基本特征：

(1) 勇气过人（courageous）。对记者来说，因为是跨国采访，必定面临更多意想不到的困难，所以，一定要勇气过人。

(2) 信息量大（heavily reported）。在信息收集方面，应该材料充分，注重抓细节。

(3) 进行平衡报道（balanced）。在报道态度和方式上，尽可能在信源的选择、信息的选择、事实的选择、新闻价值与社会公德的选择之间的达到平衡，克服主观臆断，保证事实的呈现能最大限度地忠于真相。

(4) 具有深刻见解（insightful）。在文章立意上，从独特的角度进行深度分析，提出深刻见解。

(5) 风格尖锐（sharply edged）。在写作风格上，应尖锐有利。

(6) 具有启迪意义的（illuminating/enlightening）。在报道效果上，给人以启迪。

二、课前讨论

1. Some say "war drives women away." Do you agree with this comment? Why or why not?

2. Have you heard of the "black widows" of Chechnya? What do you think motivates these young Muslim women to become "suicide bombers"?

Part Two: Exploring the text

Text A A cult of reluctant killers

The "black widows" of Chechnya—suicide bombers who stalk(悄悄地追踪) Russia—are driven by hatred, ideology, coercion and fear.

BY Kim Murphy

Los Angeles Times

February 4, 2004

GROZNY, Russia—Medna Bayrakova remembers the day a middle-aged woman showed up at her door and asked to speak to her 26-year-old daughter. They shut themselves in the bedroom for half an hour, and then her daughter left, saying she was walking the visitor to the bus stop.

An hour later, Zareta still hadn't returned and several men in camouflage(迷彩服) knocked at the door of the family's ravaged apartment in this ruined Chechen capital.

"We have taken away your daughter. She has agreed to marry one of our men," one said.

Bayrakova protested. "She's a sick girl. She has tuberculosis. She was coughing up blood only this morning."

"We will cure her," they replied quietly.

The next time Bayrakova and her husband saw their daughter's face, it was 24 days later—separatist Chechen rebels had seized Moscow's Dubrovka Theater, along with 800 hostages. Zareta's unmistakable dark eyes were visible above a black veil on the television screen. Her fingers were clasped below a belt of powerful explosives.

There was one last view, this one a postmortem photo(尸检照片) taken after federal agents gassed and stormed the theater in the early morning hours of Oct. 26, 2002, leaving all 41 hostage-takers and 129 of the captives dead. This time, Zareta's face was swollen and bruised—barely recognizable.

"They asked me, 'Is it your daughter?'" Bayrakova said. "But the face was all smashed. She looked all beaten up. And then I passed out."

In strapping the explosives belt to her waist that fall day in 2002, Zareta Bayrakova joined the cult of the "black widows," the female suicide bombers who have left much of Russia on wary watch for the mysterious, dark-eyed woman in a long fur coat who is believed to recruit them.

A nationwide alert has been issued for a middle-aged woman with a hooked nose and dark hair popularly known as "Black Fatima," who has been identified as a recruiter for the women known as shahidas, or martyrs. The woman reportedly has been seen lurking on the edges of terrorist bombings during a decade of tensions between Russia and the breakaway republic of Chechnya. Russian troops pulled out of the republic after a disastrous 1994-1996 war, and the mostly Muslim region exercises self-rule.

Seven women have launched suicide attacks against Israel, the first one in January 2002. By that time, Russia had already recorded two such attacks, and since then their numbers have grown. More than three dozen Chechen women—roughly half of the suicide bombers—have launched or attempted attacks against Russian targets since the second Chechen war began in 1999. Russian authorities say many appear to be dazed and under the influence of drugs; some would-be bombers have reported that they were forced by relatives in the Chechen resistance into attempting such attacks.

Most recently, on Dec. 9, a young woman blew herself up in front of Moscow's historic National Hotel, killing six people. An older woman in a dark coat and fur hat reportedly was seen slipping away from the scene. On Dec. 5, suicide bombers blew up a commuter train in the southern region of Stavropol, killing at least 44 others and injuring more than 150. Authorities said three women and one man were involved in the attack.

Nearly 150 people died in black-widow attacks last summer—so named in the Russian media because many of the female perpetrators(凶手) have lost husbands, brothers and fathers in the war in Chechnya.

Abu Walid, a Saudi national who is one of many Arabs who have joined the Chechen militants, is believed to be the commander of the rebels' eastern front in Chechnya. He recently explained the use of female suicide bombers in an interview with the Al Jazeera television network.

"These women, particularly the wives of the moujahedeen(圣战者) who are martyred, are being threatened in their homes. Their honor and everything are being threatened," he said. "They do not accept being humiliated and living under occupation. They say that they want to serve the cause of almighty God and avenge(为……报复) the death of their husbands and persecuted people."

Sergei Ignatchenko, spokesman for Russia's Federal Security Service, said Arab militants "have abused the idea of Chechnya's independence to suit their own ends."

Chechen commander Shamil Basayev is said to have trained a force of up to 50 black widows for suicide attacks against Russian targets. Basayev claims to have masterminded several recent terrorist operations, including the Dubrovka Theater siege and the bombing at the National Hotel.

Meanwhile, the political leader of the separatists, Aslan Maskhadov, has repeatedly disavowed any connection with terrorism and even accused Russia's secret services(情报部门) of staging the Dubrovka siege for "propaganda purposes." But Russian security officials provided *The Times* with a videotape, dated Oct. 18, 2002—a week before the siege—in which Maskhadov appeared to be referring to upcoming actions by Chechen rebels.

"We have practically accomplished a transition from guerrilla warfare to offensive combat operations," he says on the tape. "I am convinced, and I do not have a shadow of a doubt on this, that during the concluding stage of our struggle, we will definitely hold an even more unique operation, similar to jihad(圣战). And with this operation, we will liberate our land from Russian aggressors."

Another videotape, purportedly filmed at the same time, shows Maskhadov seated with Basayev, Abu Omar Seif—an Islamic spiritual leader identified by the Russians as a link to Arab funding sources—and Movsar Barayev, who led the hostage-takers at Dubrovka.

For the Russians, the tapes are proof that the moderate Chechen resistance, which has spoken out publicly against terrorism, is secretly organizing civilian terrorist operations. Russia has repeatedly sought to convince the U.S. that Moscow and Washington are facing the same enemy: the Al Qaeda terrorist network.

Maskhadov's aides have said he was talking about a strike against Russian military forces, not a terrorist act against civilians. And Chechen rebels say the Russians are ignoringthe deep domestic rage that motivates suicide attacks.

"The Chechens do not have the right to stain with their blood the streets of Russian cities, which are rear bases of the aggressors' army?" the Chechen separatist website, Kavkaz Center, asked sarcastically. "A Russian tank driver, with intestines of Chechen children on its caterpillar track(坦克的履带板), and the pilot of a low-flying warplane shelling a bus with women and infants, are just unscrupulous(肆无忌惮的) uses of force, while a Chechen widow blowing herself up together with the pilots who have murdered her children is terrorism and cannot be justified.

"According to their logic, the Chechen nation must die magnanimously(宽宏大量地) and in silence."

*

On a quiet side street in the former Cossack village of Asinovskaya in western Chechnya, there is a pile of rubble that used to be Sulumbek Ganiyev's house. It is the house in which he raised six sons and four daughters.

Only four children are alive, two of whom are in captivity. Islam was killed in a rocket attack in 1999. Daughter Petimat disappeared in July 2000 and is believed to have died in a bombing raid in Grozny. Rustam, a former rebel fighter, is in prison in North Ossetia. Hussein was fighting with the rebels when he was killed in 2000. Raisa, who resisted being recruited by her brother as a black widow, is being held by the Russian secret services at an undisclosed location. The youngest son, Tarkhan, died in a car accident last spring.

Daughters Fatima and Khadzhad died in the Dubrovka Theater siege, with unused explosives belts strapped around their waists.

A few days after the Dubrovka standoff, the family says, Russian troops arrived in the early evening and, without so much as a knock on the door, blew up their house.

Ganiyev, a former builder, says he is alive today only because he and his wife were watching television next door.

"We are not to blame. Before the war, all the children were at home. The Russians took them away from us," Ganiyev said recently.

He said the family's first encounter with Russian troops was in October 1999, not long after the beginning of the second war, when soldiers entered the village and shot the Ganiyevs' five cows, tied two of the carcasses(动物的尸体) to their vehicle and left.

In July 2000, he said, troops entered their home at gunpoint, stole their videocassette recorder, lambs and chickens, and threw a grenade into the cellar where goods for the winter were stored.

Not long after, Rustam and Hussein began fighting for the rebels. Russian soldiers came to the door in June 2002 and grabbed Tarkhan, then 21, Fatima, 23, and Raisa, 17. Ganiyev remembers daughter Khadzhad, 14, shouting defiantly, as her three siblings are being led away: "Are you really brave, when you take away girls?"

"They wanted to take her away, too, but her mother jumped in and prevented them," Ganiyev recalled.

For three agonizing days, the family knew nothing. Finally, Ganiyev said, he was able to negotiate a $1,000 ransom for his children's release. But when they came home, he says, they were different. "After that, the girls understood that they will never be in peace," he said.

"They were very angry," added his wife, Lyuba. "Otherwise, could you expect them to go to Moscow and take this death?"

Their daughters told them that they had been taken to a shed and that sometime later their brother, tied at the legs and hands and badly beaten, was thrown at their feet "like a dead body." The soldiers poured a bucket of water on him to awaken him and then led him away again.

"They tortured the girls with electric current. They put a metal spiral on their fingers and attached it to a current source, and they shocked them until they passed out," Ganiyev said. "They wanted to get information about what bandits they know, who are the rebels."

Lyuba Ganiyev tried to explain what drove Fatima, a law student who often helped her father bale hay, and Khadzhad, who had hoped to become a gynecologist(妇科医生), to join the terrorists in Moscow—and Raisa, who eventually turned herself in to Russian authorities, to nearly follow them.

"After they beat them for three days, they had had enough. They came back and said, 'We are now in shame. They held us for three days. We can't live like this anymore.' It's not that they were crying. We never saw them crying. They were just sitting down, depressed."

On Sept. 29, 2002—the same day Zareta Bayrakova disappeared—Fatima and Khadzhad left home, saying they were going to Dagestan to see their nephew. They never returned. Their parents next saw them, as Medna Bayrakova had seen her daughter, a month later in television footage of the Dubrovka siege.

"They didn't tell us," Ganiyev said. "If we had known, we wouldn't have let them. I would have broken their legs to stop them."

*

Some witnesses said they saw two women walking together just before the bombing at the National Hotel in the heart of Moscow in December.

"So, where is your parliament?" one of them asked. Then, the explosion. One witness said he saw a woman in a long coat fall to the pavement, get up and walk briskly away. Authorities believe that the woman may have been Black Fatima.

The bombing on the edge of Red Square crossed a red line of sorts for many Muscovites(莫斯科人).

"Maybe they are doing this out of religious convictions, but I think it's against our God and against the soul of every human being. No normal woman would be likely to do this," said Tatyana Yezhova, a 19-year-old medical student injured in the bombing.

Many Russians see Chechnya's drive for independence as an assault on the nation's territorial integrity, and the carnage(大屠杀)wrought by terrorists has only reinforced their support for President Vladimir V. Putin's war in the breakaway republic.

Russia has been widely criticized for atrocities(暴行)and human rights violations—Chechen men and women have been regularly kidnapped from their homes, tortured and even killed—but the Russian public sees a military body count that often reaches half a dozen a day, as soldiers are ambushed in the hills or blown up by roadside explosive devices.

Chechen terrorists have attacked rock concerts, subway stations and commuter trains full of students. At the National Hotel, horrified witnesses described seeing severed heads and limbs strewn(四处散开)on the sidewalk. Others waited in fear for the next strike.

"We were immediately told on the radio that we should stand here and watch very, very carefully over the people who come here, because there was information that there are three other suicide bombers. So I am standing here breaking my eyes over everybody who comes in here," Yevgeny Petrov, a 23-year-old security guard, said as he anxiously watched passersby at a shopping center across the street on the morning of the hotel bombing.

"They told us they are women, and they will be constantly talking on the phone, as if somebody is hypnotizing(施催眠术)them. Or we should look people in the eye, because their eyes will be weird, as if they are drugged," he said. "It's very scary. How can you uncover a terrorist if she looks like everybody else?"

After the hotel bombing, a composite drawing(罪犯等的合成图像)was distributed, purported to be a likeness of Black Fatima. By then, everyone in Moscow knew who she was, mostly thanks to Zarema Muzhikhoyeva, a would-be black widow who last July set out to blow herself up at a restaurant on Moscow's Tverskaya Street.

The 23-year-old resident of Chechnya was stopped by security guards, but her bomb later detonated(爆炸)accidentally and killed a Russian policeman trying to defuse it.

Muzhikhoyeva, whose husband was killed fighting the war while she was pregnant with their daughter, told her interrogators that she had been "a virtual slave" to rebels who convinced her that it was her religious duty to go to Moscow and detonate a bomb at a cafe on busy Tverskaya Street. Investigators told the Moscow paper Kommersant that a woman Muzhikhoyeva knew as Lyuba—Black Fatima—took her to a house near Moscow and visited her frequently during the next week. She told police that Lyuba often gave her orange juice that made her dizzy and gave her a headache.

On the last day, she said, Lyuba gave her more juice, handed her a rucksack containing a bomb and showed her how to set it off.

In a jailhouse interview published Tuesday in the newspaper Izvestia, Muzhikhoyeva said two

Chechen men prepared her for the task and dropped her off near the cafe. After being confronted by three men, she said, she went back on the street.

She said she had already decided not to pull the switch but feared that her trainers would set it off by remote control.

"Neither I nor they knew what to do," she said. "I was walking along, waiting for death."

Finally, a police officer approached and ordered her to drop her bag.

"I carried out the command and stepped away from this terrible bag," she said.

Alexei Zakharov, who heads Moscow's Research and Applied Science Center and specializes in the psychology of extreme situations, has interviewed would-be black widows in Russian custody and said many have reported having been drugged. All, he said, demonstrated signs of mental trauma.

The fact that they often are literally widows is telling, he said, because of a sense that they have become a burden on their husbands' families.

"Sometimes these women are told: 'You've been a sinner all your life. Allah(真主) punished you by taking your husband. Now it's time to restore yourself by doing your duty.'"

Zakharov says he has seen evidence of brainwashing techniques, in which religious phrases in Arabic are recited repeatedly. "They're gathered in large auditoriums, and they repeat a combination of sounds whose meaning they have no idea of. At the same time, they're making very rhythmic body motions. That, in fact, is one of the simplest and most primitive entrancing(使人神魂颠倒的) technologies."

In Grozny, whatever understanding exists of suicide bombers appears to be more instinctive than scientific.

"You must either feel terribly bad to want to kill yourself, and others in the bargain, or you must be a complete lunatic. And when you see everything that's happened around here, you know the number of lunatics has increased," said Zarema Sadulayeva, an activist with the group Save the Generation in Grozny, which works to promote the welfare of Chechen youths.

In a region where large numbers of men have either joined the rebels or fled the country to avoid arrest by the Russians, women have taken on new roles, many said.

They are the teachers trying to keep the schools open when there is no electricity. They are the mothers standing each Monday outside the Russian government headquarters, demanding to know what has happened to their missing sons. They are the stooped(驼背的) shoulders hauling buckets of water up shattered stairways to 10th-floor apartments.

And some of them are suicide bombers.

"We know now that we can take care of ourselves. But nevertheless, it's difficult. Very difficult. We are suffering every minute," said Fatima Shabazova, 37, who lives in a war-battered apartment building with 12 other Chechen war widows.

"Men die on us. And we have to be strong. We just have to be," she said. "Otherwise, we won't survive."

一、作者背景

Columbia University President Lee C. Bollinger presents Kim Murphy with a 2005 Pulitzer Prize in International Reporting.

金·墨菲（Kim Murphy）：1955 年生于美国印第安纳州首府印第安纳波利斯。1977 年以优异成绩毕业于北达科他州的麦纳特州立大学（Minot State University），主修英国文学。自 1973 年起她就开始从事新闻工作，先后担任过密西西比州报纸《北比洛克西人》（*The North Biloxian*）助理编辑、北达科他州《麦纳特日报》（*Minot Daily News*）记者、加利福尼亚州《橘郡记事报》（*Orange County Register*）都市版助理编辑。1983 年加入《洛杉矶时报》，担任时报橘郡（Orange County）版记者。在《洛杉矶时报》工作期间，除报道美国西北部地区新闻外，她还曾担任该报驻俄国、中东、巴尔干半岛、阿富汗、伦敦等地记者或分社社长，现任《洛杉矶时报》西雅图分社社长。

在三十多年的新闻生涯中，墨菲获得过很多荣誉，如因出色报道第一次海湾战争而获得 1990 年"洛杉矶时报出版人奖"（Los Angeles Times Publisher's Prize），1993 年，获得美国职业记者协会（Sigma Delta Chi）最佳国际新闻奖等。2004 年，墨菲在《洛杉矶时报》上刊登了 10 篇有关俄罗斯反恐行动以及俄国的经济、社会改革的系列报道。其报道雄辩有力（eloquent）并且内容广泛（wide ranging），因此获得 2005 年普利策国际报道奖。

二、课文背景

本单元所选的这篇报道涉及人称"黑寡妇"的自杀式爆炸的组织者，基本都是车臣分裂分子的寡妇、妻子或姐妹。他们穿着传统的伊斯兰黑色长袍，从头罩到脚，有些人蒙着脸，只露出两只阴郁的眼睛，身上绑着炸药，态度凶狠，因此叫"黑寡妇"。他们在 2002 年的莫斯科人质危机中进入公众的视野，接着，在俄罗斯其他地区接二连三地发生黑寡妇自杀性袭击事件。从此，"黑寡妇"成了车臣女恐怖分子的代名词，令人毛骨悚然。

提起"黑寡妇"，就必然会联想到俄罗斯与车臣民族之间的长期矛盾。矛盾可以追溯到18世纪沙皇对车臣的入侵，但矛盾的真正激化是在苏联解体前后开始的。1991年11月，车臣宣布成立独立共和国，杜达耶夫担任总统，采取与俄罗斯政府对抗的行为，致使车臣民族分裂主义势力恶性膨胀。为了维护国家的领土完整，俄罗斯分别于1994年和1999年与车臣当局发生了两次战争。俄罗斯的军事围剿虽然消灭了大股车臣非法武装，但车臣剩余的非法武装化整为零，在车臣内外采取游击战术，不断在俄罗斯各地制造恐怖事件。其中最残酷的是2002年的莫斯科杜布罗夫卡剧院劫持人质事件和2004年别斯兰市第一中学的人质劫持事件。

在杜布罗夫卡剧院的人质危机中，"黑寡妇"扮演了重要角色。是什么让这些原本柔弱善良的女性变成了杀人不眨眼的恶魔？墨菲对此提供了雄辩有力（eloquent）的解释。

本文通过讲述几个家庭的悲剧故事，介绍了"黑寡妇"产生的社会土壤。作者想表达的意思很清楚："黑寡妇"是被逼无奈而成杀人者的。这些年轻女子中有的是被强行拉走的，有的是出于报复心理，有的是出于对未来生活的恐惧而成为基地组织政治斗争的牺牲品。

为了帮助大家更快地抓住要点，这里对文章结构做一简要说明。文章共三个部分，没有小标题，但通过行距可以清晰分辨。第一部分讲"黑寡妇"背后的基地组织的操纵，基地组织强迫年轻女子卷入恐怖活动。文章以女孩Zareta的经历为开头，她被人从家里强行带走，成为"黑寡妇"，最后作为"人体炸弹"丧生。文章开篇就触动了读者的心。第二部分强调"黑寡妇"是出于对俄军杀死自己亲人的报复而加入恐怖组织的。作者通过讲述Ganiyev一家的经历来表明此观点。第三部分讲述经车臣恐怖活动领袖"洗脑"后的"黑寡妇"的恐惧心理。文章基本上采用了平行结构，给人视野比较开阔的感觉。文章有许多生动的细节描写，措辞雄辩有力，很值得耐心去读。

但是，值得一提的是，中国国际广播电台网站"国际纵横"上发表的刘云莉写的题为"关注车臣'黑寡妇'"一文（2003年12月12日）为我们提供了另一方面的信息。文章说："一个目前已离开车臣的寡妇米拉娜对美国记者说，女人肉炸弹在车臣受到普遍的尊敬，尤其是年轻人对她们十分崇敬。米拉娜说：'没有人让她们那样做，她们全都想进天堂，因为她们厌倦了现在的生活。'"该文作者认为对生活的绝望致使原本柔弱善良的女性变成了死神。

关于"黑寡妇"的真相究竟是什么？这是不是一个可进一步探究的问题呢？

三、作者主要观点

1. What do you think the reporter is trying to tell us in the second part of the report, which describes the tragedy of Sulumbek Ganiyev's family? In your opinion, did the reporter omit some significant information, advertently or inadvertently?

2. Can you discern the reporter's personal bias when she is telling the stories of both sides, the Chechens and the Russians? Illustrate your point with examples from the text.

四、写作风格与手法

1. What has intrigued you most about the article in terms of its writing style?

2. What, for the average American reader, is the source of interest in the story?

3. If a piece of international news is to appeal to, or better still, to touch the heart and soul of, the domestic readership, what qualities should it have? Can you identify any of such qualities in the text?

4. Find out all references to "Chechen rebels" in the text. Compare them and discuss their nuances.

5. What, if any, is the constructive purpose of the writer?

6. Comment on the reporter's use of direct accounts made by participants or eye-witnesses. What are the functions of these direct quotations?

7. In what sense is the report "eloquent" as suggested in the citation?

8. Look for examples of long sentences. Is each sentence a unified expression of a closely related group of ideas? Are the parts of sentences combined in firm, closely knit construction?

Part Three: Further exploring the text

一、语言点讲解

1. An hour later, Zareta still hadn't returned and several men in camouflage knocked at the door of the family's ravaged apartment in this ruined Chechen capital.

Ravaged 和 ruined 这两个形容词给读者带来强烈的现场感，作者用"ruined"描绘出多年战乱后车臣首府格罗兹尼的狼藉，用"ravaged"来形容一户普通人家的住宅。Ravage 和 ruin 是近义词，都表示在战争、自然灾害或疾病等的作用下"毁坏"、"蹂躏"、"劫掠"。类似的词语还有 despoil，plunder，pillage，sack，devastate，lay waste 等。请查一查英英字典，体会这些词语的细微差别。

2. Only four children are alive, two of whom are in captivity. Islam was killed in a rocket attack in 1999. Daughter Petimat disappeared in July 2000 and is believed to have died in a bombing raid in Grozny. Rustam, a former rebel fighter, is in prison in North Ossetia. Hussein was fighting with the rebels when he was killed in 2000. Raisa, who resisted being recruited by her brother as a black widow, is being held by the Russian secret services at an undisclosed location. The youngest son, Tarkhan, died in a car accident last spring. Daughters Fatima and Khadzhad died in the Dubrovka Theater siege, with unused explosives belts strapped around their waists.

作者用白描式的语言叙述了这个大家庭里多名子女的命运。这些句子的句式并不多样，用的词语也很单调，更没有什么形容词，仅仅是对一些事实的陈述，但却清晰简洁，给读者带来了强烈的震撼。一个个鲜活的生命在战乱中消逝，Ganiyev 一家人的命运也折射出一个民族的悲剧。这种以小见大的写作方法很值得我们细细体味。后文还有一些这样的例子，如：Lyuba Ganiyev tried to explain what drove Fatima, a law student who often helped her father bale hay, and Khadzhad, who had hoped to become a gynecologist, to join the terrorists in Moscow—and Raisa, who eventually turned herself in to Russian authorities, to nearly follow them.

3. For three agonizing days, the family knew nothing.

这里作者采用了移就修辞格（Transferred Epithet），即把用于形容甲事物的修饰语移用于乙事物，通常是把形容人的修饰语移用于物。这种修辞格在英语和汉语中都比较常见。Agonizing 本来是用来形容 Ganiyev 一家人盼望消息的苦苦煎熬，当用于形容 days 时，就把人的思想感情外射到客观事物里，使事物具有人的感情色彩，文字更加生动，句子表现力更强。后文还有一处这样的例子：They are the stooped shoulders hauling buckets of water up shattered stairways to 10th-floor apartments. 下面再举两个例子说明这种修辞格的使用：（1）The old man put a reassuring hand on my shoulder.（2）He said "yes" to the question in an unthinking moment.

4. Russia has been widely criticized for atrocities and human rights violations—Chechen men and women have been regularly kidnapped from their homes, tortured and even killed—but the Russian public sees a military body count that often reaches half a dozen a day, as soldiers are ambushed in the hills or blown up by roadside explosive devices.

作者用了一句话简练的交代了车臣和俄国民众对冲突根源的不同看法，对比强烈。但请注意，句子的前半段用的是被动语态，没有明说是谁在"批评"俄国。你对这个被动语态是怎么解读的?

二、中西文化比较

论"中西思维模式"

在本文第十段，作者把车臣说成是"分离出来的车臣共和国"（the breakaway republic of Chechnya），有车臣是"主权国家"的含义。这种表达绝对不可能在国内媒体出现，因为我们从来没有认为它是独立的一部分，我们认为车臣共和国仍然是俄罗斯联邦的一部分，或者更具体地说，是俄罗斯联邦的南部联邦管区的其中一个共和国。事实如何呢? 2003 年 3 月 23 日，车臣就是否赞成新的共和国宪法草案、总统选举法草案、议会选举法草案举行了车臣历史上第一次全民公决。全民公决通过的车臣新宪法规定，车臣是俄联邦领土不可分割的一部分。这从法律上确定了车臣作为俄联邦一个主体的地位，进而保证了俄联邦主权和领土完整。

为什么中美会产生如此差异呢? 大家首先考虑到的是意识形态因素。确实，这是一个非常重要的因素。美国具有独立自由的历史，独立自由是其历史发展的主流，而中国虽然并非在历史上一直是统一的国家，但统一是中华民族历史发展的主流。

我们还可以从思维模式角度来解读这种差异。通常来说，中国人擅长整体思维，而美国人更关注个体或一部分。探讨车臣问题时，我们往往从历史、地理位置、文化等各个方面进行综合思考，把车臣问题放在俄联邦这个整体框架下来分析，先整体后个体；而美国往往以个体为先，关注车臣作为个体的发展态势。中西在写信封地址上的差异也体现了这种特点。我们是从整体到个体，从街名到单位再到姓名，美国人则刚好相反。

三、语言练习

1. 请用英语解释下列句子。

...Arab militants "have abused the idea of Chechnya's independence to suit their own ends."

Russian troops arrived in the early evening and, without so much as a knock on the door, blew up their house.

The bombing on the edge of Red Square crossed a red line of sorts for many Muscovites.

...the Russian public sees a military body count that often reaches half a dozen a day...

In Grozny, whatever understanding exists of suicide bombers appears to be more instinctive than scientific.

2. 请将下列短语翻译成英文，并比较中英文表达方式的异同。

（1）把客人送到汽车站

（2）咳血

（3）昏倒

（4）鹰钩鼻、黑头发的中年妇女

（5）自我引爆

（6）从现场溜走

（7）策划近期的多次恐怖袭击活动

（8）否认与……有任何关系

（9）在枪口的威逼下

（10）路边爆炸装置

（11）精神创伤

3. 请将下面的句子或段落翻译成中文，并比较中英文表达方式的异同。

Zareta's unmistakable dark eyes were visible above a black veil on the television screen. Her fingers were clasped below a belt of powerful explosives.

In strapping the explosives belt to her waist that fall day in 2002, Zareta Bayrakova joined the cult of the "black widows," the female suicide bombers who have left much of Russia on wary watch for the mysterious, dark-eyed woman in a long fur coat who is believed to recruit them.

"We have practically accomplished a transition from guerrilla warfare to offensive combat operations," he says on the tape. "I am convinced, and I do not have a shadow of a doubt on this, that during the concluding stage of our struggle, we will definitely hold an even more unique operation, similar to jihad. And with this operation, we will liberate our land from Russian aggressors."

Many Russians see Chechnya's drive for independence as an assault on the nation's territorial integrity, and the carnage wrought by terrorists has only reinforced their support for President Vladimir V. Putin's war in the breakaway republic.

How can you uncover a terrorist if she looks like everybody else?

You must either feel terribly bad to want to kill yourself, and others in the bargain, or you must be a complete lunatic.

Part Four: Exploring beyond the text

一、自我反思

1. 我学到了什么？我要如何改进？

2. 一篇高质量的国际新闻报道的基本标准是什么？我能清楚地告诉别人吗？该篇报道的记者金·墨菲是如何达到这些标准的？我能向别人解释清楚吗？

二、知识扩展

1. 收集资料，讨论“黑寡妇”出现并存在的原因。

2. 很多人对俄罗斯处理车臣民族问题的方法提出批评，仔细分析这些评论，并得出自己的观点。

三、能力扩展

1. 请就本单元的课文撰写一篇 500 字左右的评论。

2. 请从中国文化的任意一点入手，撰写一篇 1000 字左右的新闻报道。你的目标读者是对中国了解甚少、或误解、甚至曲解的外国人。

Text B Killers set terms, a mother chooses

Militants offer a woman and her baby freedom—but only if she leaves her other child behind.

BY Kim Murphy

Times

September 3, 2004

导读：2004 年 9 月 1 日上午，一伙头戴面罩的车臣武装分子突然闯入俄罗斯南部北奥塞梯（North Ossetia）共和国别斯兰市（Beslan）第一中学，将 1100 多名学生、家长和教师赶进学校体育馆劫为人质，并在体育馆中及周围安放了爆炸物。这伙武装分子与警察对峙了 3 天，制造了俄国历史上最严重的恐怖事件，共 330 人死亡，其中 186 人是儿童。这就是媒体所谓的“别斯兰人质事件”。

墨菲的这篇报道发表于别斯兰人质危机刚刚结束之时，故事以 Zalina Dzandarova 的经历为线索，读者通过这名母亲的讲述仿佛能亲耳听到刺耳的枪声，亲眼看到悲惨的景象。读完整篇报道后，我们对人质的同情和对恐怖分子的憎恶油然而生。墨菲成功地激发了这种跨越种族、跨越文化的情感共鸣，使得这一事件的地理距离，甚至时间距离都变得不那么重要。

BESLAN, Russia—Zalina Dzandarova cradles her son Alan as he sleeps with his small face buried against her stomach. He is the child Dzandarova was able to save. The child she chose to save, really.

It is the other one, little Alana, her 6-year-old daughter, whose image torments(折磨) her: Alana clutching her hand, Alana crying and calling after her. Alana's sobs disappearing into the distance as Dzandarova walked out of Middle School No. 1 here Thursday, clutching 2-year-old Alan in her arms.

Guerrillas armed with automatic rifles and explosive belts who are holding hundreds of hostages at the small provincial school in southern Russia allowed 26 women and children to leave. About a dozen mothers, like Dzandarova, were allowed to take only one child, forced to leave another behind.

"I didn't want to make this choice," a stunned-looking Dzandarova, 27, said in the reception room of her father-in-law's house a few miles from the school. "People say they are happy that my son and I are saved. But how can I be happy if my daughter's still inside there?"

Violence often selects its victims randomly, but seldom is a mother asked to make a Sophie's choice: Save one child and leave behind another, possibly to face death. The standoff in North Ossetia republic involving about 20 guerrillas—most likely linked to the neighboring separatist republic of Chechnya or adjacent Ingushetia—has stunned a nation accustomed to war and its horrors after the many ethnic and territorial conflicts that accompanied the breakup of the Soviet Union.

Even with the downing of two Russian jetliners and two street bombings coming in just one week, the thought of schoolchildren surrounded by veiled female suicide bombers and masked guerrillas has traumatized the country. "They Have Taken Hundreds of Our Children," read a banner headline in the daily newspaper Izvestia.

And they took Alana.

"They said they would let us go only after the (Russian) troops are withdrawn from Chechnya," said Dzandarova. She said the attackers had identified themselves as Chechens. "I said we have nothing to do with that, but they wouldn't listen."

Her description provided one of the first accounts of what was happening inside the school, where Dzandarova said as many as 1,000 children and parents were being held in a gymnasium planted with explosives. Authorities officially listed the number of hostages at 354, a figure Dzandarova disputed.

"The director of the school was taken to a TV where they were saying there were 354 of us in here, and the director came back and she was in a state of shock, because there were in fact many more people there," she said.

"There were definitely 1,000 people in that one room," she said, referring to the gym. "I saw it with my own eyes."

On Wednesday, Dzandarova took her daughter to the first day of first grade. As students and parents began lining up, they saw the attackers sweeping into the school. Dzandarova ran with her children to hide in a classroom, but they were rounded up with the others and taken to the gym.

"Everyone was ordered to sit down, and they began to set up booby-traps (饵雷) around the perimeter, right in front of our eyes. They had lots of guns and explosives with them."

At first, she said, everyone was allowed to drink water from the tap. But the hostage-takers soon stopped that, she said, because they were angry that officials, including the presidents of North Ossetia and Ingushetia, had not come to meet with them.

Without water, the powdered milk the guerrillas supplied for the children had to be spooned into their mouths.

The gym was sweltering, even after the window panes were broken out.

"They were telling us, 'Your government is not allowing enough water for your kids.'"

In just two days, she said, the problem became acute. "You see, the kids won't survive these negotiations," she said. "They're not getting enough water. What we have to hope is that they'll survive this night without water."

At the beginning, 20 men in the gym were led to a different room. On Thursday, Dzandarova said, 10 of the men returned. The hostages presumed that the others were dead.

"They told us that it was 'your own side' that had executed them, who had shot them dead," Dzandarova said.

Two women who had been wearing suicide belts apparently detonated them Wednesday in an adjoining room, she said.

"They left the gym, and all of a sudden we heard two loud explosions. We thought the storming (by Russian police) had begun. But then they told us, 'Our sisters have won a victory, and there's no other cause they want to pursue.'"

The male guerrillas, she said, "took it calmly."

Much of the time, she said, the guerrillas appeared tense: running around the room, waving their guns in the hostages' faces, shouting at them to sit still and stop talking.

When Alan began to cry from hunger, Dzandarova was allowed to join several other mothers in an adjacent room, which had its own water and was several degrees cooler.

After a former local political leader visited the school Thursday, the women in the adjacent room were told there was "good news": They would be released.

"They said, 'Pack your things quickly, and take your babies with you,'" Dzandarova said.

Shortly after, she learned that she would have to choose between taking her son or her daughter.

Dzandarova had both Alan and Alana with her and made a snap decision to pass Alana to her 16-year-old sister-in-law. But the guerrillas saw through the ruse(诡计)and refused to allow her to take the older child.

"Alana was clinging to me and holding my hand firmly. But they separated us, and said: 'You go with the boy. Your sister can stay here with her.' I cried. I begged them. Alana cried. The women around us wept. One of the Chechens said: 'If you don't go now, you don't go at all. You stay here with your children... and we will shoot all of you.'"

She couldn't save both of them. She could only die with both of them—or save one of them and herself.

"I didn't have time to think what I was doing," she said. "I pressed Alan even stronger to myself, and I went out, and I heard all the time how my daughter was crying and calling for me behind my back. I thought my heart would break into pieces there and then."

Dzandarova cried as she talked. Her tears fell on Alan, who was sleeping. Even when his mother shook quietly with sobs as she cradled him, he didn't awaken.

Times staff writer Sergei L. Loiko in Moscow contributed to this report.

Unit Five Investigative Reporting

调查性报道

单元导航

本单元将讨论调查性报道。本单元只有一篇文章。文章揭露了美国纽约布鲁克林区一家州政府管辖范围内的成人精神病患者疗养所（adult home for the mentally ill）的阴暗面。

Part One：Preparing to explore

一、调查性报道

1. 定义

调查性报道的定义随着时代的变迁而发生变化。

在美国，19 世纪末，人们将以调查方式采写的新闻报道称为“侦探新闻”（detective journalism）。20 世纪初，美国总统西奥多·罗斯福对当时的调查性报道记者很反感，所以戏称他们是“扒粪者”（muckraker）。20 世纪 70 年代，调查性报道重新盛行后，“调查性新闻”（investigative journalism）才开始正式启用并广泛传播。而普利策新闻奖中始终使用“调查性报道”（investigative reporting）这个更为具体的说法。

对于调查性报道的定义有很多，但一般比较认同美国 1975 年成立的“调查性报道记者编辑协会”（Investigative Reporters and Editors）提供的权威性解释。所谓调查性报道，就是“暴露某个人或组织就一个重大的公共问题企图掩盖的信息。”后来，该协会扩展了这个概念的含义，指出调查性报道也包括“并非揭秘，而是展示公众以前未知的信息”。[①]由此看出，在美国，调查性报道不一定都是揭露性的，非揭露性的题材也是调查性报道的选择对象之一。

2. 产生与发展

虽然真正意义上的调查性报道起源于美国 20 世纪初的“黑幕揭发运动”，但调查性报道的精神早在美国的殖民时代就有了。

① James Aucoin,“Investigative journalism”, in W. David Sloan and Lisa Mullikin Parcell, ed. *American Journalism: History, principles, practices*. McFarland & Company, 2002, p. 210.

最早的调查性报道可追溯到美国殖民时期的报纸和小册子。如 1690 年出版的报纸《公共事务：国际和国内》对当时“法国和印第安人战争”期间的暴行进行了揭露。

19 世纪早期，拥有明显党派倾向的报纸编辑会通过一切手段揭露政治对手的丑闻，有时甚至会造谣。最著名的案子就是 1802 年发表的关于“美国总统汤姆斯・杰斐逊与黑人佣人萨莉・赫明斯的风流韵事”报道。事实证明，这只是一场政治争斗。

19 世纪 30 年代，废奴主义者、扩大参政权论者、劳工权利活动家、妇女、儿童、犯人和农场工人权利的倡导者就社会弱势群体艰难贫困的生活状况在报纸上进行大量曝光，以期吹起变革之风，推动社会的进步。

19 世纪后半期，调查性报道继续发展，特别是 19 世纪末 20 世纪初，美国报业大王普利策与其对手赫斯特把揭露腐败受贿等社会丑陋现象的报道看作煽动性新闻，当成了吸引读者的手段。但从客观上讲，这些报道也从此改变了美国的新闻事业，美国展开了轰轰烈烈的黑幕揭发运动。因此，20 世纪初被看作是调查性报道的第一个黄金时代。

两次世界大战期间，由于战时的新闻控制，调查性报道进入休眠期，直到 20 世纪六七十年代，调查性报道再次兴起并趋于成熟，出现第二次高潮。美国各大城市的报纸纷纷开始建立调查报道小组，愈来愈多的人力和财力被投向调查性的报道上。调查性报道的里程碑是《华盛顿邮报》披露的“水门事件”（Watergate Scandal）。从 1972 年 6 月起，该报的青年记者罗伯特・伍德沃德和卡尔・伯恩斯坦通过 22 个月的调查和报道，揭露了尼克松的政治丑闻。最初的导火索不过是一个窃听事件以及从一名嫌疑人身上搜出来的电话本。由此出发，伍德沃德和伯恩斯坦发现了事件背后的白宫官员，又发现了总统与窃听事件的关系。接着，《洛杉矶时报》、《时代周刊》、《纽约时报》和哥伦比亚广播公司相继加入，导致总统最后辞职。“水门事件”让记者们登上了影响力的顶峰。

值得一提的是，1975 年由一批富有经验的记者编辑发起成立了“调查性报道记者编辑协会”（IRE），负责具体组织、指导和协调记者和编辑关于调查性报道的工作，这个协会一直运作到现在，为训练职业化的调查性报道记者和编辑、揭发美国社会前进中存在的各式各样的问题做出了巨大贡献。

如今，调查性报道已成为一种经常性新闻报道文体，被新闻界和一般公众认为是美国新闻界发挥守望监督功能的主要手段。正如美国传播学奥库恩教授所说“调查性报道已经成为美国新闻界一个制度化的、令人景仰的传统，是衡量新闻业的标尺。”[①]

3. 普利策调查性报道奖

美国普利策新闻奖于 1985 年设立了调查性报道奖。此类获奖作品都是揭露性的，触及面很广，比如，法院、警署和监狱等执法机构、市政厅的黑暗面、高校篮球运动员的违规行为、房屋租赁机构的种族歧视现象、医疗行业的违规行为、联邦住房计划中的腐败现象、旧船报废业给工人和环境造成的危害、市长选举中的欺骗行为、中学枪杀案、食品药监局的失职行为、地方儿童福利体制的弊病、越战期间美国军队的暴行、政府官员的性丑闻、国会腐败现象、高校的腐败现象、媒体分析家与政府和公司的利益关系等，其中，揭露执法部门和食品医疗方面问题的报道相对多一些。

---

① James Aucoin, "Investigative journalism", in W. David Sloan and Lisa Mullikin Parcell, ed. *American Journalism: History, principles, practices.* McFarland & Company, 2002, p. 218.

4. 意义

第一，调查性报道对媒体本身大有益处。调查性报道需要引入大量的社会学调查方法，如问卷调查、民意调查、跟踪调查、统计和抽样调查、量化分析等，以对触及的问题进行全面、系统、科学地调查和报道，由此催生了“精确新闻学”的报道方式。这对提高媒体的专业性和锻炼记者的综合能力都有重要意义。第二，调查性报道具有重大的社会意义。一方面，此类报道不仅仅是一个收集信息和调查的过程，也是培育公民良知的过程。对社会弊端的揭露也就是界定了社会的公共道德。另一方面，调查性报道是进行舆论监督的有效方式，可以除恶驱邪，伸张正义，维护公众利益，维护社会的公平与公正。

5. 基本写作特征

从普利策奖评审委员会给予调查报道获奖作品的赞词来看，优秀调查报道作品具有以下基本特征：

(1) 具有顽强的（tenacious）、不知疲倦（indefatigable）的精神。开展调查、揭开真相不是一件容易的事情，会遇到种种困难和挫折，包括遭遇黑社会，甚至受到生命威胁，因此需要记者具备坚韧不拔的品质。

(2) 获得大量的证据（extensive documentation）。调查的目的就是获得大量真实、有效的证据。有了证据就能做到心中有数。

(3) 具有开创性（pioneering）。敢为人先，大胆探寻未触及过的重要公共问题的真相。

(4) 写作技巧超群（brilliantly written）。注意文章的结构组织，尽量简明扼要，把复杂的事情讲清楚；要把人的活动写得生动活泼，要有细节的描写；应该把事实和观点分离；应该注意平衡报道。

(5) 具有强大震撼的社会效果（powerful/compelling）。杰出的调查报道具有如此大的震撼力，以至于可以进而引发社会的变革，维护社会的公平和公正。

二、课前讨论

1. Have you ever been in touch with the mentally ill? Do you want to understand mental illness? Why or why not?

2. Which is a better solution for the people with chronic mental illness, to treat them in a psychiatric hospital or place them in a community home? Why?

Part Two: Exploring the text

BROKEN HOMES | WHERE HOPE DIES

Here, life is squalor(悲惨)and chaos

BY Clifford J. Levy

New York Times

April 29, 2002

It was the fall of 2000 and state inspectors were due to arrive at Seaport Manor, an adult home for the mentally ill in Canarsie, Brooklyn. Upstairs, some of its 325 residents, bewildered and mumbling, shuffled along the dreary hallways. Downstairs, a handful of workers hastily doctored records, they said, to make it seem as if the home was providing proper care.

The workers said they concocted case notes for manic-depressives(躁郁病患者)who holed up in their rooms for so long they became malnourished. They invented psychiatric (精神病学的,精神病治疗的)evaluations for residents who went untreated and turned suicidal. They scrawled therapy plans for women who prostituted themselves in the stairwells for cigarette money and for men who shook down(从……敲诈金钱) other residents for their $4-a-day allowance.

"We were told by the administrators at the home to be creative," said one worker, Toshua Courthan. "We were told we had to, or else we would lose our jobs. What the state wanted to see was that these people were being looked after, but they were not."

Ms. Courthan was fired after reporting the falsifying of records and other misconduct at the home to the state, and she is suing Seaport. Her account was independently supported by other current and former workers, including two who participated that evening, as well as by an examination of some of the records.

The inspectors who showed up that day in 2000, however, apparently never detected the hundreds of sham files, according to state records. Seaport, which receives more than $3.5 million annually from the government, stayed open. For its residents, life has remained as wretched as ever.

Occupying a one-acre tract(土地), the five-story brick building sits behind a row of shrubbery at 615 East 104th Street, not far from the neighborhood piers. A generation ago the home, along with dozens like it, represented a briefly entertained hope for the thousands of mentally ill people being pushed out of state psychiatric hospitals. In these homes, residents would learn to live independently and enter a mainstream community.

Just how profoundly that vision has collapsed can be appreciated in words from the state itself, which dubbed Seaport "The New Warehouse for the Insane" in a 1997 study by the Office of Mental Health. If the state gave Seaport a cynical nickname, though, records show it did nothing meaningful to improve or police it.

A portrait of life inside Seaport was gleaned(点点滴滴地收集)from more than 10 visits, more than 500 pages of state inspection reports and government documents obtained by *The New York Times*, as well as more than 50 interviews with workers and residents.

During a typical visit to the home, residents can be seen sitting for hours in the crowded smoking room, rocking back and forth, speaking only to themselves. Others can be spotted walking to the local liquor store, much to the dismay of those at the nearby day care center.

Current and former workers said two residents openly deal crack(快克,高纯度可卡

因毒品)from their rooms, contributing to the drug abuse, loan-sharking(放高利贷), prostitution and violence that have gripped the home for years. In this predatory(弱肉强食的)atmosphere, the frail quickly learn that the safest place is behind the closed doors of their rooms. Others find different ways to get by.

"It's tough around here," said a resident in her 50's who said she sells sex to workers and other residents for a few dollars. "You have to do it to survive."

Ambulances are regular visitors. In a three-month period last year, they made 93 runs to the home, city records show, sometimes to take away the dying, other times to rescue the neglected.

For years, workers said, a security guard subdued psychotic residents by beating them. Other employees are convicted drug dealers, prison records show. Several former workers said the home sometimes continued to collect the monthly disability benefits of residents after they died, or gave their Social Security numbers(社会安全号码,是"社会安全卡"上的号码,相当于美国个人身份证)to illegal immigrants the home hired.

There were dozens of numbers to choose from. From 1995 through 2001, one Seaport resident died roughly every month, according to an analysis by *The Times*. In all, at least 79 died, including at least three who committed suicide and two others whose bodies were discovered only after workers were drawn to the smell of decay.

"This is the last stop," a resident named Jerry said in his room at the home. "They are not preparing anyone for living outside of here."

For 26 years, the state has documented problems at Seaport and then averted its eyes. Since 1998, conditions have been so bad that inspection reports concluded that Seaport, as one said, "was in serious noncompliance in all major areas of operation."

The reports cited inadequate staffing and dangerous lapses in the distribution of medication. During a 1999 inspection, investigators refused to fully examine rooms because they were so fetid(有恶臭的). They also remarked in their records how workers at the home were able to walk past disheveled(凌乱的)residents without even noticing them.

Only in recent months, after The Times began an investigation of Seaport by requesting government records and questioning officials, did the state say it would crack down on the home.

Its response, however, has been erratic(飘忽不定的).

Last August, the state said it would try to revoke the operators' license. Last month, it agreed to let them surrender their license, pay a $20,000 fine and close the home. But in recent days, the state, confounded by the prospect of finding new housing for the residents, indicated it might try to keep Seaport open by installing new operators.

For now, the residents remain in Seaport under the same operators who the state has known for years have run a home of squalor and neglect. In 2001 alone, at least 18 residents died, The Times's analysis shows, 10 of whom were under 60.

Seaport's operators—Baruch Mappa, Martin Rosenberg and Emil Klein—said through their lawyer they would not be interviewed.

Before agreeing to surrender their license, the operators asserted in a disciplinary hearing before the State Department of Health that the home had undertaken renovations, overhauled medication practices and brought in more workers to increase supervision of residents.

"Seaport doesn't take the violations or alleged violations lightly," Ronald J. Aranoff, the home's lawyer, said at the hearing.

Over the years, Seaport, like many other adult homes, has often complained that the state has asked it to take responsibility for some of the most needy people while failing to provide enough money for their care. About 15,000 mentally ill adults live in more than 100 adult homes in New York.

The Department of Health said it did not take more aggressive action against Seaport in previous years because it preferred to help troubled homes improve conditions.

"Closure of a facility is disruptive to patients and residents, especially the elderly or mentally ill, and is typically pursued as a last resort after a home's repeated failures to comply with state regulations," said Robert R. Hinckley, a deputy state health commissioner.

The failures of Seaport can be witnessed in varying degrees at other adult homes in the city. State inspection reports on many of the homes are grim and interchangeable. Even so, the state seems to have grown accustomed to slapping the homes with one hand and shielding them with the other.

For the people who still live at homes like Seaport, most of whom are too sick to grasp the notion that they are entitled to something better, life is about doing what they can to endure.

Ritual Turmoil

Monthly Heightening of the Daily Disorder

Residents and workers at the home call it payday. Once a month, Seaport's administrators hand out about $120 in allowance money to each resident from the disability checks they control. Then the pandemonium(喧嚣)begins.

In-house loan sharks chase residents down the hall, intent on collecting their money, according to numerous current and former workers and residents. They said two crack dealers also opened for business, packing in(大量吸引)an assortment of fellow residents, and even the police said they have made drug arrests at the home in recent years.

Those residents unwilling to take part in either enterprise run to their rooms, fearful of the opportunistic and desperately in need of their tiny allowances. Inevitably, the strong at Seaport always know when the weak are in line to get their money.

"It would be just one big mess," Angela Peters, a former housekeeper and dietary aide, said of payday. "We couldn't do any work on the floor because it was so crazy."

From the outside, Seaport looks like a decent alternative to the homelessness that defines another portion of the city's mentally ill. From the inside, based on visits to the home and extensive interviews, it does not. If a coed(对男女都开放的) prison for the mentally ill were to exist, the inner workings of its yard might resemble Seaport. Except the prison would have security and a professional staff.

Ideally, the home is supposed to act like a bridge, helping the mentally ill return to neighborhoods where they can attain some self-sufficiency. In reality, there is nothing rehabilitative about the place—it rarely tries to help residents obtain proper therapy, job training or, at times, even get dressed, according to state inspection reports and interviews with workers and residents.

There is never enough staff, and administrators and workers typically have no mental health training. The state does not require it at adult homes, though their residents are deeply troubled.

According to the 1997 state mental health study, of about half of Seaport's population, more than 80 percent had histories of multiple psychiatric hospitalizations, 35 percent had histories of violent behavior, 32 percent had abused drugs and 13 percent had attempted suicide.

"It's just too sad a place to go to work," said Sherry Reiter, a social worker who was assigned in the late1990's to a clinic in the home run by the Kingsboro Psychiatric Center. "The sadness and the violence are part of the milieu(环境)."

Left with little supervision or treatment, residents often have psychotic episodes(精神病发作), records show. One man tried killing himself by taking an overdose of Tylenol (泰诺,畅销止痛药), burning himself with hot water and then hanging himself with a pajama top coiled into a noose. A delusional(患妄想症的) woman repeatedly stabbed herself on the back and legs.

Newcomers to the home quickly learn there is little to do. The most popular spot is the smoking room—a cluster of worn benches, bare walls, a television(always on) and a floor littered with cigarette butts, spilled coffee, ashes and discarded food.

The recreation room could offer other possibilities, but rarely does. For much of 2001, it was closed because there was no one to run it, workers and residents said. At other times, a high school student served as recreation director. For these schizophrenics (精神分裂症患者) and manic-depressives, the student liked to hold screenings of "Face/Off," a violent action movie about changeable identities.

In the late1990's, a report by a state watchdog agency, the Commission on Quality of Care for the Mentally Disabled, rated Seaport one of the worst adult homes. Yet in 1997, the state awarded Seaport $41,501.25 in bonus money intended for homes that provide quality care, state records show. The state allocated the money largely for computer training for residents. Seaport does not have computers for residents.

It barely has a laundry room. The home had a single washing machine during one inspection, and it showed. Residents had "dirty, stained or ripped clothing" and were in need of a bath or shower, the inspectors wrote in their 1999 report.

The wait to receive psychotropic(治疗精神病的) medication is sometimes half an hour or more, so some residents do not even bother. The ones who do are lucky if they get the correct pills, state inspection reports show. Peering into medication boxes, one inspector encountered dead cockroaches.

Andy Cadet, who ran the medication room for several months last year until she resigned, described the consequences of the chaos. "People were getting ill," Ms. Cadet said. "It was just a disaster."

The home itself does not provide psychiatric services, but it is expected to ensure that residents obtain them, either from the Kingsboro clinic at the home or from other psychiatrists who periodically visit. But the clinic, staffed by a psychiatrist and a few other trained workers, writes prescriptions that go unfilled. It asks that fragile residents be closely watched, and they are not, according to interviews with clinic workers and their records. The home's administrators, meanwhile, have long accused clinic workers of not doing their jobs.

At nights and on weekends, the residents are largely on their own. The clinic is closed, and the home has almost no one on duty. "Nobody wanted to take responsibility for patients who went berserk(精神错乱的) at night," said Louis Rossetti, who worked as a nurse at the clinic from 1980 until 1996 and then as a volunteer. "We would come in the morning and have to go upstairs and calm them down. It just over all got worse and worse."

Ms. Courthan, Ms. Cadet and several other workers said a security guard, Lionel Harrington, used to beat residents to subdue them. For his part, Mr. Harrington said he only tried to crack down on the drug-dealing, loan-sharking and prostitution.

He said the administrators at the home knew about the goings-on, especially the crack-dealing by one of the residents. "They are well aware that this man is destroying the residents in that building," Mr. Harrington said. He said he was fired late last year after he was late for work.

Toward the end of the month, as residents start to run out of money, the atmosphere in the home turns even worse, workers and residents said. Used condoms can be found in the stairwells and hallways, as both male and female residents trade sex for spending money, drugs or cigarettes.

"Generally, it was sex for drugs or sex for money," said Angela Johnson, a former worker at the home. "If someone wanted a dollar, it was sex for a dollar. Sex for anything was a big problem."

History

Hospital Emptied, Its Troubles Relocated

In the early1970's, Kingsboro Psychiatric Center in Brooklyn, one in the state's array of vast mental hospitals, began aggressively emptying its beds as New York undertook the process of what came to be known as deinstitutionalization.

Kingsboro was looking for places to relocate its patients when Mr. Mappa, a local real estate developer, was looking for another business enterprise. His brainchild was to open Seaport Manor in September 1975 and take in many of those who were being cast out of the hospital's wards.

Only three miles from Kingsboro, the new building had a kitchen, dining room, recreation room and 13 bedrooms on the first floor; and 40 bedrooms on each of the second through fifth floors.

The idea, shared by Mr. Mappa and the state, was that the home would make for a civilized alternative to Kingsboro. Mr. Mappa would also make money. Residents would sign over their monthly government disability checks for rent, and outside providers would pay fees to the home for the opportunity to treat residents.

Yet neither Mr. Mappa nor the two business partners he brought in had any mental health expertise. The money from the government never seemed enough, and the care that came to be provided by the medical professionals was never adequate.

As a result, a troubled psychiatric hospital was emptied and effectively recreated in a place even less equipped to deal with hundreds of seriously ill people.

In the late1970's, Seaport was a focus of an investigation into adult homes by a deputy state attorney general, Charles J. Hynes, who is now the Brooklyn district attorney. A grand jury found that at adult homes in Brooklyn, the condition of residents "was permitted to deteriorate to unconscionable(过分的) levels." Ultimately, no charges were brought against Seaport or its operators, and leading state officials brushed aside Mr. Hynes's damning portrait of the adult home system.

The state did make a few changes at Seaport, including opening a clinic in 1979, one run by workers who came over from Kingsboro. But over the years, the state has cut the number of clinic workers to roughly 8 from nearly 20, Kingsboro workers said.

For much of the past decade, the home—with more mentally ill people than most psychiatric hospitals in the nation—has been run by Esther Elizabeth Rosenberg, the daughter of one of its operators. Ms. Rosenberg, 47, graduated from Brooklyn College in 1990 with a degree in sociology and had little work experience of any kind when she took over the home, according to court records and interviews.

The state has essentially called her incompetent. "The administrator is not capable of managing this facility and correcting the problems," a 2000 inspection report said. "We recommend enforcement be pursued."

But the state's own documented dealings with Seaport show that nothing much was done. It was not until March 2001, after years of incriminating inspection reports and concerns that residents were being neglected, that the state tried to discipline the home by levying a $7,000 fine.

But while it got Seaport to remove Ms. Rosenberg, it let the operators appoint her son-in-law, Seth Fried, as administrator.

The Workers

"I Knew Jack-Diddly(完全没有)About Medicatio"

It was clear that Toshua Courthan was in over her head(超出她的理解力).

She had no mental health training yet after only a short time at Seaport, she was promoted to case manager and then director of social services, playing a pivotal role in overseeing more than 300 chronically mentally ill people.

Over her two years at the home, she said, she was pressured to commit or she witnessed a startling variety of misconduct, from the forging of records to the misreporting of deaths. She decided in her second year that she could not keep silent, she said, and began secretly telling state inspectors about problems at the home. The inspectors took her calls, but otherwise seemed uninterested, she said. The state confirmed her calls.

In early 2001, Ms. Courthan, who is black, was fired, and she sued the home in Federal District Court in Brooklyn, charging that administrators had made racially insensitive comments to her. Aaron Charles Schlesinger, a lawyer for Seaport Manor, did not respond to three phone messages seeking comment. In court papers, Seaport denied Ms. Courthan's charges.

A review of inspection reports and interviews with more than 15 current and former workers support her account of life at the home. "Seaport's thing is, 'Let's fill the beds,' "Ms. Courthan said. "'We don't care if they are psychiatrically unstable.' They don't care about these people."

Ms. Courthan was hired as a receptionist at Seaport in 1999. With low salaries and mismanagement, workers were constantly quitting, and she was rapidly promoted.

Her sister, Ms. Johnson, who had worked as a clerk for the City Board of Education, was later hired and put in charge of the medication room . Ms. Johnson found this strange, she recalled, because "I knew jack-diddly about medication ."

Soon, Ms. Courthan and Ms. Johnson were helping to run the place, at $8 to $9.50 an hour. They received strong evaluations from administrators and were popular with residents, according to records and interviews, but were swamped with work. They were supposed to meet with residents monthly, file reports and ensure the residents were being seen by psychiatrists. But they rarely did.

This was obvious to state inspectors. In a January 2000 inspection report, they noted that of 30 resident files they had examined, 14 did not have current annual evaluations, let alone monthly case notes.

Later that year, the home was expecting another inspection, and Ms. Courthan and Ms. Johnson said Ms. Rosenberg, the home's administrator, told them to put the files in order, by forgery if necessary.

Ms. Courthan and Ms. Johnson said they and other workers stayed late one night and concocted hundreds of records, making up psychiatric evaluations and signing them with the names of fictional doctors. Ms. Cadet, the former medication worker, said she witnessed the forging.

By the time the night was over, records, some of which were shown to *The Times*, reflected that many residents had seen a nonexistent Dr. Rollins and received the same diagnosis. "Everybody, if you looked at their charts, they were all paranoid schizophrenic (妄想型精神分裂症)," Ms. Courthan said.

While state inspectors evidently did not detect that documents were being faked en masse(全部地), they had previously criticized the home's record-keeping, noting that files were "altered or missing."

Ms. Rosenberg would not comment.

Ms. Courthan and Ms. Johnson said the deception did not end with the forged records.

One night in November 2000, a resident named Dorothy Clinton set herself on fire and later died at the hospital. Based in part on interviews with Seaport employees, the medical examiner's office ruled the death an accident. The home contended she had ignited herself while smoking crack in bed.

Ms. Courthan, Ms. Peters, the former housekeeper, and other workers say the tale of crack smoking was wholly invented; they tell a different story. Ms. Courthan said she had recommended that Ms. Clinton be hospitalized that day because she seemed delusional and suicidal, but that an administrator had blocked the request.

That night, Ms. Clinton, 48, got dressed up, putting on earrings and makeup, and then intentionally ignited herself while in bed, residents and workers said.

Ms. Courthan said she wrote in Ms. Clinton's file the next day that she should have been hospitalized. When Ms. Rosenberg found out, she ordered Ms. Courthan to remove those notes, Ms. Courthan said. "Esther told me, 'If you speak to the coroner(验尸官), and say anything about how depressed she was, it is going to be a problem for us and it will be a problem for you,'" Ms. Courthan said.

Ms. Clinton's death was one of the few the state has investigated at adult homes. But while it cited the home for having inadequate staffing, state records show, it does not appear that it addressed the question of whether Ms. Clinton had been suicidal and whether her death could have been prevented.

Three months later, Ms. Courthan was dismissed, and she said she tried to unburden (吐露真相) herself to inspectors one final time. She faxed them a letter on Feb. 6, 2001, repeating and elaborating on many of her allegations. An examination of the letter shows she wrote of how she and other workers had forged the records, saying that they made up "those forms A to Z."

Again, she said, inspectors did nothing.

Asked about Ms. Courthan and Ms. Johnson, Robert Kenny, a spokesman for the State Department of Health, at first said that the two had talked to inspectors only in early 2000 and complained only about administrators' stealing money from residents. Mr. Kenny said the inspectors cited the home 18 months later for failing to manage residents' accounts properly.

Pressed further, Mr. Kenny acknowledged that the inspectors had talked to the two women more regularly and that they had received the faxed letter from Ms. Courthan.

He said her allegations "were not new to inspectors."

After Ms. Courthan was dismissed, the home had Ms. Johnson arrested and charged with stealing \$200 from residents. She was fired. The charges were later dropped.

The Deaths

Invisible Lives End Without Notice

The final indignity for many of Seaport's residents comes with a shovel full of dirt at potter's field(公共墓地). Nearly one out of every four residents who died from 1995 through 2001 was sent to the island cemetery in the East River, without headstones(墓碑) to mark their graves or eulogies(悼词) to recall how they weathered their troubled lives.

Seaport, after profiting from them, made no effort to find them proper burial. In a way, it was almost fitting, given that the residents' deaths came with the same invisibility that surrounded their lives at the home.

Of the 79 people who died in the seven-year period, the average age of death was 58. Twenty-four of the dead were under 50.

"People were dying like flies," Ms. Peters said. "They have nobody who is looking after those people."

It will probably never be known how many of the deaths could have been avoided. The home almost always either failed to notify the state about deaths or left out details pointing to deficient care, records show.

In turn, the State Department of Health could provide documentary evidence that inspectors looked into only three deaths at Seaport—Ms. Clinton's and two others. Those three inquiries, in fact, were the only ones that appeared to have been done by state inspectors at 26 of the largest and most troubled adult homes in the city in the seven-year period, when at least 946 residents died, according to the Times's analysis.

Elayne Silverman, once a promising student who wanted to be a social worker, was only 39 when she took her life in April 1995 at Seaport. It was just after breakfast when she climbed the stairs to the roof, according to state records and interviews. No workers at the home noticed. Then again, it was a Saturday, and few were on duty. Either the alarm on the door to the roof was broken, or it went off and was disregarded.

Ms. Silverman walked around for a while before taking off her clothes, folding them into a neat pile and then jumping, according to a Kingsboro clinic record.

Even that failed to get anyone's attention. A neighbor eventually called the home and said a naked body was in the parking lot. When the clinic asked about the death, Seaport administrators could not explain how a home that sheltered numerous people with histories of suicidal behavior could allow such access to the roof, clinic records show.

The state never investigated her death, or those of numerous others, according to interviews and records: Stephen Willner, 60, who succumbed(死亡) to dehydration and malnourishment in 1999; Lewis Howard, 45, who died of kidney failure last year after no one responded when he passed out; and Albert Jarrell, 44, who had a heart attack in 1997 and was dead before workers thought to call 911.

While residents are free to come and go from the home during the day, the home is required by law to keep track of them. Bed checks are mandatory, but rarely done, residents and workers said. If a resident is missing for more than 24 hours, a report must be filed with the state and the police.

Artie Washington had not been seen for longer than that. Not only did Seaport not fill out a form, it did not even notice his absence.

Mr. Washington was known around the home for wearing an assortment of silly hats, from a Santa's cap to a Burger King crown. He was last seen on the Friday morning before Labor Day weekend in 1998. Early Monday afternoon, workers concerned by "a foul odor" entered Room 333, according to state records. "We found him dead, just sitting in the bathtub," said Mr. Rossetti, the nurse at the Kingsboro clinic.

An autopsy determined that Mr. Washington, 54, had died of a seizure. It is unclear whether he could have been saved had he been discovered earlier. Inspectors, in one of the three death inquiries they performed, criticized Seaport for allowing him to remain at the home even though he was unstable. Yet the state took no action to safeguard against similar deaths.

So in July 2001, Rosendo Velez, 77, was found dead. Mr. Velez, nicknamed Keebler because he walked like the elves in the cookie commercial, had returned to the home in a drunken fog(酩酊大醉), workers said. He was left in his room unattended anyway, and was found drowned an hour later in his bathtub, fully clothed. It was not until three months later, in October, that the state cited the home for failing to supervise Mr. Velez.

In the meantime, Martin Rochlitz, 51, was found decomposing in his sweltering room days after dying of a heart attack during an August heat wave, according to the coroner. Unlike the deaths of Mr. Washington and Mr. Velez, Mr. Rochlitz's did not even warrant a question by the state, its records show.

Holding On

Expecting Trouble, Fearing Even Worse

Kevin Johnson sees death all around him, and fears that his will be the next.

He has seizure disorder(癫痫症), schizophrenia and cerebral palsy(脑瘫). He is mildly retarded(轻度智障)and cannot perform basic arithmetic. At a recent lunch, he had difficulty pulling the wrapper off a straw. Yet, sadly, even he understands that at Seaport, the odds are against him.

Mr. Johnson, 39, cannot forget all the seizures that have sent him tumbling to the floor of Room 106 during the past three years. Dazed and bruised, he is eventually found by a worker and taken to Brookdale University Hospital and Medical Center.

Each time, Mr. Johnson is admitted to the hospital for a few days. In vain, it calls the home for his medical and psychiatric history. "They could not provide more information on the patient," a nurse wrote one day. As always, he is sent back to the home.

His latest wound is a jagged gash on his forehead. He needed stitches to close it after banging his head on the floor during a convulsion. Still, he considers it a minor injury.

What he dreads is a repeat of what happened on a Sunday morning in July 1999. He was left alone to shower, had a seizure and passed out. It is not known how long he lay there as he was scalded(烫伤) by water that inspectors have repeatedly warned is too hot. He needed two skin-graft(植皮)operations to heal huge swaths on his chest, back and arms.

Seaport never notified the state about his injuries, as was required, and Mr. Johnson was once again returned to the home. Left to himself, he has devised his own way of dealing with the seizures. "I sit on the bed and try to take it easy," he said the other day.

Ill since he was a teenager, Mr. Johnson is 5-foot-8 and beefy, with a mustache, a round face and no family. He has a kindly disposition, but often reverts to long silences, as if he learned long ago that the way to make it through the day is by shutting everyone out. He sits in his room for hours, listening to oldies on the radio and worrying that if he walks around the home, someone will harass him for money, or worse.

With the turmoil over Seaport's fate, Mr. Johnson's future is uncertain. For now, he soothes himself against his surroundings by reading the paperback King James Bible that he hides in the top drawer of his dresser.

Sitting on his flimsy mattress as mice scamper by, he opens to the same chapter and mouths the words, over and over. Second Corinthians, Chapter 5: Do not despair, for there is a better place in the afterlife.

一、作者背景

Columbia University President Lee C. Bollinger (left) presents Clifford J. Levy with the 2003 Pulitzer Prize in Investigative Reporting.

克利福德·J·莱维(Clifford J. Levy):1967 年生于美国纽约州新罗谢尔市(New Rochelle),1989 年从普林斯顿大学毕业,获得公共政策与国际事务学位。毕业后,莱维在合众国际社(UPI)纽约分社做了一年记者。1990 年,莱维加入《纽约时报》,从新闻助理做起,1992 年成为正式记者。此后,他曾做过该报驻纽瓦克记者、专门报道纽约市政府事务的记者、政治新闻记者、《纽约时报》奥尔巴尼记者站主任等职务。2000 年,莱维成为《纽约时报》都市版的专题报道记者。2007 年起,他成为该报莫斯科记者站记者。

1998 年莱维曾因成功报道纽约州高级官员的竞选经费问题获得著名的乔治·波克新闻奖(George Polk Award)。2003 年,他撰写的系列报道又获得普利策调查报道奖。

二、《纽约时报》

The New York Times

CLINTON IS VICTOR, DEFEATING OBAMA; McCAIN ALSO WINS

The January 9, 2008 front page

《纽约时报》在纽约出版，全世界发行，是美国最负盛名的报纸，以报道国内国际大事和严肃的社会新闻著称，有“档案记录报”的美称。该报属苏兹伯格家族拥有。

《纽约时报》于 1851 年创刊。其创办人是记者兼政治家亨利·贾维斯·雷蒙德（Henry Jarvis Raymond）和银行家乔治·琼斯（George Jones）。该报在相当长的时期内版面风格严肃，拘谨保守，一片灰色，因此曾被戏称为“灰贵妇”（Gray Lady）。

1896 年，阿道夫·奥克斯（Adolph Ochs）收购了《纽约时报》，并确定了该报的新闻报道原则：“力求真实，无畏无惧，不偏不倚，并不分党派、地域或任何特殊利益。”他还提出了著名的报道格言：“一切适宜刊印的消息”（All the news that's fit to print），以与煽情新闻为主的《纽约日报》和《纽约世界报》抗衡。

1935 年，奥克斯的女婿苏兹伯格（Sulzberger）接管报纸。在他任内的 20 多年，该报的新闻采访范围进一步扩大，广告收入翻了一倍，技术设备得到极大的更新。

《纽约时报》第四代发行人是苏兹伯格的独子阿瑟·奥克斯·苏兹伯格（Arthur Ochs Sulzberger）。他励精图治，选拔麦森、罗森索等优秀编辑和经营人才，引进先进技术，开拓多元化经营。在他任内的 30 年，该报走出了濒临崩溃的困境，积累了雄厚的物质基础，1963 年该报的总收入为 1 亿美元，到 1991 年，该报总公司的收入已达 17 亿美元，在这一过程中，《纽约时报》也完成了由家族式经营向市场式经营的转型。

《纽约时报》的现任发行人是小阿瑟·奥克斯·苏兹伯格。该报至 2013 年为止已获得 112 次普利策新闻奖，是获普利策奖总数最多的报纸，其中仅 2002 年，就一举获得了 7 个奖项，也是单次获奖数量最多的报纸。

三、课文背景

由于抗精神病药物的发明及社区心理卫生运动的提倡，自 20 世纪六十年代开始，美国政府针对慢性精神病患者提出“去机构化”（deinstitutionalization）政策，是指逐步关闭大规模的封闭管理式的州立精神病医院，将患者接回社区，在社区正常的环境中疗养，帮助他们回归家庭或社区生活。但在政策执行过程中，出现了资金不到位，医疗和康复专业人力以及设施不足等种种问题。因此，许多精神病人离开医院后在疗养院得不到应有的康复，有些患者流向仅供食宿的收容所，甚至流浪街头。此外，犯罪、吸毒和酗酒等问题也层出不穷。莱维的系列调查性报道就为我们展示了精神病人在疗养所的悲惨境遇以及主管部门的冷漠与失职。

普利策奖评审委员会对莱维作品的赞词是：语言生动（vivid）、写作技巧超群（brilliantly written）。

在写作技巧上，文章的结构组织尤为值得注意。文章共分为六个部分，除了第一个部分外，其他部分都有小标题，像路标一样，引导读者，读者不会因为文章篇幅长而迷失方向。第一部分侧重总体描写精神病疗养院的糟糕状况及其原因；第二部分具体展现了疗养院里的混乱嘈杂情景；第三部分重点批评政府管理者的冷漠与无为；第四部分反映工作人员的不称职问题；第五部分讲述了一个个在疗养院里悄无声息消失的生命；第六部分体现了患者的绝望。“死后就有希望了。”这是何等的绝望！越往后读，越会感到沉重和压抑。

四、作者主要观点

1. List all the malpractices Levy has spotted in Seaport Manor. What factors have led to such malpractices?

2. "Sitting on his flimsy mattress as mice scamper by, he opens to the same chapter and mouths the words, over and over. Second Corinthians, Chapter 5: Do not despair, for there is a better place in the afterlife." Why do you think Levy closes the story with this paragraph?

五、写作风格与手法

1. What has intrigued you most about the article in terms of its writing style?

2. What evidence does the story give of the methods by which the news was obtained and/or verified? What are, if any, some unusual sources?

3. Are there signs indicating the difficulties of the reporter in getting the details of the story? How does the author explain such difficulties in his writing?

4. What measures has the reporter taken to convince the readers that such information is accurate and valid?

5. Does the story seem to be fair or unbiased? Explain.

6. How does the reporter strike a balance between narration and explanation? In what order does he organize the materials?

7. Is there variety in sentence length and sentence construction? Look for examples in the text.

8. Study the reporter's choice of words and comment on his style of writing.

9. In what way is the story "vivid" and "brilliantly written" as suggested in the citation.

Part Three: Further exploring the text

一、语言点讲解

1. It was the fall of 2000 and state inspectors were due to arrive at Seaport Manor, an adult home for the mentally ill in Canarsie, Brooklyn. Upstairs, some of its 325 residents, bewildered and mumbling, shuffled along the dreary hallways. Downstairs, a handful of workers hastily doctored records, they said, to make it seem as if the home was providing proper care.

这是一个非常成功的导语，作者用文字实现了电影蒙太奇的效果。在这段话中，我们看到了精神病人的神态、表情、语言和动作（bewildered and mumbling, shuffled along），看到了精神病疗养院的环境（dreary hallways），更看到了员工为应付上级检查而篡改文件的慌张（hastily doctored records）。这几句话为整篇文章定下了基调，并迅速激发了读者的好奇——这个精神病疗养院到底是怎样的？员工为什么要篡改文件？问题的根源在哪里？Upstairs 和 Downstairs 很自然地带出了本文的两大主人公：精神病患者和疗养院的工作人员。这两句话的结构类似，对比强烈。

2. The workers said they concocted case notes for manic-depressives who holed up in their rooms for so long they became malnourished. They invented psychiatric evaluations for residents who went untreated and turned suicidal. They scrawled therapy plans for women who prostituted themselves in the stairwells for cigarette money and for men who shook down other residents for their ＄4-a-day allowance.

动词是句子的灵魂，选用恰当的动词无疑可以增加语言的魅力。我们看看这里介绍疗养所工作人员篡改文件时一串排比结构中使用的动词：concocted，invented，scrawled。Concoct 表示“编造”、“捏造”。Invent 是“创造”，带点讽刺意味，Scrawl 本身虽然没有编造谎言的意思，但“匆忙、潦草地书写”这个含义却与上面两个动词呼应，入木三分地刻画了工作人员大规模造假的行为。在这篇文章中表示造假、伪造文件的词或短语还有以下几个：doctor，creative，falsify，sham，forge，forgery，misreport，make up，fake，alter，deception 等。请找到它们在文章中的位置，利用英英字典查出这些词语的具体含义、使用场合和常用搭配。在这篇文章中，作者还使用了一系列表示“肮脏”、“恶臭”的词或短语，也请大家找出来并比较学习。另外，“＄4-a-day allowance”写得也很巧妙，这涉及数据的表现方法。从后文中，我们得知每名精神病患者每月可以领到大约 120 美元的微薄津贴，作者在这里按天计算出病人的津贴，金额更少，给读者的印象也更深刻。

3. A portrait of life inside Seaport was gleaned from more than 10 visits, more than 500 pages of state inspection reports and government documents obtained by *The New York Times*, as well as more than 50 interviews with workers and residents.

这句话解释了记者的信息来源，让读者相信记者讲述的故事。类似的句子在文章中还有几处。当然，我们也可以通过这句话一窥调查报道记者的艰辛。

4. If a coed prison for the mentally ill were to exist, the inner workings of its yard might resemble Seaport. Except the prison would have security and a professional staff.

这里作者使用了类比的写作方法，先是假设存在专门关押精神病犯人的监狱，然后说 Seaport 的运作应该与监狱差不多，最后说监狱还有保安人员和专业人员，言外之意是 Seaport 连监狱都不如。在为读者描述一个他们不是特别熟悉的环境时，使用这样的类比写法是很有必要的。

5. In the late 1990's, a report by a state watchdog agency, the Commission on Quality of Care for the Mentally Disabled, rated Seaport one of the worst adult homes. Yet in 1997, the state awarded Seaport ＄41,501.25 in bonus money intended for homes that provide quality care, state records show. The state allocated the money largely for computer training for residents. Seaport does not have computers for residents.

作者在这段话里罗列了大量互相矛盾的事实，言外之意是州政府对 Seaport 监管不力，应当对精神病患者的悲惨境遇负责。但是，作者并没有把这个观点表述出来并强加于读者，而是让读者自然的得到这个结论。这样的处理方式值得我们学习。

二、中西文化比较

论“同情心”

在本文中，莱维把精神病疗养院看作是“破碎的家”（broken home）、“悲惨和被忽略的家”（home of squalor and neglect），并充满了“弱肉强食的气氛”（predatory atmosphere）。同时，在描写精神病患者的状况时，莱维说“他们病得太严重，以至于不知道自己还拥有改善生活条件的权利。对他们来说，生活就是忍受。”在文章末尾，他描写了强生先生的悲惨境地和无望的生活，与老鼠为伴，以一遍遍重复《圣经》中的“不要绝望，因为死后就可以到一个更好地方”而度日。从字里行间，我们可以感受到莱维对这些精神病患者的同情与悲悯。

所谓“同情心”，就是对他人痛苦的感同身受。同情心是人性中固有的，它是人类社会全部道德的开端和基础。古人说“恻隐之心人皆有之”。西方也有许多这方面的论述。如：

1. The value of compassion cannot be over-emphasized. Anyone can criticize. It takes a true believer to be compassionate. No greater burden can be borne by an individual than to know no one cares or understands. （Arthur H. Stainback）

2. Compassion will cure more sins than condemnation. （Henry Ward Beecher）

3. Compassion is the antitoxin of the soul：where there is compassion even the most poisonous impulses remain relatively harmless. （Eric Hoffer）

4. Compassion is the basis of all morality. （Athur Schopenhauer）

三、语言练习

1. 请用英语解释下列句子。

For its residents,life has remained as wretched as ever.

The failures of Seaport can be witnessed in varying degrees at other adult homes in the city.

Even so,the state seems to have grown accustomed to slapping the homes with one hand and shielding them with the other.

From the outside,Seaport looks like a decent alternative to the homelessness that defines another portion of the city's mentally ill.

The idea,shared by Mr. Mappa and the state,was that the home would make for a civilized alternative to Kingsboro.

An examination of the letter shows she wrote of how she and other workers had forged the records,saying that they made up “those forms A to Z.”

In a way,it was almost fitting,given that the residents' deaths came with the same invisibility that surrounded their lives at the home.

2. 请将下列短语翻译成英文，并比较中英文表达方式的异同。

（1）龟缩在自己的屋子里

(2) 对伪造文件进行举报
(3) 在所有主要环节都有严重违规现象
(4) 人手不足
(5) 严厉整顿
(6) 吊销经营者的执照
(7) 不把……当成一回事
(8) 忙得不可开交
(9) 整理文档
(10) 把衣服整齐地叠成一堆
(11) 前额处一道很深的、锯齿状的伤口

3. 请将下面的句子或段落翻译成中文，并比较中英文表达方式的异同。

Her account was independently supported by other current and former workers, including two who participated that evening, as well as by an examination of some of the records.

A generation ago the home, along with dozens like it, represented a briefly entertained hope for the thousands of mentally ill people being pushed out of state psychiatric hospitals. In these homes, residents would learn to live independently and enter a mainstream community.

Just how profoundly that vision has collapsed can be appreciated in words from the state itself, which dubbed Seaport "The New Warehouse for the Insane" in a 1997 study by the Office of Mental Health. If the state gave Seaport a cynical nickname, though, records show it did nothing meaningful to improve or police it.

The most popular spot is the smoking room—a cluster of worn benches, bare walls, a television (always on) and a floor littered with cigarette butts, spilled coffee, ashes and discarded food.

The final indignity for many of Seaport's residents comes with a shovel full of dirt at potter's field. Nearly one out of every four residents who died from 1995 through 2001 was sent to the island cemetery in the East River, without headstones to mark their graves or eulogies to recall how they weathered their troubled lives.

He has seizure disorder, schizophrenia and cerebral palsy. He is mildly retarded and cannot perform basic arithmetic. At a recent lunch, he had difficulty pulling the wrapper off a straw. Yet, sadly, even he understands that at Seaport, the odds are against him.

Ill since he was a teenager, Mr. Johnson is 5-foot-8 and beefy, with a mustache, a round face and no family. He has a kindly disposition, but often reverts to long silences, as if he learned long ago that the way to make it through the day is by shutting everyone out. He sits in his room for hours, listening to oldies on the radio and worrying that if he walks around the home, someone will harass him for money, or worse.

Sitting on his flimsy mattress as mice scamper by, he opens to the same chapter and mouths the words, over and over. Second Corinthians, Chapter 5: Do not despair, for there is a better place in the afterlife.

Part Four：Exploring beyond the text

一、自我反思

1. 我学到了什么？我要如何改进？

2. 一篇高质量的调查性新闻报道的基本标准是什么？我能清楚地告诉别人吗？该篇报道的记者克利福德·J·莱维是如何达到这些标准的？我能向别人解释清楚吗？

二、知识扩展

1. “去机构化”是本课文的重要社会背景。请收集资料，更多地了解该政策的利弊及其在全球范围内的推广情况。

2. 请阅读两本相关著作：

● *Watchdog Journalism*：*The Art of Investigative Reporting* by Stephen J. Berry，USA：Oxford University Press，2008.

● *The Evolution of American Investigative Journalism* by James L. Aucoin，University of Missouri Press，2007.

三、能力扩展

1. 访问普利策奖官方网站，阅读莱维在2002年撰写的“破碎的家”系列报道（http：//www.pulitzer.org/works/2003，Investigative+Reporting）。读完这六篇报道后，请写一篇500字左右的评论。

2. 就自己生活环境中一个让你感触颇深的问题撰写一篇2000字左右的调查报道。报道中的人物和事件应该是真实的。

Unit Six　Feature Writing

特稿写作

单元导航

本单元将讨论特稿写作。本单元有两篇文章。课文 A 讲述了人称“心如黄金”的黑人洗衣老妇奥莎拉·麦卡迪（Oseola McCarty）的故事。课文 B 是关于美国海军少将斯蒂夫·贝克（Steve Beck）以伤亡援助官（casualty assistance officer）的身份帮助在伊拉克战争中阵亡战士的家人走出丧子之痛的故事。

Part One：Preparing to explore

一、特稿写作

1. 定义

在美国新闻里，编辑一般把新闻分成三大类：spot news story/breaking news story（突发新闻），news feature（新闻特写）和 feature（特稿）。突发新闻是对重大事件的报道，其基本特点是以快取胜，内容包括新闻五要素，一般篇幅短；新闻特写是比突发新闻更详尽的新闻，即在新闻五要素之外，补充具有“人情味”的重要细节来完善新闻事实，让新闻更具可读性；特稿则是比新闻特写更详尽的新闻，作者使用大量有趣但未必重要的信息，以打动和感染读者，进一步增加可读性，增强传播效果。

美国的丹尼尔·威廉森教授为特稿写作下的定义是：特稿写作是一种带有创作性的，有时也带有主观性的文章，旨在给读者以精神享受，并使他们对某件事、某种情况或对生活中的某个侧面有所了解。

2. 产生与发展

在 18 世纪美国新闻早期时代，特稿写作并没有受到重视。美国第一张定期发行的报纸《波士顿新闻报》的发行人理查德·德雷伯（Richard Draper）曾在其报上公开宣称：“只有在新闻缺乏的情况下才能用特稿”。进入 19 世纪，一些保守的编辑仍然对特稿嗤之以鼻，认为有辱新闻的崇高使命，只适用于面向工人阶层的廉价报纸。比如，1841 年，贺拉斯·格里利（Horace Greeley）在创办《纽约论坛报》（*New York Tribune*）时，宣布其报纸将避免刊登不道德的和不体面的警署报道，广告以及那些已使主要廉价报刊专栏质量下降的其他新闻体裁。

但是，19世纪末，特稿写作备受欢迎。为了吸引读者，赫斯特的《纽约日报》（*New York Journal*）与其对手普利策的《纽约世界报》（*New York World*）打破老套的新闻报道方式，开创了被称为“黄色新闻”（yellow journalism）的报道方式，即在犯罪新闻、体育、社会和科技等新闻报道中添加了许多耸人听闻的、甚至纯属捏造的细节。特稿从此成了增加报纸销量的有力武器。

然而，第一次世界大战后，特稿写作又一度转入沉寂状态。面对战争带来的后果以及后来的经济萧条，有些报纸把特稿写作看成是琐碎之事，开始转向严肃题材报道。而坚持此报道方式的报纸开始走下坡路。比如，赫斯特的报业集团从22份报纸减少到了8份。又如，1947年，《纽约先锋论坛报》的城市版编辑约瑟夫·赫兹伯格（Joseph G. Herzberg）主编并出版了《新近城市版》（*Late City Edition*）一书，共29章，包括该报编辑记者写的一系列文章，但没有任何一章涉及特稿写作。

第二次世界大战后，特稿写作卷土重来。一方面，面对美国战后出现的麦卡锡主义、民权运动、越南战争、水门事件等事件，教育程度越来越高的公众想了解这些问题，并期望新闻界树立严肃的态度，帮助找到解决问题的方法；另一方面，报刊编辑们意识到严肃新闻并不意味着单调沉闷。他们重新发现了2300年前希腊剧作家们的一种共识，即几乎所有的新闻事件都具有人情味的一面。而正是人情味使事件具有新闻价值。正像希腊剧作家阿里斯多芬在其讽刺喜剧《青蛙》中的一句台词暗示的那样：你应该让人像人一样说话。因此，充满人情味的新闻特写和特稿在报纸新闻版大量出现，改变了传统新闻写作较为刻板的叙事方式，受到公众欢迎。特稿写作从此日趋成熟。

3. 普利策特稿写作

特稿写作奖是普利策新闻奖中比较新的项目，1979年才加入。1979年，《巴尔的摩太阳晚报》（*Baltimore Evening Sun*）记者乔恩·富兰克林发表了一篇关于大脑手术、读起来像短篇小说的题为“凯利太太的妖怪”（*Mrs. Kelly's Monster*）的医学报道，意外地得到了普利策奖评审委员会的赏识。从此，特稿写作重新走向繁荣并成熟起来。

普利策特稿奖作品大多是对普通人的生活和命运的关怀，如黑人、军人、父亲、农场工人、贫困大学生、移民、火灾幸存者、大屠杀幸存者、中毒性休克综合征患者、盲童、畸形儿等等。这些作品都是文学性新闻报道的纯正典范，作者运用文学手法为新闻事实注入了强烈的情感内容，让戏剧效果和情节自然展开，在叙事中巧妙地运用冲突，凸显了事实的张力，使每篇都成了让人感动、让人恐惧、让人痛苦的新闻。

关于普利策特稿写作奖项，还有两个小插曲。1981年，该奖得主、《华盛顿邮报》记者珍尼特·库克（Janet Cooke）因被发现杜撰了8岁的海洛因受害者吉米的故事而被退还普利策奖，从此声名狼藉。2004年，入围的三篇作品最后均未被评上，普利策特稿写作奖空缺。这是很少发生的事情，这三篇作品的话题皆涉及国家大事，分别是：2003年美国哥伦比亚号航天飞机坠毁的原因；从伊拉克战场回美的伤残战士的生活状况；州政府采取的企图终止家长权利的强硬政策。

4. 意义

特稿的最高要求是“讲一个好故事及讲好一个故事”。特稿不但可以提供知识，而且可以帮助人们认识和理解自身的存在状态。作为故事化模式新闻，特稿写作往往体现了人对自身命运的关注。无论是讲故事的，还是听故事的，都表现了对过去和他人的好奇，建立起了过去和现在、他人和自己的联系，通过这种联系产生命运观以及对命运的关怀，从而借此来体验和领会自身的生存状态。

5. 基本写作特征

从普利策奖评审委员会给予特稿写作获奖作品的赞词来看，优秀特写作品具有以下基本特征：

（1）文学性（literary quality）。运用文学的叙事手法，让情融于事中；在真实性的原则上，运用多种描绘手法，生动而集中地再现场景与人物；巧妙运用冲突，产生悬念，避免平铺直叙。

（2）新颖性（originality）。确立和提炼深刻而新颖的主题；在写作方法、技巧、结构、语言上都有独到之处，能给人耳目一新的感觉。

（3）精确性（concision）。语言生动、形象，同时准确、简洁，不妄加虚拟。

二、课前讨论

1. What kind of life do you wish to lead and what legacy would you want to leave behind? What kind of impact would you want to make on society?

2. Often those who give the most are those who have the least. Have you had such an experience as seeing those who have little but give substantially? If so, why do you think this could happen?

Part Two: Exploring the text

Text A All she has, $ 150,000, is going to a university

BY Rick Bragg

New York Times

August 13, 1995

Oseola McCarty spent a lifetime making other people look nice. Day after day, for most of her 87 years, she took in bundles of dirty clothes and made them clean and neat for parties she never attended, weddings to which she was never invited, graduations she never saw.

She had quit school in the sixth grade to go to work, never married, never had children and never learned to drive because there was never any place in particular she wanted to go. All she ever had was the work, which she saw as a blessing. Too many other black people in rural Mississippi did not have even that.

She spent almost nothing, living in her old family home, cutting the toes out of shoes

(削足适履)if they did not fit right and binding her ragged(破旧的)Bible with Scotch tape(透明胶带)to keep Corinthians(基督教《圣经· 新约》中的《哥林多书》)from falling out. Over the decades, her pay—mostly dollar bills and change—grew to more than ＄150,000.

"More than I could ever use," Miss McCarty said the other day without a trace of self-pity. So she is giving her money away, to finance scholarships for black students at the University of Southern Mississippi here in her hometown, where tuition is ＄2,400 a year.

"I wanted to share my wealth with the children," said Miss McCarty, whose only real regret is that she never went back to school. "I never minded work, but I was always so busy, busy. Maybe I can make it so the children don't have to work like I did."

People in Hattiesburg (哈蒂斯堡,密西西比州城市)call her donation the Gift. She made it, in part, in anticipation of her death.

As she sat in her warm, dark living room, she talked of that death matter-of-factly, the same way she talked about the possibility of an afternoon thundershower. To her, the Gift was a preparation, like closing the bedroom windows to keep the rain from blowing in on the bedspread.

"I know it won't be too many years before I pass on(去世)," she said, "and I just figured the money would do them a lot more good than it would me."

Her donation has piqued(激起)interest around the nation. In a few short days, Oseola McCarty, the washerwoman, has risen from obscurity to a notice she does not understand. She sits in her little frame house(木屋), just blocks from the university, and patiently greets the reporters, business leaders and others who line up outside her door.

"I live where I want to live, and I live the way I want to live," she said. "I couldn't drive a car if I had one. I'm too old to go to college. So I planned to do this. I planned it myself."

It has been only three decades since the university integrated. "My race used to not get to go to that college," she said. "But now they can."

When asked why she had picked this university instead of a predominantly black institution, she said, "Because it's here; it's close."

While Miss McCarty does not want a building named for her or a statue in her honor, she would like one thing in return: to attend the graduation of a student who made it through college because of her gift. "I'd like to see it," she said.

Business leaders in Hattiesburg, 110 miles northeast of New Orleans, plan to match her ＄150,000, said Bill Pace, the executive director of the University of Southern Mississippi Foundation, which administers donations to the school.

"I've been in the business 24 years now, in private fund raising," Mr. Pace said. "And this is the first time I've experienced anything like this from an individual who simply was not affluent, did not have the resources and yet gave substantially. In fact, she gave almost everything she has."

"No one approached her from the university; she approached us. She's seen the poverty, the young people who have struggled, who need an education. She is the most unselfish individual I have ever met."

Although some details are still being worked out, the $300,000—Miss McCarty's money and the matching sum—will finance scholarships into the indefinite future. The only stipulation is that the beneficiaries be black and live in southern Mississippi.

The college has already awarded a $1,000 scholarship in Miss McCarty's name to an 18-year-old honors student from Hattiesburg, Stephanie Bullock.

Miss Bullock's grandmother, Ledrester Hayes, sat in Miss McCarty's tiny living room the other day and thanked her. Later, when Miss McCarty left the room, Mrs. Hayes shook her head in wonder.

"I thought she would be some little old rich lady with a fine car and a fine house and clothes," she said. "I was a seamstress(女裁缝师) myself, worked two jobs. I know what it's like to work like she did, and she gave it away (捐赠)."

The Oseola McCarty Scholarship Fund bears the name of a woman who bought her first air-conditioner just three years ago and even now turns it on only when company comes. Miss McCarty also does not mind that her tiny black-and-white television set gets only one channel, because she never watches anyway. She complains that her electricity bill is too high and says she never subscribed to a newspaper because it cost too much.

The pace of Miss McCarty's walks about the neighborhood is slowed now, and she misses more Sundays than she would like at Friendship Baptist Church. Arthritis(关节炎) has left her hands stiff and numb. For the first time in almost 80 years, her independence is threatened.

"Since I was a child, I've been working," washing the clothes of doctors, lawyers, teachers, police officers, she said. "But I can't do it no more. I can't work like I used to."

She is 5 feet tall and would weigh 100 pounds with rocks in her pockets. Her voice is so soft that it disappears in the squeak of the screen door and the hum of the air-conditioner.

She comes from a wide place in the road called Shubuta, Miss., a farming town outside Meridian, not far from the Alabama line. She quit school, she said, when the grandmother who reared her became ill and needed care.

"I would have gone back," she said, "but the people in my class had done gone on, and I was too big. I wanted to be with my class."

So she worked, and almost every dollar went into the bank. In time, all her immediate family(直系家庭成员) died. "And I didn't have nobody," she said. "But I stayed busy."

She took a short vacation once, as a young woman, to Niagara Falls. The roar of the water scared her. "Seemed like the world was coming to an end," she said.

She stayed home, mostly, after that. She has lived alone since 1967.

Earlier this year her banker asked what she wanted done with her money when she passed on. She told him that she wanted to give it to the university, now rather than later; she set aside just enough to live on.

She says she does not want to depend on anyone after all these years, but she may have little choice. She has been informally adopted by the first young person whose life was changed by her gift.

As a young woman, Stephanie Bullock's mother wanted to go to the University of Southern Mississippi. But that was during the height of the integration battles, and if she had tried her father might have lost his job with the city.

It looked as if Stephanie's own dream of going to the university would also be snuffed out(扼杀), for lack of money. Although she was president of her senior class in high school and had grades that were among the best there, she fell just short of getting an academic scholarship. Miss Bullock said her family earned too much money to qualify for most Federal grants but not enough to send her to the university.

Then, last week, she learned that the university was giving her ＄1,000, in Miss McCarty's name. "It was a total miracle," she said, "and an honor."

She visited Miss McCarty to thank her personally and told her that she planned to "adopt" her. Now she visits regularly, offering to drive Miss McCarty around and filling a space in the tiny woman's home that has been empty for decades.

She feels a little pressure, she concedes, not to fail the woman who helped her. "I was thinking how amazing it was that she made all that money doing laundry," said Miss Bullock, who plans to major in business.

She counts on Miss McCarty's being there four years from now, when she graduates.

一、作者背景

里克·布莱格（Rick Bragg）：1994年10月成为《纽约时报》驻亚特兰大分社的记者，负责报道国内新闻。之前，他曾在多个报社工作过，包括阿拉巴马州的《安尼斯通星报》(*Anniston Star*)、《伯明翰新闻报》(*Birmingham News*)、《洛杉矶时报》(*Los

Angeles Times）以及《泰晤士报》（*The Times*）。

布莱格先生于1959年7月26日出生于阿拉巴马。1980年，他毕业于杰克斯威尔州立大学（Jacksonville State University）。1992—1993年，他获得哈佛大学的尼曼奖学金（Nieman Fellow），在该校继续深造学习。

他获得过许多新闻奖，如：美国报纸编辑协会颁发的优秀写作奖，还有其他31项国家、州和地区级的写作奖。他写的新闻故事被收入《1991年最佳报刊写作》、《1988年最佳报刊写作》，以及两本新闻专业的教科书中。

他还曾在多个大学教授写作，包括哈佛大学（Harvard University）、潘特传媒学院（Poynter Institute for Media Studies）、波士顿大学（Boston University）、南佛罗里达大学（University of South Florida）和其他一些学院。现在他在阿拉巴马大学教授新闻写作。

布莱格因于1995年间在《纽约时报》发表6篇反映当代美国社会的特稿而获得普利策特稿写作奖。他的文章的关注点都是普通小人物的生活和命运，比如黑人洗衣妇、美国印第安人、地方治安官、罪犯等。他的作品风格细腻优雅（elegantly written），语言简洁生动，具有很强的感染力。

二、课文背景

对美国经济来说，20世纪90年代至21世纪初是一个繁荣的年代，美国创造了一个经济史上的奇迹。美国出现了历史上最长的经济扩张期，还出现了高经济增长率、高生产率和低失业率与低通货膨胀率并存的新特征。但是，虽然经济上强大了，可人们的生存状态令人忧思。人性受到压抑，人们的精神生活受到破坏。人们普遍不相信还有什么无私或爱心这些美好事物。用美国人自己的话说："People are suspicious of things too good to be true"。在此背景下，《纽约时报》记者里克·布莱格用细腻的笔触，把情融于事中，优雅地讲述了一个平凡中见伟大的故事。

奥莎拉·麦卡迪（Oseola McCarty，1908—1999）是一位终生为人洗衣服和烫衣服的黑人老妇。1995年，只有小学文化程度的她把一生的积蓄十五万美元作为"礼物"捐给了南密西西比大学，用作青年学子的奖学金。她的爱心奉献使她获得了许多赞誉。《纽约时报》称她为"心如黄金"的洗衣妇（1999年9月28日）。2001年，第100期《价值》杂志把奥莎拉列于100名最有价值人物的第六位。哈佛大学和南密西西比大学授予奥莎拉·麦卡迪荣誉博士学位。克林顿给她颁发了总统公民奖。对这一切，她泰然处之，并说"这个礼物是一种准备，就像关上卧室的窗子，不让雨吹到床单上。"

三、作者主要观点

1. What do you think is the main message of the feature story?

2. "To her, the Gift was a preparation, like closing the bedroom windows to keep the rain from blowing in on the bedspread." (para. 7) What implications arise from this sentence?

3. She counts on Miss McCarty's being there four years from now, when she graduates. (last para.) What implication arise from this sentence?

四、写作风格与手法

1. What has intrigued you most about this story in terms of its writing style?

2. How much would the story interest the average reader? Why?

3. What, if any, is the constructive purpose of the writer?

4. In what way is the feature story "elegantly written"? Explain.

5. Is the description detailed or suggestive? Is it effective? Why?

6. How are the details arranged in the body of the essay?

7. Where do you think is the climax of the feature story? Explain.

8. What is the average length of the paragraphs?

9. What is the average length of the sentence?

10. Is the diction original or hackneyed?

11. Are informal expressions found in the story? What is the effect of them?

12. Is there any humor or pathos in the story? How is the humorous or the pathetic effect secured?

Part Three: Further exploring the text

一、语言点讲解

1. *All she has, $150,000, is going to a university* (title)

可译成"她所有的15万美元都捐给了大学"。这个题目朴实无华，简洁明了，但主题突出，意义深刻，让人过目难忘。

2. take in bundles of dirty clothes (para. 1)

意思是"（为了赚钱）把一包包的脏衣服拿回家来洗"。"Take in"在本文的意思是：accept work to be done in one's house for pay，即为赚钱把活拿回家做。如take in typing，（别人付钱让你打字）你把打字活拿回家做。这是一个比较口语化的表达方式。

3. She spent almost nothing, living in her old family home, cutting the toes out of shoes if they did not fit right and binding her ragged Bible with Scotch tape to keep Corinthians from falling out.

作者选择了两个方面的事实说明本句主旨，"spent almost nothing"，无论从物质用品，还是精神用品，麦卡迪都是能省就省，自己几乎不花钱。Cutting the toes out of shoes，是"削足适履"的意思。这是一个夸张的修辞手法，说明麦卡迪本人非常节俭，即使鞋子不合适了，也不买新的。在后半句话中，作者继续告诉我们麦卡迪如何省钱，《圣经》是"破旧不堪的"，其中的《哥林多书》部分是用透明胶带粘在一起的。可以看出，作者观察得非常仔细，写作手法非常细腻。这种修辞和描写相结合的表达手法很值得体味和学习。

4. ...she talked of that death matter-of-factly, the same way she talked about the

possibility of an afternoon thundershower. To her, the Gift was a preparation, like closing the bedroom windows to keep the rain from blowing in on the bedspread. (para. 7)

本段涉及麦卡迪对待死亡的态度，从中看出主人公的鲜明形象特征。

本句中连用了两个比喻：她说到死就像说到下午可能有暴雨一样；把积蓄作为“礼物”捐给大学就像关上卧室窗户以免雨吹到床单上一样。由于运用了恰当的修辞，作者在此寥寥两笔就把一个淡定自若、温和优雅的人物形象勾勒了出来。

值得一提的是，作者接着描写了麦卡迪坐在自己的小木屋里耐心地接见在门外排着长队慕名而来的记者和企业界领袖的场景，通过动作描写进一步加深了读者对麦卡迪的印象。

作者用很优雅的手法刻画了一个普通人的形象，尤其值得学习。

5. People in Hattiesburg call her donation the Gift. (para. 6)

当地人把麦卡迪的捐款叫做“礼物”。“Gift”的首字母是大写的，说明这是一份大礼物或特殊礼物，体现了当地民众对这份礼物的敬意。

在本文中，用“礼物”一词替代捐款还出现过两次，均在麦卡迪表达自己心愿的场合。在第13段中，麦卡迪表示希望参加一位因为她的“礼物”而完成学业的毕业典礼；在第31段中，她表示希望由第一位因为她的“礼物”而改变了生活的年轻人来“领养自己”。从其语言中，我们可以看出麦卡迪的谦卑和慈爱。首先，“礼物”的首字母都变成了小写，因为也许在她眼里，这就是一份普通的礼物，是在与年轻人一起分享而已。她曾说：“我希望与年轻人分享财富……我想我能做到，因此他们就不必像我一样辛苦工作了。”其次，她没有直接说捐款，也体现了她对被接受人的尊重和体贴，在一定程度上保护了他人的自尊。

通常说，语言是心灵的镜子。谦卑慈爱的人说话让人如沐春风。

6. Her donation has piqued interest around the nation. (para. 9)

Piqued interest，激起兴趣。“pique”是“激起”的意思，是一个习惯用语，使故事读起来更加生动活泼，富有趣味。

7. She counts on Miss McCarty's being there four years from now, when she graduates. (last para.)

“今后四年直到毕业，她都要依靠麦卡迪女士了。”作者似乎想说：一个学商科的大学生要依靠一位黑人洗衣女的资助完成学业，那是一个多么了不起的洗衣女。文章这句话点题，并且呼应和延伸第一段中的第一句话：“洗衣女的一生不但能够让别人的外表更加好看，而且还能让别人更有知识和智慧。”这就是麦卡迪的价值所在，也是为什么她被评为美国最有价值的人之一的原因吧。读完本文，我们禁不住惊叹作者的深刻思想和高超表达。他对主题的提炼实在是既深刻又让人感到新颖。

二、中西文化比较

论“无私”

课文中有这样一句话：She is the most unselfish individual I have ever met.

这是南密西西比大学基金会执行主任 Bill Pace 说的话。其实，作者布莱格在用别人的话表达了他自己的观点，当然，这也是民众的心声。他在写一个高尚无私的普通人的故事，实际上也在传播这种无私的精神。

无私奉献是人类最纯洁、最崇高的道德品质。她像冰山雪莲，洁白无瑕；她像满山杜鹃，情暖人间；她像大树绿叶，挡风遮雨。

无论在西方文化，还是在中国文化里，无私奉献精神都是十分重要的价值观，有许多关于无私奉献的名人名言。

(1)The unselfish effort to bring cheer to others will be the beginning of a happier life for ourselves. (Helen Keller)

(2)Be unselfish. That is the first and final commandment for those who would be useful and happy in their usefulness. If you think of yourself only, you cannot develop because you are choking the source of development, which is spiritual expansion through thought for others. (Charles W. Eliot)

(3)One great, strong, unselfish soul in every community could actually redeem the world. (Elbert Hubbard)

(4) 丈夫贵兼济，岂独善一身。(白居易)

(5) 捧着一颗心来，不带半根草去。(陶行知)

(6) 春蚕到死丝方尽，蜡炬成灰泪始干。(李商隐)

(7) 先天下之忧而忧，后天下之乐而乐。(范仲淹)

(8) 鞠躬尽瘁，死而后矣。(诸葛亮)

三、语言练习

1. 请用英文解释以下短语或句子。

(1)All she ever had was the work, which she saw as a blessing.

(2)...cutting the toes out of shoes if they did not fit right...

(3)More than I could ever use,"Miss McCarty said the other day without a trace of self-pity."

(4)As she sat in her warm, dark living room, she talked of that death matter-of-factly, the same way she talked about the possibility of an afternoon thundershower. To her, the Gift was a preparation, like closing the bedroom windows to keep the rain from blowing in on the bedspread.

(5)I know what it's like to work like she did, and she gave it away.

(6)Now she visits regularly, offering to drive Miss McCarty around and filling a space in the tiny woman's home that has been empty for decades.

(7)She counts on Miss McCarty's being there four years from now, when she graduates.

2. 请将下列短语翻译成英文，并比较中英文表达方式的异同。

(1) 辍学

(2) 削足适履

(3) 去世

(4) 订阅报纸

（5）声名鹊起
（6）激起兴趣
（7）赠送
（8）排队
（9）上完大学
（10）预见
（11）实事求是地
（12）以表示对她敬意而建的雕塑

3. 请将下面句子或段落翻译成中文，并比较中英文表达方式的异同。

（1）People in Hattiesburg call her donation the Gift. She made it, in part, in anticipation of her death.

（2）As she sat in her warm, dark living room, she talked of that death matter-of-factly, the same way she talked about the possibility of an afternoon thundershower. To her, the Gift was a preparation, like closing the bedroom windows to keep the rain from blowing in on the bedspread.

（3）"I know it won't be too many years before I pass on," she said, "and I just figured the money would do them a lot more good than it would me."

（4）Her donation has piqued interest around the nation. In a few short days, Oseola McCarty, the washerwoman, has risen from obscurity to a notice she does not understanShe sits in her little frame house, just blocks from the university, and patiently greets the reporters, business leaders and others who line up outside her door.

Part Four: Exploring beyond the text

一、自我反思

1. 我学到了什么？我要如何改进？
2. 一篇高质量的特稿的基本标准是什么？我能清楚地告诉别人吗？该篇报道的记者里克·布莱格是如何达到这些标准的？我能向别人解释清楚吗？

二、知识扩展

1. 如对奥莎拉·麦卡迪感兴趣的话，可以浏览南密西西比大学的网页，了解更多关于她的情况，还可以阅读她本人写的书 *Simple Wisdom for Rich Living*，以及美国作家艾芙琳·科勒曼写的 *The Riches of Oseola McCarty*。

2. 在美国，捐款的并不仅仅是盖茨和巴菲特这样的大款，像麦卡迪一样生活节俭的普通老百姓也很慷慨。而且根据慈善机构的报告，这种挑战自己财政极限的捐助越来越多，捐助人的年龄也越来越小。你如何解读这种“穷人捐款”现象？

3. 如果你喜欢本文作者里克·布莱格的作品和写作风格，还可以欣赏他的其他四本书：*All Over but the Shoutin'* 和 *Ava's Man*，这两本都是畅销书，都以爱和赎罪为主题。*The Prince of Frogtown* 是关于家庭题材的。*I Am a Soldier Too*：*The Jessica Lynch Story* 是关于美国战俘 *Jessica Lynch* 的人物传记。

三、能力扩展

1. 围绕一点展开，就此文写一篇 500 字左右的新闻评析。
2. 关注当前新闻中的“小人物”，写一篇细腻优雅的特稿。

Text B Final salute

BY Jim Sheeler

Rocky Mountain News

November 9, 2005

导读：2003 年 3 月 20 日，以美国和英国为主的联合部队正式宣布对伊拉克开战，这是一场旷日持久的战争。美国海军陆战队以机动灵活和骁勇善战著称，被称为美国“第四军种”，是美国海外用兵的一支重要力量，也是伤亡人数较多的部队。对于每一位在伊拉克阵亡的战士，海军陆战队的“伤亡援助官”都要访问其家人，亲自把悲痛的消息告诉他们，与他们一起面对不幸，并且帮助他们重新鼓起生活的勇气。《洛基山新闻报》的特约撰稿人杰姆·席勒向我们讲述了这些鲜为人知的伤亡援助官的故事。

作者背景

杰姆·席勒（Jim Sheeler）：2004 年成为《洛基山新闻报》特约撰稿人。在此之前，他在多家报刊工作过。1991 年，他在科罗拉多州圆石市（Boulder）的一家地方报社就职，开始从事写作；1996 年至 2000 年，换到该市另一家周报工作，担任高级特约撰稿人；1999 年至 2004 年成为《丹佛邮报》的自由撰稿人。

席勒出生并生活在得克萨斯州。1990 年，他毕业于科罗拉多州立大学，并获得新闻学士学位。他与人合写了有关讣闻写作的书，书名为《讣闻写作生涯》（*Life On the Death Beat*）。

Part One

Inside a limousine parked on the airport tarmac（停机坪），Katherine Cathey looked out at the clear night sky and felt a kick（感到肚子里的胎儿在踢）.

"He's moving," she said. "Come feel him. He's moving."

Her two best friends leaned forward on the soft leather seats and put their hands on her stomach.

"I felt it," one of them said. "I felt it."

Outside, the whine（哀鸣声）of jet engines swelled（增大）.

Part one.

"Oh, sweetie," her friend said. "I think this is his plane."

As the three young women peered through the tinted windows(贴膜车窗), Katherine squeezed a set of dog tags(身份识别牌) stamped with the same name as her unborn son:

James J. Cathey.

"He wasn't supposed to come home this way," she said, tightening her grip on the tags, which were linked by a necklace to her husband's wedding ring.

The women looked through the back window. Then the 23-year-old placed her hand on her pregnant belly.

"Everything that made me happy is on that plane," she said.

They watched as airport workers rolled a conveyor belt to the rear of the plane, followed by six solemn Marines(海军陆战队员).

Katherine turned from the window and closed her eyes.

"I don't want it to be dark right now. I wish it was daytime," she said. "I wish it was daytime for the rest of my life. The night is just too hard."

Suddenly, the car door opened. A white-gloved hand reached into the limousine from outside-the same hand that had knocked on Katherine's door in Brighton five days earlier.

The man in the deep blue uniform knelt down to meet her eyes, speaking in a soft, steady voice.

"Katherine," said Maj. Steve Beck, "it's time."

Closer than brothers

The American Airlines 757 couldn't have landed much farther from the war.

The plane arrived in Reno on a Friday evening, the beginning of the 2005 "Hot August Nights" festival-one of the city's biggest-filled with flashing lights, fireworks, carefree music and plenty of gambling.

When a young Marine in dress uniform had boarded the plane to Reno, the passengers smiled and nodded politely. None knew he had just come from the plane's cargo hold(货舱) after watching his best friend's casket(棺材) loaded onboard.

At 24 years old, Sgt. Gavin Conley was only seven days younger than the man in the coffin(棺材). The two had met as 17-year-olds on another plane—the one to boot camp (海军新兵训练营) in California. They had slept in adjoining top bunks, the two youngest recruits in the barracks(兵营).

All Marines call each other brother. Conley and Jim Cathey could have been. They finished each other's sentences, had matching infantry tattoos etched on their shoulders, and cracked on each other as if they had grown up together—which, in some ways, they had.

When the airline crew found out about Conley's mission, they bumped(提升) him to first-class. He had never flown there before. Neither had Jim Cathey.

On the flight, the woman sitting next to him nodded toward his uniform and asked if he was coming or going. To the war, she meant.

He fell back on the words the military had told him to say: "I'm escorting a fallen Marine home to his family from the situation in Iraq."

The woman quietly said she was sorry, Conley said.

Then she began to cry.

When the plane landed in Nevada, the pilot asked the passengers to remain seated while Conley disembarked alone. Then the pilot told them why.

The passengers pressed their faces against the windows. Outside, a procession walked toward the plane. Passengers in window seats leaned back to give others a better view. One held a child up to watch.

From their seats in the plane, they saw a hearse(灵车) and a Marine extending a white-gloved hand into a limousine, helping a pregnant woman out of the car.

On the tarmac, Katherine Cathey wrapped her arm around the major's, steadying herself. Then her eyes locked on the cargo hold and the flag-draped casket.

Inside the plane, they couldn't hear the screams.

Part two

Each door is different.

Some are ornately carved hardwood, some are hollow aluminum. Some are protected by elaborate security systems, some by loose screen doors.

During the past year, the 40-year-old Marine major in the white gloves has stood at the front doors of homes in three states, preparing to deliver the message no family wants to hear.

It is a job he never asked for and one for which he received no training. There are no set rules, only impersonal guidelines. It is a mission without weapons.

Steve Beck trained to fight as a Marine, winning accolades(勋章) as the most accomplished marksman(快枪手) of his class-a man who later earned two master's degrees in a quest to become a leader on the battlefield. He had hoped to deploy(部署) during the Persian Gulf War and definitely thought he would get his chance this time.

Instead, he found himself faced with an assignment that starts with a long walk to a stranger's porch(门廊) and an outstretched hand. It continues with a promise steeped in (渗透在) the history of the Corps(海军陆战队) that most people associate only with the battlefield:

Never leave a Marine behind.

In combat, men have been killed while retrieving their comrades' bodies, knowing that the dead Marine would have done the same for them. It's a tradition instilled in boot camp, where Marines are steeped in 230 years of history and the sacrifices of tens of thousands of lives.

For Beck, that promise holds long after the dead return home.

In the past 12 months, he has seen inside the caskets, learned each Marine's name and nickname, touched the toys they grew up with and read the letters they wrote home. He has held grieving mothers in long embraces, absorbing their muffled cries into the dark blue shoulder of his uniform.

Sometimes he's gone home to his own family and found himself crying in the dark.

When he first donned(穿上) the Marine uniform, Beck had never heard the term "casualty assistance calls officer." He certainly never expected to serve as one.

As it turned out, it would become the most important mission of his life.

Each door is different. But once they're open, Beck said, some of the scenes inside are inevitably the same.

"The curtains pull away. They come to the door. And they know. They always know," he said.

"You can almost see the blood run out of their body and their heart hit the floor. It's not the blood as much as their soul. Something sinks. I've never seen that except when someone dies. And I've seen a lot of death."

"They're falling-either literally or figuratively-and you have to catch them."

"In this business, I can't save his life. All I can do is catch the family while they're falling."

"We have a casualty"

Hours before Beck's first call, a homemade bomb exploded.

Somewhere in the Iraqi desert, in the midst of the rubble, lay the body of a Marine from Colorado.

The information from his dog tags was checked. Double-checked. And then the name began its journey home.

During World War I, World War II and the Korean War, the message arrived in sparse sympathy letters or in the terse language of telegrams, leaving relatives alone to soak in the words. Near the end of the Vietnam War, the military changed the process, saddling stateside troops with the knock at the door(让美国本土部队承担上门拜访的责任).

On that day in October 2004, inside an office at Buckley Air Force Base in Aurora, Beck's phone rang.

"We have a casualty in your area," the voice said.

At the time, Beck wasn't sure what came next. He did know that he didn't have much time. Once the call is received, the goal for notification(通知) is four hours.

Troops in the field now often have access to e-mail and satellite telephones. So when a service member dies, his commander is directed to shut off communications back home to keep rumors from reaching the family before the notification officers.

Still, the pressure is palpable(明显的). The call often comes in the middle of the night. Officers must retrieve vital information from headquarters-the Marine's next of kin(近亲), the basic circumstances surrounding the death, addresses and phone numbers and there is no room for error.

With each step, they get closer to the door.

Answering the call

Beck looks like the job: hard and soft. His white cotton gloves cover calloused(起老茧的) hands. They lead to thick, regular-guy arms shaped by work instead of weightlifting, and a round, pale face with big cheeks that turn red when he hasn't had enough sleep, which is most of the time.

Beck's bookshelf is packed with titles ranging from the History of the Peloponnesian War to the 9 • 11 Commission Report. He can quote Clausewitz(克劳塞维茨,《战争论》作者) and Sun Tsu(孙子) in regular conversation.

But he never strays far from his roots.

Born in Sand Springs, Okla., he still pronounces his home state "O-koma." He'll describe another Marine's muscles as "hard as a woodpecker's(啄木鸟) lips," and when he wants something done with precision, he'll require his troops to get it "down to the gnat's ass."

His car radio is eternally tuned to country stations because, he insists, "a day without country music is like a day without sunshine."

It's an Everyman quality that can't be faked, one that has become a crucial component in helping the families of fallen Marines.

After receiving that first call last fall, Beck grabbed for a thick, acronym-studded(充满首字母缩写词的) manual(手册), The Casualty Assistance Calls Officer's (CACO) Guide. It offered only the basics:

"In cases of death, the following is suggested and may be modified as follows," it reads, in part.

"The Commandant of the Marine Corps has entrusted me to express his deep regret that your (relationship), (name), (died/was killed in action) in (place of incident), (city/state or country) on (date). (State the circumstances). The Commandant extends his deepest sympathy to you and your family in your loss."

When he began the job as site commander at Marine Air Control Squadron 23, Beck knew that death notification was a possibility. The previous commander already had supervised three funerals in the region that includes Colorado and parts of Wyoming, Kansas, South Dakota and Nebraska.

Until that first call, however, Beck had plenty of other worries.

From their base among the top-secret radar installations at Buckley, Beck and his

Marines are highly trained to support aircraft and missile operations. They also are continually training Marine Reservists and sending them to Iraq.

Since the beginning of the war, the Marines stationed at Buckley have made 19 notifications following the deaths of active-duty(现役)Marines. Fifteen of those were killed in action in Iraq and four died in stateside traffic accidents.

Beck personally has notified five families, but even when he isn't the one who delivers the message, he is involved.

Before leaving on his first notification, Beck asked for advice from two men in another branch of the service.

"One of the first things they said was, 'Don't embrace them. If they embrace you, keep your distance,'" he said, shaking his head.

"I didn't have much use for them."

No fork in the road(没有岔路口)

Different services have different guidelines for notification. In the Army, one officer is responsible for the knock, while another steps in to handle the aftercare(安置).

In the Marines, the same person who knocks on the door is the family's primary contact for the next year or more.

There is no group of Marines whose primary task is death notification. Just as every Marine is a rifleman(步枪兵)-expected to be able to handle a weapon and head to the front if tapped-any officer also may be called to make the walk to the door.

For Beck, that door is the "LOD"-the line of departure. The point of no return.

After all of the racing, all of the frantic scramble, it's the point where time freezes.

"Once I get to the porch, I stand there and take a deep breath. At that point, you can wait 10 seconds, wait 30 seconds, wait an hour-it's not going to go away," he said.

"There's no option. There's no fork in the road. You just stare down that straight path. You step up because there is no fork."

"I pick myself up, gather my thoughts and ring the bell."

Part three

There were no footprints in the snow.

That struck Beck as he sat across the street in his government SUV that night, outside a house in Laramie blanketed by cold and quiet.

In his briefcase was a sheet of paper: "INITIAL CASUALTY REPORT," it read. "LCPL. KYLE W. BURNS."

Every second he waited would be one more second that, for those in the house, everything was still all right. He stared at the front door, at the drifting snow, then looked at his watch.

When he left Denver, it was still Nov. 11; now it was well past midnight.

Veterans Day was over.

Inside the house, the lights were still on.

All during the drive to Laramie, Beck imagined what would happen at the door and what he would say once it opened. This was his second notification. He had easily memorized the words in the manual. There was no script for the rest.

He talked it out with his passenger, Gunnery Sgt. Shane Scarpino. In the truck, the two men played out scenarios the same way they would if headed into battle. What if the parents aren't home? What if they become aggressive? What if they break down? What if, what if, what if.

Two Marines are required for every visit, not just for emotional support, but for each other's protection. While most parents eventually grow close to their casualty assistance officer, the initial meeting tests all emotions. One of the Buckley Marines had been slapped by a mother. Last year, a group of Marines in Florida had their van set on fire by a distraught(发狂的)father.

Amid sheets of blowing snow just outside Laramie, Beck had pulled the truck into a gas station and the two Marines grabbed their garment bags.

When they emerged from the restroom, their spit-shined black shoes clicked on the floor. Their dark blue pants, lined with a red stripe signifying past bloodshed, fell straight. Their jackets wrapped their necks with a high collar that dates back to the Revolutionary War, when Marines wore leather neck straps to protect them from enemy swords.

As they walked out of the gas station, Beck felt the eyes of the clerk.

He knows, Beck thought.

Once they drove into the family's neighborhood, the modest white house found them first, beckoning with the brightest porch lights and biggest house numbers on the block.

Beck pulled to the curb and cut his headlights. He looked at Scarpino.

Then the two men climbed out of the truck, and walked into the pristine(洁白的) snow.

From then on, every step would leave footprints.

The man nobody wants to see

Down in the basement of their home in Laramie, Kyle Burns' parents didn't hear the doorbell.

The couple had spent most of the snowy night trying to hook up(连接)a new television. It was nearly 1 a. m. when the dog leapt into a barking frenzy.

Jo Burns looked out the window and saw the two Marines.

"I thought, 'Go away! Get the hell away from here!'" she said. "Then I just started screaming."

Down in the basement, Bob Burns assumed that someone was trying to break in. He grabbed a flashlight and flew up the stairs.

"When I got up there, I saw Major Beck and the (gunnery) sergeant (军士)," he said. "I'll never forget Major Beck's profile (轮廓)."

It was a silhouette (轮廓，尤其侧面影像) their son had warned them about.

"When Kyle left, he sat us down and told us that if he didn't come back, the Marines would come," Jo said. "So when I saw them standing there..."

Beck and Scarpino spent hours with the family, telling them the little information they knew, promising they would take care of everything they could.

Over the next few weeks, Beck found a way to bring home two Marines who had enlisted alongside Kyle. He helped organize a memorial service and Kyle's burial at Fort Logan National Cemetery in Denver. He helped the Burnses navigate the piles of paperwork dealing with insurance and benefits.

The whole time, Marines from Buckley watched over Kyle's body.

That first night, as the two men prepared to leave, Jo Burns gave each a hug. Bob Burns shook their hands.

"I don't know why, but even then I felt compassion for them," Bob Burns said. "I've done a lot of reflecting on that first night and that's what comes back: compassion."

"I don't know how Major Beck does this," Jo Burns said. "Because nobody wants to see him."

"You know, he feels every one of these like they were his own. He does. I tried to talk to him about that once, but he just put his hand up and turned around to face the wall."

"He had tears in his eyes. And he just said, 'I know.'"

Part four

Although Beck had no training as a casualty assistance officer (伤亡援助官), in a way he had trained for it all of his life.

His earliest memory begins with a needle.

As a toddler, he learned to hold a syringe to inject his diabetic (患糖尿病的) mother with insulin (胰岛素). His parents had divorced when he was 1. Sometimes, he was the only one there to help.

As he grew up, the family scraped by. Some days he wore Salvation Army (基督教的救世军) clothes to school. Things got harder from there.

When he was 13, Beck and his mother watched his 3-year-old brother die after being hit by a car. Months earlier, young Steve had taught the little boy to play catch.

Before the funeral, Beck stood at the open casket and placed his brother's baseball glove inside.

It took years for Beck and his mother to recover. She retreated and he rebelled, leaving home early.

Eventually, Beck channeled his anger into books, even planning to go to medical school, where he hoped to find a cure for his mother's diabetes.

But the stirrings of the Persian Gulf War shook him as he prepared to take his medical school entrance exams. His father had been a Marine and Beck had long thought of joining. He figured this would be the war of his generation and he didn't want to miss it.

His mother died while he was attending officer training school. When he lost her, he also lost his reason for studying medicine. He never went back.

Though his relationship with his father—a cop and former Drug Enforcement Administration agent—wasn't as close as that with his mother, they eventually reconciled. Then his father was diagnosed with cancer.

"On my last trip out to see him, I took a drive with him and asked him if there was anything I could do," Beck said.

"He asked me if I could get a color guard at his funeral. That's all he asked for: a Marine color guard."

"I said", Dad, that's easy.

"I didn't get to talk to him again."

Witnesses to sacrifice

On a winter night, Beck pulled his SUV into Denver International Airport and looked into the sky, staring at all the lights that were not stars.

A limousine pulled in behind him, followed by an empty hearse.

It was early December, nine months before he would stand on the tarmac in Reno alongside a 23-year-old widow.

There is no rule requiring airports to allow a family into a secure area to receive the body of a fallen service member, and some airports around the country have refused, Beck said, shaking his head.

"In my mind, this is the first time that a Marine is back on Colorado soil, and (the family) deserves to be there," Beck said. "If I had my way, they'd know which frickin' light in the sky is him, which plane is bringing him in all the way."

Inside the SUV, his phone rang. He looked at the number and smiled.

"Hi, babe," he said. "We're at the airport, getting ready to bring one of our guys home. How are the kids?"

For Beck's wife, Julie, and their three young children, his job has sometimes meant his absence on birthdays and anniversaries. He spent last Thanksgiving at a funeral.

Still, when he wakes up in the middle of the night to an ominous call, Julie wakes with him and remains nearby until he heads off to knock on another door. He talks about her the way the families he cares for talk about him: She's his rock.

"Hang in there," he said into the phone. "I'll be home late."

Then another call. Again, he recognized the number: another one of his families.

The contact list on Beck's cell phone is programmed with the numbers of grieving parents and spouses from Rapid City to Reno.

But he's not the only one, he insists, over and over. He said he takes his cues from his Marines, the men and women who get involved to the point where many of their families say they might as well have been deployed overseas.

"This job is all about sacrifice," Beck said. "We sacrifice our family stability. Many of us sacrifice income. We sacrifice our bodies. We break things. We're hard on ourselves. We break each other. And we're asked to make the ultimate sacrifice."

Outside the car, a Denver police officer's walkie-talkie crackled and he motioned to Beck.

The cortege(随从)pulled behind the police escort, heading toward the tarmac.

"There are moments in this experience that energize you, and there are moments that suck you dry (耗尽)" Beck said. "Those moments are short, but they're so defining."

"And you're about to see one of them."

As jet engines roared around him, Beck looked at the plane. The Marines marched to the cargo hold, toward the casket.

"See the people in the windows? They'll sit right there in the plane, watching those Marines," Beck said. "You gotta wonder what's going through their minds, knowing that they're on the plane that brought him home."

Commercial airplanes transport caskets every day-including service members killed in action. For the most part, the passengers have no idea what lies below.

Most people will never see the Transportation Security Administration officials standing on the tarmac with their hands over their hearts as a body is unloaded. They won't see the airport police and firefighters lined up alongside their cars and engines, lights flashing, saluting the hearse on its way out.

Occasionally, a planeload of passengers is briefly exposed to the hard reality outside the cabin.

"They're going to remember being on that plane for the rest of their lives," Beck said, looking back at the passengers. "They're going to remember bringing that Marine home."

Part five

Before graduating from boot camp, every Marine masters the blank stare: the focused but distant look that glares down from recruiting posters, the one meant to strike fear in enemies, the one intended to convey more than two centuries of tradition.

Marines are taught to hold the stare no matter what. If a fly crawls(爬行)on their face, or in their ear, they are ordered to remain steady.

No training could prepare them for the funerals.

According to protocol(规定)—an extension of their sacred "never leave a Marine behind" mandate—a fallen Marine's body must be guarded by another Marine whenever it is accessible by a member of the public.

During the past year, the 60 active-duty Marines stationed at Buckley have taken turns standing guard over the caskets. Inevitably, they get to know the person inside.

Underneath their formal white caps, or "covers," many of the Buckley Marines keep the funeral brochures of every Marine they have watched over.

"Now they're watching over us," said Sgt. Andrea Fitzgerald, as she turned over her cap, revealing a photo tucked inside. "I call them my angels."

At the visitation(探望), Marines hear the families talk to the body. At the memorial services, they hear the eulogies(赞词). During the burials, they see the flag presented to the grieving mother or widow.

Through it all, they try to hold the stare.

"They can stand there for hours," Beck said. "Their feet fall asleep up to their knees. The pain we're feeling drives us. It drives us for the family because the pride is bigger than the pain. But the pain-you gotta eat it, you gotta live with it, you gotta take it home and cry in the dark. What else are you going to do?"

For Sgt. Kevin Thomas, of Aurora, it starts when the Marines first meet the casket at the airport.

"You always hear all these statements like 'freedom isn't free.' You hear the president talking about all these people making sacrifices," he said.

"But you never really know until you carry one of them in the casket. When you feel their body weight. When you feel them, that's when you know. That's when you understand."

Thomas said he would rather be in Iraq or anyplace he doesn't feel so helpless.

Still, he said, he has learned lessons from funeral duty that he knows combat can't teach.

"I'll be sitting in front of the computer and I'll see the news: Another service member killed. It's enough to choke me up, tighten my chest. That's another hundred people that are about to be affected," Thomas said.

"It's almost enough to wish that you could take his place, so these people wouldn't hurt so much."

"There's no way that doing one of these funerals can't make you a better person. I think everyone in the military should have to do at least one."

Still, it doesn't end at the cemetery(墓地).

"People think that after the funeral, we're finished," Beck said. "It's not over. It's not over at all. We have to keep taking care of the families."

"He only got halfway through"

The sound of strapping tape ripped through the living room in Laramie.

"Now for the hard part," Jo Burns said, after opening one of the cardboard boxes from Iraq filled with her son's possessions.

Then she corrected herself.

"It's all hard."

It had been more than a month since Beck's midnight drive to the white house with the biggest numbers on the block. Beck wasn't required to personally deliver the boxes to Laramie. He didn't have to stay with the family for two hours more as they sifted through them, either.

But actually, Beck said, he had no choice.

"I know that Kyle Burns is looking at me, making sure I'm squared away—with his family and with him," he said during the drive to Wyoming. "I know I'm going to have to answer the mail on that one day—not with God, but with Kyle."

Inside the living room, Bob Burns began lifting Ziploc bags from the box, cataloging the contents in a shaky voice.

"Here's his wallet," he said, as he looked inside. "A fishing license. A hunting license. A Subway Club card? Good grief."

"They're things that reminded him of home," Jo Burns said.

A few minutes later, she pulled out a list in her son's handwriting and started to cry.

"What is it, Jo?" Bob Burns asked.

"It's everyone he wanted to call. And write."

"Well," Bob said, "now we've got a list, don't we, Jo?"

They found more. A camouflage Bible. A giant clothespin. Pens with their tops chewed up.

Corporal's stripes.

"He already bought them," Bob said. "He only had a couple more tests to take."

Kyle's older brother, Kris, pulled out a book, Battlefield Okinawa, and feathered the pages, then placed his finger at a wrinkle on the spine.

"Looks like he only got to about here," he said. "He only got halfway through."

Jo Burns never wanted Kyle to be a Marine. When he invited a recruiter over to meet her, she was openly hostile.

"I have to be honest," she said later. "I didn't believe all that brotherhood bull—I thought it was just a bunch of little boys saying things that boys say."

"I never believed it until after he died."

In the midst of it all, they found a little snow globe with a typical Wyoming scene: trees, an elk, a bear and a coyote.

Jo Burns shook it up and watched the flakes fall.

She then grasped Beck's hand.

"He told us several times, 'You won't be alone through this-we'll be here,'" she said.

"I guess I didn't understand what that meant."

Part six

Throngs of raucous, face-painted fanatics filled the Stevens High School gymnasium in Rapid City, S. D., preparing for the biggest basketball game of the season.

As the time for tip off neared, some of the kids cheered and others stomped their feet on the stands. But when the lights dimmed, the teams didn't take the court.

"Good evening, ladies and gentlemen," said a uniformed Marine major, as the gym fell to murmurs, then silence.

Eight Marines from Buckley marched to the front of the gym floor, along with a dozen members of the Stevens High School football team and the family of Lance Cpl. Joe Welke.

"For some of you, this is a surprise," Beck said. "For others, you knew we had something special. For everyone, I promise you, this will be a memorable night."

In the gym rafters hung the retired jerseys of former Stevens High football players who later turned pro. On Feb. 5, the crowd's attention was drawn to a special display case for three more uniforms, all worn by the same man.

"Keep Joseph Welke long in your memories, for his sacrifice and that of others should never be forgotten," Beck said. "For if it is, none of us deserve our freedom."

The spotlight swept across the line of football players as they passed the jersey of No. 36 from player to player, across the gym, until it rested with Joe Welke's mother.

Then the light shone on the Marines. Many of them had been the last to carry Welke's body, the last to feel the weight.

This night, they carried his empty uniforms.

"The Marine dress blue uniform is the only uniform in use today that is comprised of all the colors of the American flag," Beck said to the crowd, as the suit was passed along, through white-gloved hands, until it also rested with Betty Welke.

A Marine then held up a desert camouflage uniform—one that had arrived in the U. S. only a few days earlier.

"The Marine combat utility uniform has seen duty around the globe in the toughest of environments," Beck said. "Joe's combat uniform is with us tonight and comes directly from the deserts of Iraq."

The Marines passed the uniform along until it reached Beck. He turned, cradling it with the same reverence he showed months earlier at the funeral when he presented Betty Welke with the folded American flag that had covered her son's casket.

The lance corporal's mother buried her face in the uniform. Her sobbing lifted into the silence of the gym.

In the stands, the face paint smeared into tears. Beck whispered in Betty Welke's ear.

"I said, 'Do you want to hold that for a little while?' And she said, 'Yes.'"

"She was crying into it pretty good. And for me, that was kind of perfect. Because his combat uniform from Iraq has her tears in it. Her tears are in those threads. Forever."

'Was it worth his life?'

The day after the ceremony in the gym, the Welke home in Rapid City filled with Marines Joe Welke never knew. Around the country, as people prepared for Super Bowl Sunday(超级球碗星期日，美国橄榄球联盟年度冠军赛的日子), the Marines prepared for a birthday party.

"Today he would be 21," said Joe Welke's older brother, Nick. "He'd be back in town now. His battalion(连队)just got back."

"Twenty-one," he said. "The one you look forward to."

When the Colorado Marines arrived, they were met the way Joe Welke would have welcomed them with backslaps and beer.

"The Marines were so adamant(坚决地)about coming up here with me on this," Beck said. "They were the ones who carried Joe. That funeral touched them so deeply."

After the start of the football game, the Marines and Joe Welke's high school buddies headed for the big-screen TV in the basement. Betty Welke remained upstairs, looking through photo albums as Beck hovered nearby.

When they were alone, she pressed an album closed and looked up at the major.

"I want to know what's really happening over there," she said.

For the next hour, Beck spoke passionately about the scenes he said not enough people see: the Iraqi elections, the small, successful everyday missions, and the positive days he saw ahead for Iraq—turning points he said her son helped make possible.

He then explained how he believes it could take more than a decade until the sacrifices made by the military pay off. The American public, he said, would have to learn to be patient.

She remained quiet, soaking it all in.

"But is it worth it?" she asked him finally. "Was it worth his life?"

He looked her in the eyes.

"Betty, with all you've been through, that's not something I can answer for you," Beck said.

"That's something for you to decide."

Part seven

Casualty notification isn't always conducted with the same care.

In May, the parents of an Army private first class were stunned when their son's casket was delivered to them on a forklift(叉式机)in a cargo area of a St. Louis airport where employees on break smoked nearby. They also thought it insensitive that, when informing them of their son's death, the casualty assistance officer literally read from a script.

Others have watched their casualty officers "drop off the radar," or end up in Iraq, with no replacement provided. In some cases, the military has taken months to pay for a funeral or left families alone to navigate the morass of paperwork that follows the death of a loved one.

Recently, the governor of Illinois met with Army officials to voice the concerns of military families in his state. Other cases surfaced in February, during congressional testimony by war widows.

"Successful casualty assistance is not the rule, it is quite the exception," one Marine widow told the congressional committee. "This is certainly not the military taking care of its own."

Some branches now offer daylong courses on casualty notification. Next week, the Marine Corps is holding a large symposium in Quantico, Va., where casualty assistance calls officers—including Beck—will convene to share stories and advice.

Many problems could be solved, Beck said, if everyone followed a simple principle:

"To do this right, to do it properly, you have to look at these women as if they were your mother or your wife, and these men as if they were your father or your brother. And you have to ask, 'What would I want someone to do if it were me?'"

Remembering the brave

Inside a ballroom at an Aurora hotel in April, Beck adjusted a line of medals on a banquet table, struggling with all they reflected.

"When you think about what these guys did, it's not easy to look at these medals," he said. "What's the trade-off? What's the exchange? How do you say (holding up a medal), 'This is for your son?'"

At the beginning of the year, Beck realized there were a number of medals due the Marines whose families he watched over. Instead of mailing the medals to them, which often occurs, he decided to hold a formal ceremony to present them to the families personally.

He called the ceremony "Remembering the Brave."

Beck considered the medals again, feeling their weight.

"It's not a trade, but in the minds of the mothers, I wonder if they think it is a trade, and that they're thinking, 'I don't want this medal. I want my son,'" he said.

"The only way I can dispel that is through something like this. By showing them the honor. By honoring their son."

After the lights dimmed in the ballroom, more than 500 people fell silent.

"You are about to hear the descriptions of individual acts of courage," Beck said.

"Listen closely."

"Listen. Closely."

For nearly an hour, they heard detailed accounts of rocket-propelled grenade attacks and improvised explosive devices, of ambushes and assaults-each with the same ending.

Slowly, methodically, the Marines brought out the medals and citations and kneeled before a mother or father they had first met on a doorstep. For each family, the Marines also presented a vase of yellow roses, one rose for every year of the Marine's life.

After it was over, Beck sat back and took another deep breath.

"Even some of our Marines say, 'Why are we doing this to the families? Why do you have to keep reminding them?'"

Beck shook his head.

"This isn't about reminding them they don't need reminding. These families think about this every day of their lives."

He looked up, addressing every person who hasn't felt what those families have.

"This isn't about reminding them," he said.

"This is about reminding you."

Part eight

On the tarmac in Reno, the white glove reached into the limousine, but Katherine Cathey couldn't move.

"Katherine," Beck said, "it's time."

"I'm not ready for this," she said. "I'll never be ready."

Her mother leaned into the car and spoke to her daughter.

"Katherine," she said. "Jim would want you to see this."

Katherine looked at her mother, then at Beck, and took his hand. After climbing from the car, she steadied herself, her arm intertwined with Beck's. Then she looked toward the plane.

At the sight of the flag-draped casket, Katherine let loose a shrill, full-body wail that gave way to moans of distilled, contagious grief.

"NO! NO! Noooooo! Not him! Noooooo!"

She screamed as the casket moved slowly down the conveyor belt. She screamed until she nearly collapsed, clutching Beck around the neck, her legs almost giving way.

At the base of the luggage ramp, the screams hit the pallbearers(抬棺者).

Of all the Marines they had met or trained with, Jim Cathey was the one they considered invincible, built with steel—cable arms and endless endurance—a kid who had made sergeant at 19 and seemed destined to leapfrog through the ranks.

Most of the Marines who would serve as pallbearers had first met "Cat" at the University of Colorado, while enrolled in an elite scholarship program for enlisted infantrymen taking the difficult path to becoming officers. They partied with him, occasionally got into trouble with him, then watched him graduate with honors in anthropology and history in only three years.

When they lifted his casket, they struggled visibly with the weight, their eyes filling with tears as they shuffled to the white hearse.

After they placed the flag-draped coffin inside, Katherine fell onto one corner, pressing her face into the blue field of stars.

Beck put a hand on her back as she held the casket tight. By then, he was close enough to her to know that she wouldn't let go. He kept his hand on her back until he found a solution.

"Would you like to ride with him?" he finally asked. She looked up, dazed, and replied with a sniffling nod. She took his hand again as he guided her to the front seat of the hearse, where the surprised funeral directors quickly moved papers to make room for her.

Jim Cathey's mother, father and sister took their own time with the casket, caressing the flag, remembering.

His mother, Caroline, thought of the baby who used to reach out to her from the crib. His father, Jeff, saw the boy he watched grow into a man on long hunting trips through the barren landscape nearby.

His sister, Joyce, saw the kid who became her protector. The day after she learned of his death, she had his face tattooed on the back of her neck, so "he will always be watching my back."

Last of all, the young Marine who had escorted his friend home walked up to the casket and came to attention.

Only a few months before, Gavin Conley had stood before his best friend at the formal commissioning ceremony in Boulder, where Cathey received his brass lieutenant's bars.

For Cathey, it was one of the most important days of his life, and Conley knew the best way to share his pride.

At the end of the ceremony, Conley walked up to the new lieutenant and snapped his arm to his brow, giving the new officer his first salute.

In front of the casket on the tarmac, Conley again brought his hand to his face, this time in one slow, sweeping movement. As the family wept, his hand fell to his side.

His job as escort was officially over.

Before climbing into the hearse with Katherine, Beck took one last look at the scene, fixing on the plane. By then, the passengers had moved on, leaving the Marines and the family alone with the casket-and everything that was about to follow.

Strangers at the door

Five days before Jim Cathey returned home, two uniformed men sat in a government SUV, several blocks from Katherine Cathey's home in Brighton, and bowed their heads.

Beck and Navy chaplain Jim Chapman closed their eyes in prayer as the chaplain asked for "words that will bring the family peace."

This time, Beck was dressed in a drab green uniform in accordance with a controversial new mandate from the top brass not to wear dress blue uniforms to notifications, based on concerns that the distinctive blues had become too associated with tragedy.

It was a warm, blue-sky Sunday afternoon. Nearby, a neighbor mowed his lawn.

When the knock came, Katherine Cathey was taking a nap. Her stepfather saw the Marines first and opened the door.

"We're here for Katherine," Beck said quietly.

"Oh, no," Vic Leonard said.

At first, Katherine's mother thought it was someone trying to sell something. Then she saw her husband walking backward and the two men in uniform.

"Oh, no," she said.

"She's pregnant!"

Leonard suggested to his wife that she wake up Katherine. Vicki Leonard shook her head. She couldn't speak.

When her stepfather opened the door to her bedroom, Katherine could hear her mother crying. She thought something had happened to someone in her mother's family. She had never heard her mother cry like that.

"What's going on?" Katherine asked her stepfather.

"It's not good," he told her. "Come with me."

Her own screams began as soon as she saw the uniforms.

Katherine ran to the back of the living room and collapsed on the floor, holding her stomach, thinking of the man who would never see their baby. Finally she stood, but still couldn't speak.

As Beck and the chaplain remained on their feet, she glared at them. She ran to the back of the house and drew a hot bath. For the next hour, she sat in the tub, dissolving.

Shortly after their arrival, Beck had ducked back outside to make a quick phone call.

Inside a government SUV in Reno, just around the corner from the home where Jim Cathey grew up, another phone rang.

"Tell me it's not my son"

The toolbox was a mess.

Jim Cathey's mother stood in the garage, trying to find the right wrench to fix a sprinkler head in her front yard.

What a frustrating morning, she thought.

As she prepared to leave for the hardware store, the family dog started to howl a howl like she had never heard before. She put the dog in the house and drove off.

When the silver SUV pulled up, the Marines inside assumed someone was home. A lawn mower sat outside and it looked as if someone was doing yard work.

No one answered the door.

A neighbor drove up, looked at them and pulled into an adjacent driveway. The Marines started to get nervous. The neighbor looked out a window at them. Their orders were to remain parked at the house until the parents returned.

When Caroline Cathey drove up, she saw the strange government vehicle, then fixed her eyes on the man in the driver's seat.

"She saw me; she pulled in," Capt. Winston Tierney said. "And I hate this, but I think she might have suspected when she saw me. She got out of her vehicle and I told my guys, 'Time to go.'"

Caroline Cathey's hands went to her face.

"As I made my way up the driveway, we didn't say anything," Tierney said. "I wanted to wait until I was there. She looked at me and it looked like she was going to collapse. I supported her and tried to give her a hug."

He recounted the conversation from there:

"Please don't let it be," she said.

"I'm sorry to have to be here today. Can we go inside and sit down? There are some things we need to confirm."

"Please tell me it's not Jimmy, please tell me it's not my son."

The Marines stayed with the Catheys for the next 10 hours. With Caroline's help, they contacted Jim Cathey's 9-year-old daughter, Casey, who was born while he was still in high school. Casey, along with Katherine, had pinned the lieutenant's bars on her father only a few months before.

Casey's mother and stepfather drove the little girl from Carson City, Nev., to Reno, where another one of the Marines—an operations chief who had children of his own—told her that her daddy had been hurt in the war and wouldn't be able to come back. He asked her if she understood. She answered with tears.

The Marines held fast until Jim Cathey's father, Jeff, returned from a trip he had taken to his son's favorite hunting grounds, where he was scouting for game birds.

When it was all over, the Marines climbed back into the silver SUV. A staff sergeant looked at Tierney.

"Sir," he said. "Please don't take me on another one of these."

Part nine

From the moment his body departed Iraq, the sturdy, heavyweight cotton flag remained nearby, following him from the desert to Dover Air Force Base, Del., where a mortuary affairs team received his body.

According to the Department of Defense, Cathey was killed in Al Karmah, Iraq, on Aug. 21. Members of his unit later told family members that Cathey was leading the search of an abandoned building when a booby-trapped door exploded. The explosion was so fierce it blew off an arm and leg of the Marine directly behind Cathey. That man, now in recovery, credits his lieutenant with saving his life.

Once Cathey's remains arrived at Dover, the mortuary affairs team began the delicate task of readying his body for the final trip home. When possible, military morticians prepare a body for viewing by the family. In Cathey's case, that wasn't an option.

Specialists at Dover wrapped his body in a white shroud and covered it with a satin body-length pillow and his dress blue uniform before closing the casket lid and securing the flag nearby.

When the plane landed in Reno, the same flag was draped over the casket, which was loaded into the hearse to continue its journey to the funeral home.

After all the noise at the airport—the screaming, the crying, the whining of jet engines—inside the funeral home each footstep echoed.

The pallbearers carried their friend's body to the front of an enormous empty room, then faded into the background. Beck posted himself at the head of the casket, his face frozen in the Marine stare.

His eyes trained forward, he still saw everything.

Inside the room, Cathey's mother, Caroline, bent down to hug Katherine. They squeezed each other for a long time.

"You give me strength," the young widow said.

Other family members sat on couches and some sat on the floor—hugging, holding hands, their eyes locked on the casket, for nearly half an hour.

Finally, Beck broke the silence.

"I'm sorry," he said, excusing the family from the room. "There are some things I need to do."

Last watch

Beck motioned to the pallbearers and began the instructions that would hold for the next three days.

Although the Marines are required to stand watch over a comrade's body, once the casket is safely inside a locked mortuary or church, they usually leave at night and return when the mortuary reopens.

This time, however, the watch would not end.

"Katherine and Caroline have both expressed concerns about Jim being left alone," Beck told the Marines. "So we won't leave him alone."

He then explained how to guard the casket. They all had posted watch before. They had stood at attention for hours as part of basic training, but nothing like this.

They were to take shifts of about an hour at a time, Beck instructed, standing watch 24 hours a day. When changing the guard, they were to salute Cathey's casket first, then relieve the other Marine the same way.

He showed them the slow salute—the one they aren't taught in basic training—

three seconds up, hold for three seconds and three seconds down.

"A salute to your fallen comrade should take time," he said.

For Beck, that salute embodies more than the movement itself. Earlier in the day, someone had asked him about the arrival of "the body." He held up his hand with a firm correction.

"'The body' has a name." he said. "His name is Jim."

In the room, he walked up to the casket and paused.

"Now, this is important, too," he said. "If a family member wants you to break, you can break. They may want to hug you or kiss you. That's OK. Hug them. If someone wants to shake your hand, shake their hand. I'll take my glove off when I shake their hand—you don't have to, it's up to you. But then go back to position."

"Everyone understand?"

"Yes, sir," they responded. "Roger that."

"This is a serious business," he said. "Jim is watching you."

As the other Marines filed into the hallway, closing the door behind them, Beck walked back to the casket. For the first time, he and Jim Cathey were alone.

It was time for the final inspection.

No detail too small

Beck walked up to the casket and lifted the flag back, tucking it into neat pleats and leaving just enough room to open the heavy wooden lid. He walked around the flag several times, making sure each stripe lined up straight, smoothing the thick stitching with his soft white gloves.

Then he lifted the lid.

For the past five days, Beck had spent hours looking at pictures of Jim Cathey, listening to the family's stories, dabbing their tears. When he looked inside, they were no longer strangers.

For the next 10 minutes, Beck leaned over the open casket, checking the empty uniform that lay atop the tightly-shrouded body, making sure every ribbon and medal was in place. Occasionally, he pulled off a piece of lint or a stray thread and flicked it away.

Although casualty assistance officers receive an advisory from military morticians(殡仪业者) about whether a body is "viewable," some families insist on looking. The casualty assistance officer is often the one to make last-minute recommendations, since by then he knows the family and—after the final inspection—knows exactly what the family will see.

Whether or not the family decides on a viewing, Beck said, the procedure is no less meticulous.

In Cathey's case, the family decided not to look under the shroud. But Katherine wanted a few minutes alone with the open casket, to give her husband a few of the things they had shared and one he never got to see.

Beck ran his hand alongside the shroud, taking one last look at the uniform.

He closed the lid and turned toward the door.

"I'm always kissing you, baby"

Katherine draped her body over the smooth wood, pressing her pregnant belly to the casket, as close to a hug as she could get.

Beck placed a hand on her back.

"Tell me when you're ready," he said. "Take your time."

He stepped back.

The air conditioner clicked on, filling the room with a low hum. Ten minutes passed. It clicked off, leaving the room to her soft moans.

She moved only to adjust her feet, continuing to rub her belly against the wood. She closed her eyes and whispered something.

Then she looked up at Beck.

"OK," she said.

As she stood at his arm, he opened the casket.

She didn't cry. She didn't speak. He gave her a few seconds, then took her hand and brought it to the middle of the empty uniform. He held her hand there and pressed down.

"He's here," he told her. "Feel right here."

She held her hand on the spot, pressing the uniform into the shrouded body beneath. She dragged her hand the length of all that was there.

Beck walked back to get the personal belongings Katherine had brought with her from Colorado.

"Where do you want to start?" he asked.

"With the picture of us kissing," she said.

She placed the picture at the top of the casket, above the neck of the uniform. She bent down and pressed her lips to it.

"I'm always kissing you, baby," she whispered.

She took several other photos of their lives together and placed them around the uniform. She gently added a bottle of her perfume, then picked up the dried, fragile flowers of her wedding bouquet.

Before Jim Cathey had left for officer training, they were married by a justice of the peace in Denver, planning a big wedding on his return from Iraq. Her wedding dress still hangs in her closet at home, unworn.

She placed the flowers alongside the uniform, then turned again to the major.

"The ultrasound(超声波图)," she said.

The fuzzy image was taken two days after her husband's death. Katherine had scheduled the appointment for a day when Jim was supposed to call, so they could both learn the baby's gender together. He had a feeling it was a boy, he had told her. If it was, she suggested they name the child after him.

She stood cradling the ultrasound, then moved forward and placed it on the pillow at the head of the casket. She stood there, watching for several minutes, then removed it.

She walked the length of the casket, then stepped back, still holding the only image of James J. Cathey Jr..

She leaned in and placed it over her husband's heart.

Part ten

In the house where Jim Cathey grew up, a tattered stuffed animal still peers from a heavy wooden chest.

"This is Floppy Floyd," his mother said. "The last time he was here he said he wanted to take Floyd back, for the baby."

She held the stuffed animal to her face. Elsewhere in the house, she still has all of Jim's baby teeth and every award he ever won.

On his bookshelf, encyclopedias are shelved near the Louis L'Amour novels she used to read to him, next to a collection of Thucydides' writings.

"These are the things that made him who he is today," she said, then caught herself in present tense.

"Who he was today," she corrected herself softly.

Later, in the kitchen, she paused at a note that has hung on the refrigerator since the day Jim left home.

"See you all later. You know I love you and will be thinking about you every minute of every day. I miss you. Don't worry about me too much. I'll be back May 8th as a Marine! Write as much as you can. I will look forward to the letters. With all my love, J. C.."

She looked away from the note and at the things that made Jim Cathey who he was.

"Maybe now I know why my son was always in a hurry," she said.

A father's memories

Jeff Cathey almost didn't make it to his son's funeral. From the moment he saw the Marines at the door, he was thinking of his own.

Jeff, who suffers from clinical depression, spiraled deeper the day the Marines came to the house, to the point where his family worried more about him than their own grief. His wife hid all of his guns. Even so, the day after he found out about his son's death, he insisted on going back to the hunting grounds where he and Jim had spent their best times together.

"Before he left, I made him swear on his son's life that he would come back to me," Caroline said.

"I thought about doing it. Ending it," Jeff said, breaking into tears. "I really did. I want to be with him."

As he sat on the couch, he tried to compose himself.

"Good thoughts," he told himself. "Good thoughts."

And then found plenty.

"One of my finest memories was when we were hunting and he came back to the car, overturned a pail, sat down and started doing his homework."

"I wish I had a picture of that."

"You do," his wife said, rubbing his back, pointing to his head. "Right up here."

Part eleven

Inside the mortuary(太平间)the night before Cathey's funeral, two Marines stood near the casket, unfurling(展开)sheets on a makeshift bed.

"Make it look nice, dude, make it look nice," one of them said.

"Who are you, Martha Stewart?" the other shot back with a grin.

Another looked at the blanket.

"If you're pregnant, do you get hot or cold?"

One of the Marines who has a child of his own looked at the bed.

"She's going to need another pillow," he said. "Since she's pregnant, she'll need to put a pillow between her legs."

Then they saw car lights outside and took their positions.

Earlier that day, Katherine had told them she couldn't bear to spend the last night away from her husband. She said she would sleep on a pew(长凳子)if she had to. The Marines found her an air mattress instead and promised to be ready.

Arriving exhausted, she almost immediately crawled onto the bed they had made for her. Her stepfather helped tuck her in.

"Do you have another pillow?" she asked. "I need one to put between my legs."

One of the Marines crouched down and asked if they should continue to post guard in the room.

"We can do whatever you want," he said. "We can stay or we can give you some privacy."

"I think it would be kind of nice if you kept doing it," she said. "I think that's what he would have wanted."

After one of the Marines dimmed the lights, Katherine opened a laptop computer on the floor. In the blue glow of the screen, she listened to the songs they would have played at the wedding they never held.

She swayed, then closed her eyes.

As drowsiness set in, she picked up an old T-shirt—the last shirt Jim Cathey wore before changing into his cammies to leave for Iraq. She hadn't washed it. It still smelled like him.

She held the shirt to her face and breathed in.

"Selfish of us to die"

Just past midnight, Staff Sgt. Andrew Price walked to the back of the room and, like a watchful parent, dimmed the lights further. Then he closed Katherine's computer.

For the next hour he stood, barely illuminated by the light behind the altar, until another Marine approached from the shadows, paused before the makeshift bed and raised his hand in slow salute.

As each man was relieved, he walked into a spare room next to the chapel. In the darkness, one by one they spoke:

1:37 a.m. Staff Sgt. Andrew Price

The lanky Marine had stood watch at dozens of funerals at Arlington National Cemetery, but none prepared him for this.

"We would have stayed as long as Katherine wanted us there tonight. Even if she wanted us to go, I would have stayed there for her. I would have walked around in the shadows. Some way or another, we're always going to try to take care of her."

Of all the hours he has walked sentry, the last hour and a half was the hardest.

"It's almost selfish of us to die. James won't have to see her like that. They train us as warriors. They don't teach us how to take the pain away."

2:28 a.m. 2nd Lt. Charlie Loya Jr.

They call him the joker of the group: a massive man with a massive laugh.

"(After Cathey got killed) People would ask me how I'm doing and I'd say, 'I'm fine.' And I was. Then (at the airport)... we picked the casket up off the conveyor belt and all I heard was Katherine screaming. I thought, 'My wife would be doing the same thing.' Then all I could think about was my son."

When he heard about Cathey's death, he was scheduled to leave for Iraq in two weeks. Inside the room, he realized there were only eight days left.

"(Before Cathey died) people would ask how I felt about going over there. I'd say, 'I'm confident, I'm prepared and my boys are ready.'"

"Now I'm scared."

3:19 a.m. Staff Sgt. David Rubio

"Cat" would have wanted them to laugh, he said, so he did.

"He was the smartest dumb guy I knew. I used to always tell him that. He was just a big oaf. I keep seeing that face, that big cheesy face."

He got up, paced the floor, holding the grin, the way the big oaf would have wanted.

"I got a call from him a couple months ago... The last thing he said was, 'Mark time, dude. Mark time. I'll see you in the fleet.'"

"It just basically means, 'I'll be waiting for you.'"

4:23 a.m. 2nd Lt. Jon Mueller

He looked at the dark wall and thought of the casket on the other side.

"I'm still going to go when they ask me to go. But I also want people to know what I am doing. I'm not a very emotional guy. I don't show emotion, but I know that it's important for people to know how much you care for them. I'm not the kind of guy who can say, 'I love you.' It's not easy for me."

"I'll make it so that my loved ones know that I love them."

5:19 a.m. 2nd Lt. Jason Lindauer

"Cat was doing what he loved. I suppose that makes it a little easier, but... I called my (4-year-old) son on the phone, and he said, 'Daddy, my friend Cat got killed.' (My wife had told him.)"

"I said, 'Yeah, I know buddy. Cat's in heaven.'"

The Marine began to cry.

"(My son) said, 'Well, when's he coming back?'"

He lowered his head.

"I said, 'He's not, buddy.'"

"Angels looking over me"

As the sun rose in Reno, the casinos continued to chime. Diners began to fill. In the newspapers that hit the porches, Iraq had been pushed to the back pages again.

While the city churned, the sun found the building where Katherine Cathey awoke.

"It's the best night of sleep I've had," she said, surprised. "I really slept."

As she sat, wrapped in a blanket, her eyes bleary, she looked at the casket.

"You take for granted the last night you spend with them," she said. "I think I took it for granted. This was the last night I'll have to sleep next to him."

Behind her, the next Marine approached, preparing to take over the watch.

"I feel like they're my angels looking over me," Katherine said.

She placed her hand on her belly.

"Looking over us," she said.

Part twelve

It starts in slow motion.

At a windswept cemetery near 2nd Lt. Jim Cathey's favorite hunting grounds, the Marines moved as if underwater, a precision slowness, allowing everyone in the cemetery to study each move, each frame, holding it as long as possible until it's gone.

Beck stood back and started the ritual again.

"Present military honors," he commanded.

In the distance, seven members of the rifle guard from Reno readied their weapons. Because the Reno unit was so small—with many of its members in Iraq—they called in recruiters and other Marines from across the state to help with the duty.

"Ready. Aim. Fire."

With each volley, almost everyone in the shelter flinched.

"Ready. Aim. Fire."

The Marines at the casket held steady.

"Ready. Aim. Fire."

They knew the hard part was still to come:

Taps.

As the bugler played, the Marines held onto the flag. Second Lt. Loya blinked almost continuously, trying to hold back the tears.

After the last note, they began to fold.

The afternoon before, the pallbearers spent more than an hour with Beck as he instructed them on how to fold the flag. For such a seemingly simple task, there are hundreds of ways to get it wrong. Especially when you're folding it for your friend's pregnant wife—especially when you're folding his flag for the last time.

The Marines took their time, stretching one fold after another, until the flag strained, a permanent triangle. A sergeant walked up and slipped the still—hot shells from the rifle salute into the folded flag.

Beck took the flag, cradling it with one hand on top, one hand below, and carried it to Katherine.

He bent down on one knee, looking at his hands, at the flag, his eyes reddening.

Before his tears could spill, his face snapped up and he looked her in the eyes.

"Katherine," he said.

Then he said the words meant only for her—words he had composed. When he was done, he stepped back, into the blank stare.

Capt. Winston Tierney walked forward, carrying another flag for Caroline Cathey. The night before, the Marines had used the flag to practice, draping it over the casket—not only for themselves, but also so that Jim Cathey's mother would know that it had covered her son.

The captain bent down on one knee, passed the flag into Caroline Cathey's hands, then faded into the background.

For a group of Cathey's friends, there was one more task.

The Marines, many of whom had flown in from Okinawa the night before, walked up to the casket. One by one, they removed their white gloves and placed them on the smooth wood. Then they reached into a bag of sand the same dark gray shade as gunpowder.

A few years ago, while stationed in the infantry in Hawaii, Jim Cathey and his friends had taken a trip to Iwo Jima, where nearly 6,000 Marines had lost their lives almost 60 years before. They slept on the beach, thinking about all that had happened there. The day before they left, they each collected a bag of sand.

Those bags of sand sat in their rooms for years. Girlfriends questioned them. Wives wondered what they would ever do with them.

One by one, the young Marines poured a handful of sand onto the gloves atop the casket, then stepped back.

Sgt. Gavin Conley, who had escorted his friend's body to Reno, reached into the bag, made a fist and drizzled the grains onto the casket.

Once again, he slowly brought his bare hand to his brow.

A final salute.

"(The day after sleeping on the beach), we all did a hike up Mount Suribachi, where our battalion commander spoke, and we rendered honors to all the fallen on Iwo Jima," Conley said.

He looked over at the sand.

"Now they can be part of him, too."

"Let them in"

Minutes after the ceremony ended, a windstorm blew into the cemetery, swirling the high desert dust.

Beck was one of the last to leave, giving his final commands to the cemetery caretakers in the funeral shelter: Make sure the sand on the casket doesn't blow away.

"It's important," he told them.

As he drove away from the cemetery, Beck replayed the last few hours in his mind, looking for lessons for the next time, hoping there wouldn't be one, but knowing there would.

He thought back to the latest funeral—from the moment he rang the doorbell in Brighton until he handed the flag to Katherine and said those words that usually begin, "On behalf of a grateful nation..."

"You know, everyone always wants to know what the words are, what it is that I say," he said. "I don't say it loud enough for everyone to hear."

There are scripted words written for the Marines to follow. Beck has long since learned that he doesn't always have to follow a script.

"I'm basically looking into that mother, father or spouse's eyes and letting them know that everyone cares about them," he said. "But the words are nothing compared to the flag."

He then drove several miles without speaking.

In his mind, the subject had not changed.

"You think about the field of cotton somewhere in Mississippi, and out of all of it comes this thread that becomes this flag that covers our brave. Think about it."

"I had a cotton field right behind the house when I was going to command and staff college. Imagine being that farmer who owned the cotton field. Imagine if one of these parents was able to take a flag back to him and say, 'That flag came out of your field and escorted my son home. ' "

He shook his head.

"The things you think about," he said.

It's usually on these long drives that he allows himself to step back from it all, or at least tries to. He still hasn't learned how to step back far enough.

"One morning after burying a lance corporal, all I wanted to do was come home and play with my children. Just take them into a corner with all their things and play with them," he said. "But you know, all I was thinking about while I was playing with them were all those guys out there in harm's way, making all that possible."

"Here we are, while they're out there. Someone could be under attack right now. Someone could be calling for an airstrike..."

Someone could be standing at a door, preparing to knock.

"This experience has changed me in fundamental ways," Beck said. "I would not wish it on anyone, but at the same time, I think that it's important that it happened to me. I know it's going to have an impact on someone's life that I'm going to meet years from now."

In a year, he said, so many scenes return. The doors and doorbells. The first time he completed a final inspection. Sand on a casket.

The scene he sees the most, however, is not of a single moment but the entire journey, viewed through someone else's eyes.

"One thing keeps coming back to me," he said. "It was during the memorial service for Kyle Burns."

The service came only a week after Beck first parked in front of that little white house in Laramie, watching the perfect snow, preparing to walk through it all.

During that memorial service, Kyle Burns's uncle, George Elsom, recounted the call from his devastated sister, who phoned him after she first saw the Marines at the door.

"At Kyle's memorial service, his uncle talked about all they had learned since that night." Beck said. "Then he looked at us and said something I'll never forget."

"He said, 'If these men ever come to your door, don't turn them away.' "

"He said, 'If these men come to your door...' "

"Let them in."

Unit Seven Explanatory Reporting

解释性报道

单元导航

本单元我们将讨论解释性报道。本单元有三篇文章。课文 A 阐述海洋生态恶化的问题；课文 B 反映美国蒙大拿州的酗酒问题；课文 C 讲述一对美国夫妇利用胚胎干细胞治疗儿子的肌无力症及其引发的道德争论。

Part One：Preparing to explore

一、解释性报道

1. 定义

解释性报道指对某一复杂现象或科学原理进行解释说明的报道。它重在阐述事件发生的原因和背景，或剖析事件发生的来龙去脉，以预测其趋势。美国报人罗斯科·德拉蒙德曾形象地说，解释性报道是“把今天的事件置于昨天的背景之下，从而揭示出它对明天的含义”。

从报道性质上讲，解释性报道与调查性报道（investigative reporting）相对；从文体上讲，解释性报道把叙事和议论有机地结合起来，介于侧重叙述事实的纯新闻与侧重分析和议论事物的评论之间。

2. 产生与发展

解释性报道产生于 20 世纪 20 年代，由美国《时代》(*Times*) 杂志率先采用。该杂志将一周重大新闻分门别类，加以综合改写，并补充材料，略加分析，同时配上照片，使其报道条理清晰，又有一定的深度。这种文体很适合当时战后生活节奏加快的多数美国人，因此，受到读者欢迎。

此后，解释性新闻逐步发展起来。第一，经济因素。在经历了 1923—1929 年经济发展黄金期后，美国于 1929 年爆发了空前的经济危机。10 月 29 日开始的一周内，美国人在证券交易所内失去的财富达 100 亿美元。农业资本家和大农场主大量销毁“过剩”的产品，把牛奶倒进密西西比河，以维持农产品的价格。到 1932 年，钢铁工业下降了近80%，汽车工业下降了95%，至少13万家企业倒闭，占全国劳工总数1/4的人口失业，1929—1933年，社会处于剧烈动荡之中。人们对此感到困惑，希望了解更多真相，获得某种解释与答案。解释性报道正好满足了大众的需求，因而迅速地发展起来。

第二，科技发展也是推动解释性报道发展的重要原因。20世纪40年代中期，新科技的出现使社会生产与生活发生了重大变化。1945年7月美国试爆第一颗原子弹成功，并在日本广岛、长崎显示了震撼世界的毁灭之力。1946年2月，电子计算机在宾夕法尼亚大学问世。同时，被称为“新三论”的系统论、信息论与控制论的综合性基础理论出现。这些新的科技发展使新闻事件更趋复杂与难于理解。在这种背景下，解释性报道得到了进一步发展。

第三，解释性报道的发展还是媒体竞争的结果。20世纪20年代广播出现，20世纪30年代电视发明，随着这两种电子媒介的日益发展和普及，传统报纸受到前所未有的挑战。面临以快速敏捷为优势的新兴媒介，报纸采取了包括解释性报道在内的挖掘新闻深度的报道手段，通过利用自己的强项与电子媒介形成了共存与发展的局势。报纸将挑战变成了机遇，促进了解释性报道的发展。

第四，推动解释性报道发展的另外一个重要因素是报业本身对20世纪50年代“客观报道”原则的反思。当时，美国报纸依据“客观报道”原则，对诬陷和清洗共产党人和进步人士的麦卡锡主义言论进行报道和传播，但实际上起到了帮凶的作用。人们由此反思，如果新闻界知道麦卡锡的言论是虚假的还要借“客观报道”的名义广为传播，这显然是助纣为虐；但如果他们不能看透其虚假，那么新闻工作者的专业水准就要受到质疑，因为新闻界理应消息灵通，判断力强，这样不合格的新闻工作者没有资格拥有作为社会公器的大众传媒。无论是哪种情况，新闻界都难逃其责，处境尴尬。在这种背景下，新闻界选择了客观报道之外的另外一种新的报道方式，即解释性报道。从此，解释性报道得以长足发展。

3. 普利策解释性报道奖

1985年，普利策评奖委员会设立“解释性报道”奖，取名为“explanatory journalism”，但从1998年至今，一直用“explanatory reporting”。

解释性报道的获奖文章触及广泛而深刻的话题，特别是医学研究等科学话题，如药品安全、DNA检测引起的尴尬和道德问题、干细胞研究、动脉瘤、人类基因组多样性研究、分子精神病理学、基因疗法、伊波拉病毒、抗生素和杀虫剂疗效的减退问题等，其他话题还包括股市大崩盘、美国公司丑闻、亚洲经济危机对美国的影响、高额筹资带来的人力损失等经济问题，还有美国对也门的内政干涉、阿富汗政局等政治问题、酗酒、贫困、犯罪、临终关怀等社会问题、航空安全和美国航空计划问题、海洋生态破坏问题、美国战略国防问题以及全球恐怖活动网络问题等。

4. 意义

首先，解释性报道可以帮助读者了解事物的本质和意义。因为这类报道突出“为什么”和“如何”，追根究源，讲清来龙去脉，深挖新闻背后的新闻，所以它不仅提供信息，而且引导受众，这在当今信息爆炸的时代显得尤为重要。其次，通讯社和纸质媒体可以利用解释性报道提升竞争力。广播、电视的普及，因特网等新型媒体的迅速崛起，把各类新闻迅速带给受众，这对报纸、杂志等纸质媒体构成了巨大的挑战。但是电子媒体在内容深度的开发上仍有一些局限性，因此仍然难以满足受众的需求。通讯社和纸质媒体正好能填补这方面的空缺，取长补短，胜过竞争对手。再次，解释性报道还有助于科学技术的传播与普及。比如，1985 年的普利策解释性报道获奖者琼·富兰克林（Jon Franklin）通过对 50 多位科学家的采访，介绍了分子精神病理学（molecular psychiatry），并展望了它对精神病患者的治疗疗效，使更多的人了解了这门新学科。

5. 基本写作特征

从普利策奖评审委员会给予解释性报道获奖作品的赞词来看，优秀的解释性新闻报道作品以下基本特点：

（1）复杂而深刻的选题的了解与把握（complex subject）。

（2）所选话题（mastery of subject）。关键是掌握背景材料，包括历史性事实，与新闻事件相关的社会或自然因素，与新闻人物相关的材料、相关数据等。

（3）通俗易懂的语言（lucid writing）。

（4）清晰明了的表达手法（clear presentation）。

二、课前讨论

1. Albert Schweitzer, Nobel Peace Prize winner in 1952, said: "Man has lost the capacity to foresee and to forestall. He will end by destroying the earth." Do you agree? Explain.

2. What do you see in the picture below? Explain.

Part Two: Exploring the text

Text A　Plague of plastic chokes the seas

BY Kenneth R. Weiss

Los Angeles Times

August 2, 2006

On Midway Atoll(中途岛),40% of albatross chicks(小信天翁)die,their bellies full of trash. Swirling masses of drifting debris pollute remote beaches and snare(诱捕) wildlife.

Young Casualty:One of the 200,000 albatross chicks that die yearly on Midway Atoll. (Rick Loomis/*Los Angeles Times*)

MIDWAY ATOLL—The albatross chick jumped to its feet, eyes alert and focused. At 5 months,it stood 18 inches tall and was fully feathered except for the fuzz(绒毛)that fringed its head.

All attitude,the chick straightened up and clacked its beak at a visitor(向一位过客啪嗒啪嗒地咂嘴),then rocked(摇摆)back and dangled(摇晃) webbed(有蹼的)feet in the air to cool them in the afternoon breeze.

The next afternoon,the chick ignored passersby. The bird was flopped on its belly(肚子朝下扑落在地),its legs splayed awkwardly(笨拙地张开). Its wings drooped(低垂)in the hot sun. A few hours later,the chick was dead.

John Klavitter,a wildlife biologist(野生动植物学家),turned the bird over and cut it open with a knife. Probing its innards(内脏) with a gloved hand, he pulled out a yellowish sac(囊)in its stomach.

Out tumbled(翻滚出)a collection of red,blue and orange bottle caps,a black spray nozzle(喷雾嘴),part of a green comb,a white golf tee(高尔夫球座)and a clump(块)of tiny dark squid beaks(鱿鱼嘴)ensnared in a tangle of fishing line.

“This is pretty typical,” said Klavitter,who is stationed at the atoll(环状珊瑚岛)for the U. S. Fish and Wildlife Service. “We often find cigarette lighters,bucket handles(桶柄),toothbrushes,syringes(注射器),toy soldiers—anything made out of plastic. ”

It’s all part of a tide of plastic debris(碎片)that has spread throughout the world’s oceans,posing a lethal hazard(致命的危害)to wildlife,even here,more than 1,000 miles from the nearest city.

Midway,an atoll halfway between North America and Japan,has no industrial centers,no fast-food joints with overflowing trash cans,and only a few dozen people.

Its isolation would seem to make it an ideal rookery(群居地)for seabirds,especially

Laysan albatross, which lay their eggs and hatch(孵化) their young here each winter. For their first six months of life, the chicks depend entirely on their parents for nourishment (营养). The adults forage(寻找食物) at sea and bring back high-calorie takeout: a slurry (浆) of partly digested squid and flying-fish eggs.

As they scour the ocean surface for this sustenance, albatross encounter vast expanses of floating junk. They pick up all manner(各式各样的) of plastic debris, mistaking it for food.

As a result, the regurgitated payload(回流的载重物) flowing down their chicks' gullets(食道) now includes Lego blocks(乐高积木块), clothespins(晾衣绳上夹衣服的夹子), fishing lures(鱼饵) and other pieces of plastic that can perforate(打孔) the stomach or block the gizzard(砂囊) or esophagus(食管). The sheer volume of plastic inside a chick can leave little room for food and liquid.

Of the 500,000 albatross chicks born here each year, about 200,000 die, mostly from dehydration(脱水) or starvation. A two-year study funded by the U. S. Environmental Protection Agency showed that chicks that died from those causes had twice as much plastic in their stomachs as those that died for other reasons.

The atoll is littered with decomposing remains(腐烂的遗体), grisly wreaths of feathers(可怕的一圈圈羽毛) and bone surrounding colorful piles of bottle caps, plastic dinosaurs(恐龙), checkers(棋子), highlighter pens(荧光笔), perfume bottles, fishing line and small Styrofoam(聚苯乙烯泡沫塑料) balls. Klavitter has calculated that albatross feed their chicks about 5 tons of plastic a year at Midway.

Albatross fly hundreds of miles in their search for food for their young. Their flight paths from Midway often take them over what is perhaps the world's largest dump: a slowly rotating mass of trash-laden water about twice the size of Texas.

This is known as the Eastern Garbage Patch, part of a system of currents(水流) called the North Pacific subtropical gyre(亚热带旋流圈). Located halfway between San Francisco and Hawaii, the garbage patch is an area of slack(不流畅的) winds and sluggish(流速很慢的) currents where flotsam(漂浮物) collects from around the Pacific, much like foam piling up in the calm center of a hot tub(浴盆).

Curtis Ebbesmeyer has been studying the clockwise swirl(顺时针方向流动的旋涡) of plastic debris so long, he talks about it as if he were tracking a beast.

"It moves around like a big animal without a leash(束缚)," said Ebbesmeyer, an oceanographer(海洋学者) in Seattle and leading expert on currents and marine debris. "When it gets close to an island, the garbage patch barfs(呕吐), and you get a beach covered with this confetti of plastic(五颜六色的塑料)."

Some oceanic trash washes ashore at Midway—laundry baskets, television tubes(显像管), beach sandals, soccer balls and other discards(废弃物).

Nearly 90% of floating marine litter is plastic—supple(柔软的), durable materials such as polyethylene(聚乙烯) and polypropylene(聚丙烯), Styrofoam, nylon and saran

(涉纶). About four—fifths of marine trash comes from land, swept by wind or washed by rain off highways and city streets, down streams and rivers, and out to sea.

The rest comes from ships. Much of it consists of synthetic floats(人造纤维漂流物) and other gear(物品) that is jettisoned illegally to avoid the cost of proper disposal in port.

In addition, thousands of cargo containers fall overboard(掉到船外) in stormy seas each year, spilling their contents. One ship heading from Los Angeles to Tacoma, Wash., disgorged(吐出) 33,000 blue-and-white Nike basketball shoes in 2002. Other loads lost at sea include 34,000 hockey gloves and 29,000 yellow rubber ducks and other bathtub toys.

The debris can spin(旋转) for decades in one of a dozen or more gigantic gyres around the globe, only to be spat out and carried by currents to distant lands. The U. N. Environment Program estimates that 46,000 pieces of plastic litter are floating on every square mile of the oceans. About 70% will eventually sink.

Albatross are by no means the only victims. An estimated 1 million seabirds choke or get tangled in plastic nets or other debris every year. About 100,000 seals, sea lions, whales, dolphins, other marine mammals(海洋哺乳动物) and sea turtles suffer the same fate.

The amount of plastic in the oceans has risen sharply since the 1950s. Studies show a tenfold increase every decade in some places. Scientists expect the trend to continue, given the popularity of disposable plastic containers. The average American used 223 pounds of plastic in 2001. The plastics industry expects per-capita usage to increase to 326 pounds by the end of the decade.

The qualities that make plastics so useful are precisely what cause them to persist as trash.

Derived from petroleum, plastics eventually break down into carbon dioxide(二氧化碳) and water from exposure to heat and the sun's ultraviolet rays.

On land, the process can take decades, even centuries. At sea, it takes even longer, said Anthony L. Andrady, a polymer(聚合物) chemist at the Research Triangle Institute in North Carolina who studies marine debris. Seawater keeps plastics cool while algae, barnacles and other marine growth block ultraviolet rays.

"Every little piece of plastic manufactured in the past 50 years that made it into the ocean is still out there somewhere," Andrady said, "because there is no effective mechanism to break it down."

Oceanographers have counted on beachcombers(海滩流浪汉) around the world to help them plot the course of plastic flotsam as it circumnavigates(环行) the globe. Ebbesmeyer has found that some debris gets hung up for decades in gyres before being spun out into different currents, flung ashore or picked up by animals.

A piece of plastic found in an albatross stomach last year bore a serial number that was traced to a World War II seaplane shot down in 1944. Computer models re-creating the object's odyssey showed it spent a decade in a gyre known as the Western Garbage Patch, just south of Japan, and then drifted 6,000 miles to the Eastern Garbage Patch off the West Coast of the U. S., where it spun in circles for the next 50 years.

The Hawaiian archipelago(群岛), which stretches from the Big Island of Hawaii westward for 1,500 miles to Kure Atoll, acts like 19 unevenly spaced teeth of a giant comb, snagging debris drifting around the Pacific. Most of the archipelago's atolls are awash in plastic junk, as are some beaches on the main islands.

Native Hawaiians, seeking wood for dugout canoes(独木舟), used to go to Kamilo Beach at the southernmost tip of the Big Island to collect enormous logs that had drifted from the Pacific Northwest. Now, locals like Noni Sanford pick through the debris for novelties to enter in a trash-art show in Hilo every fall.

Sanford, 58, a free-spirited great-grandmother with long gray hair pulled back in a ponytail, once won second place for a mobile fashioned out(制造) of fishing line, floats and a colorful palette(调色板) of plastic toothbrushes.

As a lifelong beachcomber, she is fascinated and horrified by the transformation of Kamilo Beach since she first set foot there in 1959. She was searching for driftwood with her father, a sculptor.

She remembers seeing a few tires back then. Now, plastic debris litters the crescent-shaped(新月形的) beach for more than a mile.

"This is nothing," Sanford said, stepping over a pile of twisted lines and nets. "This used to be 8 and 10 feet high. Of course, that was three or four cleanups(清除) ago."

Sanford and her husband, Ron, have joined in regular cleanup efforts, organized most recently by Bill Gilmartin, a retired wildlife biologist who studied monk seals.

"The rule is, don't pick up anything smaller than your fist," Gilmartin told a team of volunteers. "Otherwise, it'll take forever. We'll never be done."

Noni Sanford reached down, scooped up a handful of beach sand and let it trickle through her fingers. Most of the grainy mix was bits and pieces of plastic. The beach itself, it seemed, was turning into plastic.

Cleanup efforts in Hawaii and elsewhere have focused on "ghost nets," tangles of abandoned fishing lines, nets and traps that snare and kill marine life.

The National Oceanic and Atmospheric Administration dispatches scuba divers(佩戴水肺的潜水员) every year to cut tons of these death traps off Hawaiian coral reefs(珊瑚礁). It's dangerous and costly work. In July 2005, a 145-foot charter vessel brought in to haul away nets ran aground on the reef at Pearl and Hermes Atoll, about 100 miles from Midway. The ship was lost. The Coast Guard flew the 23 divers and crew 1,200 miles back to Honolulu(火奴鲁鲁,即檀香山).

If it were easier to find them, it would make sense to round up(使聚拢) the medusas(水母体) of nets and synthetic lines at sea before they snagged on coral reefs and endangered monk seals and other coastal wildlife.

But the Pacific spans millions of square miles, and even the debris circulating in the Eastern and Western garbage patches is often diffuse(散开的)and hard to see, bobbing(上下或来回地动)just below the surface.

Connecting the two patches is a ribbon of oceanic highway that stretches 6,000 miles, an extension of Japan's Kuroshio Current heading east. Oceanographers call this the Subtropical Convergence Zone, where the cold, green, heavier waters from the north slide under the warm, blue waters of the south.

A team of scientists working on NOAA's GhostNet Detection Project(美国国家海洋大气局的"鬼网搜寻计划")suspected that flotsam collected along this line, making it an ideal place to concentrate cleanups. Yet they couldn't be sure. They needed to see it.

The team got its chance last year, after persuading NOAA to lend them an instrument-packed, four-engine reconnaissance plane(侦察机)often deployed to study hurricanes. Wearing life jackets while flying 1,000 feet above the ocean's surface, observers were positioned at windows to spot nets and floats. They were to call out each sighting over the plane's intercom. Others were poised to jot down the location of each sighting.

"When we got into it, we couldn't write fast enough," said Tim Veenstra, an Alaskan pilot and private researcher working with government scientists. The meandering(蜿蜒的)line of buoys(浮标), nets, life rings(救生圈), buckets and other castoffs stretched for hundreds and hundreds of miles until the airplane had to turn back.

"It was sort of a bittersweet feeling," Veenstra said. "Sweet in the fact that what we had postulated(假定)was proven true. Bitter in the fact that there was actually that much debris floating around."

Tuna fishermen have long known about the convergence zone and the debris. They know that fish like to congregate(聚集)beneath anything that floats.

Off the southern tip of the Big Island of Hawaii, recreational fishermen like Guy Enriques will race miles offshore to fish beneath the flotsam.

It's important to get close to the trash, but not too close, Enriques explained, or the nets and lines will wrap around a boat's propeller(螺旋桨).

He said the best fishing was around what looked like an enormous metal garage door floating just below the water's surface. Even some charter boat skippers(包船船长)learned of that one, Enriques recalled, and took fishermen there day after day, until it vanished.

But it wasn't a garage door. He and other fishermen were looking at the top of an 8-by-40-foot cargo container that fell off a ship. Such containers can float for as long as nine months. Until they sink, they are the bane(祸害)of sailors in fiberglass boats who watch for them like icebergs on the high seas.

Nursery:Midway Atoll is a major rookery for millions of birds,including white tern (top),albatross and other species. The remote atoll,the focus of a major World War II battle,is now under siege from drifting debris. Plastic mistaken for food by foraging albatross is found filling the bellies of dead chicks,hundreds of thousands of which die each year on the island. (Rick Loomis/*Los Angeles Times*)

Charles Moore,a member of the Hancock Oil family,was on his way home from the Los Angeles to Hawaii Transpacific Yacht Race in 1997 when he took a shortcut through the Eastern Garbage Patch. It's a place that sailors usually avoid because it lacks wind.

As he motored through on his 50-foot catamaran(筏),Moore was startled by what he saw thousands of miles from land. "Every time I came on deck, there was trash floating by," he said. "How could we have fouled(弄脏)such a huge area? How could this go on for a week?"

The experience changed Moore's life, turning him from an adventurer into a self-taught scientist and environmental activist.

Two years later,he returned to the garbage patch with a volunteer crew to survey its contents. He knew he would collect plenty of plastic bags,bottle caps,nets and floats.

He didn't expect what turned up in a special net,one with a tight mesh for collecting plankton(浮游生物),the bottom link in the oceanic food chain. Instead of plankton,it was choked with a colorful array of tiny plastic fragments.

"It blew my mind,"Moore said. "We are filling up the oceans with this confetti stuff,and nobody cares."

Over the last decade, Moore, 59, who lives in a waterfront home in Long Beach, has spent his own money and some from a family foundation on a quest to track the plume of plastic(塑料堆) so he can figure out how to stop it.

On a cloudless spring day, Moore waded(涉水) up to his knees into the Los Angeles River in Long Beach wearing shorts, sandals and a white hard hat. He was tethered to a volunteer standing on the dry riverbank, in case he slipped on the slick concrete channel.

The Los Angeles River carries enough trash each year to fill the Rose Bowl two stories high, and despite efforts to corral(阻拦) some of it near the river mouth, most slips through to the ocean.

Moore adjusted a trawlnet(拖捞网) to collect trash flowing downriver. At Moore's signal, a crane operator lifted the net out of the water. Volunteers swarmed around the trawlnet, extracted the contents and loaded them into more than a dozen jars.

The jars were filled with plastic pellets(小团) the size and shape of pills. They come in all colors and are the raw material for a vast array of plastic products, from trash bags to medical devices.

About 100 billion pounds of pellets are produced every year and shipped to Los Angeles and other manufacturing centers. Huge numbers are spilled on the ground and swept by rainfall into gutters; down storm drains, creeks and rivers; and into the ocean.

From his river sampling, Moore estimated that 236 million pellets washed down the Los Angeles and San Gabriel rivers in three days' time. Also known as "nurdles" or mermaid tears(美人鱼眼泪), they are the most widely seen plastic debris around the world. They have washed ashore as far away as Antarctica.

The pellets, like most types of plastic, are sponges for oily toxic chemicals that don't readily dissolve in water, such as the pesticide DDT and polychlorinated biphenyls, (多氯化联二苯) or PCBs. Some pellets have been found to contain concentrations of these pollutants 1 million times greater than the levels found in surrounding water.

As they absorb toxic chemicals, they become poison pills. Wildlife researchers have found the pellets, which resemble fish eggs, in the bellies of fish, sea turtles, seabirds and marine mammals.

Over time, plastic can break down into smaller and smaller pieces, eventually turning to powder and entering the ocean in microscopic fragments. Some plastic starts out as tiny particles, such as the abrasives in cleaning products that are washed down the sink, through sewage systems and out to sea.

The chemical components of plastics and common additives can harm animals and humans. Studies have linked the hormone-mimicking phthalates(邻苯二甲酰化), used to soften plastic, to reduced testosterone(睾丸激素) and fertility in laboratory animals, and to subtle changes in the genitals of baby boys. Another additive, bisphenol A(双酚 A), used to make lightweight, heat-resistant baby bottles and microwave cookware, has been linked to prostate cancer(前列腺癌).

Moore has tried, without success, to get manufacturers to improve their efforts to clean up spills of pellets that wash off lots and into storm drains. He considers beach cleanups a waste of time, except to raise public awareness of the problem. In his view, the cleanup has to start at the source—many miles inland.

River Runoff: Tons of garbage that swept down the Los Angeles River after a storm is corralled by a boom in Long Beach. Most trash runoff ends up in the sea, joining more floating debris from ships—nets, gear, even cargo containers. (Rick Loomis/*Los Angeles Times*)

To make that point, Moore tromped through rail yards in Vernon and La Mirada. On the side of a rail car a faded decal read "Operation Clean Sweep." It had three check boxes:

"Keep Plastics Off Ground."

"Close and Lock Caps When Outlets Not in Use."

"Pick Up All Spills."

Beneath the sign was a cone-shaped pile of pellets, as white as freshly fallen snow. Moore shuffled his sandaled feet through another drift nearby.

"This is a plastic s and dune(塑料沙丘)," he said. "It's very slippery, very roly-poly. What makes them so good for the factory makes them good for getting into the ocean."

一、作者背景

肯尼斯·R·伟斯（Kenneth R. Weiss）：1957 年 5 月 28 日出生于加利福尼亚。自 1990 年起，他成为《洛杉矶时报》的记者和编辑，报道过教育、政府和政治等话题，现在

主要从事环境报道。他还是国家科学作家协会会员，环境记者协会会员。

供职于《洛杉矶时报》前，他曾在多家新闻机构工作过，包括《纽约时报》、前美国新闻社、《巴尔的摩太阳报》、《加利福尼亚日报》等。

伟斯获得过许多重要的新闻奖项，如 2006 年获哥伦比亚大学授予的约翰·欧克斯优秀环境新闻奖；2000 年分别获教育作家协会颁发的佛雷德·海切格大奖、调查新闻报道一等奖、特写一等奖。

伟斯先生还与人合作出版著作《知识链接：中学和大学的伙伴关系》。该书于 2001 年由教师大学出版社出版。

伟斯先生 1981 年毕业于加利福尼亚大学伯克利分校，获得文学学士学位。

二、课文背景

2007 年，普利策奖评审委员会把解释性报道奖授予了《洛杉矶时报》一组关于海洋生态恶化的文章，共五篇，其中三篇由肯尼斯·R·伟斯（Kenneth R. Weiss）独立完成，一篇由阿莎·李·麦克法林（Usha Lee McFarling）独立完成，另外一篇由这两位作者和里克·密鲁斯（Rick Loomis）共同完成。这五篇报道揭示了海洋生态恶化给海洋物种和人类本身带来的恶果，并因丰富的描写（richly portrayed）获得普利策奖。

“原始毒潮”（Primeval tide of toxins）一文主要讲海洋有机废物的爆炸性增长及其危害。由于人类大量向海洋排放有机废物，使海洋繁殖了大量的有毒海藻，从而导致了海洋生物消失，同时也影响了人类本身。比如，一种叫鞘丝藻的（ Lyngbya）有毒海藻使大量鱼类死亡，也使渔民染上皮肤病。

“受袭击的哨兵”（Sentinels under attack）一文主要讲有毒海藻对海洋哺乳动物的影响。海洋哺乳动物的神经系统因有毒海藻而受到破坏，导致了越来越多的动物搁浅，或者大量的动物尸体被冲上海滩。

“化学失衡”（Chemical imbalance）一文侧重海水酸性度的提高及其危害。海水的 PH 值变得越来越小，即酸性程度越来越高，使珊瑚、鱼类和其他生物难以生存。

“黑潮毒风”（Dark tides，ill winds）阐述有毒海藻对沿岸居民的威胁。有毒海藻随风传播，正在向近海和沿岸地区发展，使沿岸居民纷纷逃离家园。

“塑料瘟疫令海洋窒息”（Plague of plastic chokes the seas）是本文所选的课文。它揭示了海洋中的塑料垃圾瘟疫对信天翁幼仔及其他生物的危害。文章虽然篇幅较长，但结构清晰。作者首先运用大量细节描写了因吞食塑料而惨死的信天翁，接着极其专业地阐述了塑料垃圾的来源、形成、数量上的增长与危害，然后全面详尽地描述人类为了解决海洋塑料垃圾所作出的种种努力。看得出来，作者对该话题非常熟悉和了解，其语言通俗易懂，表达手法清晰明了，读后令人难忘，使我们对世界上最大的海洋鸟类信天翁以及其他海洋受害者的命运感到刻骨铭心的伤痛。

三、作者主要观点

1. What is the message that the writer tries to get across to the readers in the first five paragraphs of the article in which he gives a detailed description of the death of the

albatross chick?

2. What does the title"plague of plastic chokes the seas" tell you about the writer's attitude towards the sea pollution?

四、写作风格与手法

1. What has intrigued you most about the article in terms of its writing style?
1. How much would the essay interest the average reader? Why?
2. What, if any, is the constructive purpose of the writer?
3. Do you think this explanatory report is richly portrayed? Explain.
4. Has the author demonstrated a full command of the subject? Explain.
5. How are facts presented? Are they presented clearly?
6. What's your comment on the language of the article?
7. What kinds of people has the author interviewed?

Part Three：Further exploring the text

一、语言点讲解

1. Plague of plastic（title）

翻译成“塑料瘟疫”。Plague 的意思是：anything that afflicts and harasses，任何折磨或烦扰人的东西，尤指灾害、祸害、流行病、瘟疫等。

Plague of plastic 是本文的核心词。为了说明塑料垃圾像瘟疫般地蔓延，作者提供了大量的证据，并且层层深入，把“塑料瘟疫”这个概念深深印刻在读者的脑海里，如：一只受害的信天翁幼仔肚子里的各种塑料垃圾，包括塑料瓶盖，梳子等；成年信天翁用来喂幼仔的反胃物，如衣服夹等；中途岛上信天翁尸体腐烂后暴露出来的塑料垃圾，如塑料玩具、荧光笔等；“东部垃圾堆”中的五颜六色的各种塑料垃圾；20 世纪 50 年代以来塑料垃圾的飞速增长以及它们的不易腐烂性；夏威夷群岛上的塑料垃圾；“亚热带回合区”的塑料垃圾；最终将流入海洋的洛杉矶河流里的小白球似的塑料产品。可以说，只有通过艰苦的实地考察才能如此丰富地描写“垃圾瘟疫”。

值得一提的是，文章首尾呼应，产生了强烈的效果。从文章开头描写的信天翁幼仔肚子里的各种塑料垃圾到文章末尾描写的海滩上的塑料垃圾堆积成的沙丘，敏感的读者从头到尾读来会产生一种非常不愉快的感觉，甚至是窒息的感觉。

2. The albatross chick jumped to its feet... Its wings drooped in the hot sun. A few hours later, the chick was dead.（para. 1-3）

这三小段描写了一只活泼可爱的小信天翁死亡的过程。头一天还在活蹦乱跳，第二天就“趴在地上，两腿张开，翅膀垂落”，不久，一个小生命转眼就消失了。从作者对这只信天翁生命的细致描述，我们似乎看到了他对自然界小生命的悲悯情怀。作为记者，也只有具备这种情怀，才有如此细腻的笔触。

3. Eastern Garbage Patch（para. 15）

“东部垃圾堆”，位于北太平洋，在夏威夷和加利福尼亚之间，经过一个 6000 英里长的水域（通常叫 subtropical convergence zone，亚热带汇合区），与西部垃圾堆（western garbage patch）相连，成为世界上最大的垃圾场，被戏称为“塑料汤”（plastic soup）或“太平洋垃圾涡流”（Pacific trash vortex）。

4. The qualities that make plastics so useful are precisely what cause them to persist as trash.（para. 24）

这句话的意思是：塑料的耐用性也正是导致塑料垃圾不容易腐烂的原因。这与课文最后一句话表达了同样的意思：What makes them so good for the factory makes them good for getting into the ocean。最后作者引用的是 Moore 的话，最后用别人的话，特别是权威人士的话来表达自己的观点是常用的写作手法，可以加强可信度，从而加强效果。

5. Derived from petroleum, plastics eventually break down into carbon dioxide and water from exposure to heat and the sun's ultraviolet rays.（para. 26）

The chemical components of plastics and common additives can harm animals and humans... Another additive, bisphenol A, used to make lightweight, heat-resistant baby bottles and microwave cookware, has been linked to prostate cancer.（para. 70）

前一段话讲塑料的成分和特征，后一段讲塑料中的化学成分和其他常用添加剂的危害。这两段里面有许多专业术语，大家读起来比较困难。但这却体现了作者对报道话题有很好的专业准备。这是报道专业性较强的题材时必须做好的功课。

二、中西文化比较

1. 论“志愿精神”

在课文中，有这样一句话：“The rule is, don't pick up anything smaller than your fist,” Gilmartin told a team of volunteers. “Otherwise, it'll take forever. We'll never be done.”（para. 37）

从这句话中，我们可以了解到有关海滩垃圾清扫方面的知识：一是只清除一些比拳头大的塑料物品，因为塑料垃圾太多，人们还顾不上小物件。二是有许多环保志愿者参与海洋塑料垃圾的清除工作。

借此我们来谈一谈志愿者的话题。

志愿者是具有志愿精神，不计报酬而主动承担社会责任的人。在美国，志愿者无处不在——公共图书馆、公园、医院、法院、老人服务中心、家庭与儿童保护服务机构和无家可归者庇护所等。有调查显示，约 1/4 的美国人当过志愿者。可以说，没有志愿者，美国社会难以正常运转。在中国，志愿者概念自 20 世纪 80 年代引入后，志愿者的队伍也越来越庞大，其影响也越来越大，特别是奥运会志愿者、汶川地震志愿者等。如今，我们的青年志愿者行动的服务领域不断扩大，在农村扶贫开发、城市社区建设、环境保护、大型活动、抢险救灾、社会公益等领域都发挥了强大的作用。可见，无论在美国还是中国，志愿者已是社会的一个高频词汇。

志愿服务几乎是每个文明社会不可缺少的一部分。它是个人对生命价值、社会、人类和人生观的一种积极态度，能够提高个人的自主性，为社会做贡献，能够促进社会进步，推动整个社会的健康发展。

志愿服务起源于19世纪西方国家宗教性的慈善服务，在世界上已经存在和发展了100多年。它的核心精神是"自愿、利他、不计报酬"。

如果说，中国传统文化中"先公后私"、"公而忘私"是志愿者的行动源泉，那么肯尼迪的至理名言"不要问你的国家为你做了什么，而要问一问你为你的国家做了什么"（Ask not what your country can do for you; ask what you can do for your country）就是志愿者的至理名言。

三、语言练习

1. 请用英文解释下列短语或句子。

(1)Plague of Plastic Chokes the Seas.

(2)...about 200,000 die,mostly from dehydration or starvation.

(3)chicks that died from those causes had twice as much plastic in their stomachs as those that died for other reasons.

(4)Curtis Ebbesmeyer has been studying the clockwise swirl of plastic debris so long,he talks about it as if he were tracking a beast.

(5)The qualities that make plastics so useful are precisely what cause them to persist as trash.

(6)As a lifelong beachcomber,she is fascinated and horrified by the transformation of Kamilo Beach since she first set foot there in 1959.

(7)"It blew my mind," Moore said. "We are filling up the oceans with this confetti stuff,and nobody cares."

(8)What makes them so good for the factory makes them good for getting into the ocean.

2. 请将下列短语翻译成英文，并比较中英文表达方式的异同。

（1）塑料瘟疫

（2）戴着手套的手

（3）翻滚出

（4）引发致命的危害

（5）把……错认为

（6）将……聚拢

（7）撮起（一把沙）

（8）由……组成

（9）掉到船外

(10) 依靠
(11) 使淹没
(12) 使我惊讶
(13) 使……布满了
(14) 提高公众对这个问题的意识

3. 请将下面句子或段落翻译成中文，并比较中英文表达方式的异同。

(1) Out tumbled a collection of red, blue and orange bottle caps, a black spray nozzle, part of a green comb, a white golf tee and a clump of tiny dark squid beaks ensnared in a tangle of fishing line.

(2) Its isolation would seem to make it an ideal rookery for seabirds, especially Laysan albatross, which lay their eggs and hatch their young here each winter. For their first six months of life, the chicks depend entirely on their parents for nourishment. The adults forage at sea and bring back high-calorie takeout: a slurry of partly digested squid and flying-fish eggs.

As they scour the ocean surface for this sustenance, albatross encounter vast expanses of floating junk. They pick up all manner of plastic debris, mistaking it for food.

As a result, the regurgitated payload flowing down their chicks' gullets now includes Lego blocks, clothespins, fishing lures and other pieces of plastic that can perforate the stomach or block the gizzard or esophagus. The sheer volume of plastic inside a chick can leave little room for food and liquid.

(3) This is known as the Eastern Garbage Patch, part of a system of currents called the North Pacific subtropical gyre. Located halfway between San Francisco and Hawaii,

the garbage patch is an area of slack winds and sluggish currents where flotsam collects from around the Pacific, much like foam piling up in the calm center of a hot tub.

Part Four: Exploring beyond the text

一、自我反思

1. 我学到了什么？我要如何改进？

2. 一篇高质量的解释性报道的基本标准是什么？我能清楚地告诉别人吗？本篇报道的记者肯尼斯·R·伟斯是如何达到这些标准的？我能向别人解释清楚吗？

二、知识扩展

1. 建议阅读其他四篇 2007 年普利策解释性报道获奖作品。

2. 寻找一本你感兴趣的有关环境题材的书阅读，更多地了解环境问题。如果暂时找不到，建议阅读 Rachel Carson 的《寂静的春天》(*Silent Spring*)。最好阅读英文原版。

三、能力扩展

1. 围绕一点展开，就此文写一篇500字左右的新闻评析。
2. 就你关注的某一个比较复杂的问题写一篇解释性报道。

Text B Alcohol flowing through our daily lives

BY Eric Newhouse

Great Falls Tribune

January 31,1999

导读：蒙大拿州位于美国西部地区，面积排在全美第4位，人口总数排在第44位，属于地广人稀的州。其经济主要以农业、伐木和采矿为主。爱酒是该州的另一个特点，有些人适度地喝一点，有些却酗酒成性，毁了前程。《大瀑布论坛报》记者艾里克·纽豪斯生动地记录了一个星期五所发生的一些不该发生的事情。

作者介绍

艾里克·纽豪斯（Eric Newhouse）：1988年加入《大瀑布论坛报》，现担任该报项目编辑（projects editor）。

在此之前，他曾就职于多家新闻单位，包括数家美联社分社，并出版著作《分解中东石油的并行性》（*Disintegrating Parallelism in Middle East Oil*）。

自1988年起，纽豪斯一直是大瀑布大学的兼职教师，他教授英语、大众传播学、职业写作和写作策略。

他本科就读于威斯康星大学，并获政治学学士学位，后来分别在马里兰大学和哥伦比亚大学读研，获国际关系和新闻学硕士学位。

A brisk(凛冽的)December breeze greeted people Friday,Dec. 11,as they left their homes and dashed for their cars. Shivering kids waited for the school buses. It was too chilly to pack a good snowball.

Unseen to most was how alcohol was flowing through the community,affecting even those who hadn't touched a drop.

Liquor is a common commodity in Montana. Most people drink in moderation(适度). Friends share a story over beer,and a bartender(酒吧男招待)pockets tips that help pay for his college textbooks.

Some Montanans abstain(戒酒). Others are addicted(酗酒). Those who abuse alcohol often pay the price with their health,their finances,their families,their social lives and their jobs.

The flow of alcohol can be traced as it courses through everyday life on any given day. Following is a diary of that Friday in Great Falls(大瀑布城).

5:30 A. M.

It's wake up time at the Great Falls Rescue Mission(救援机构), which has been called the final pit stop(最终逗留地) before the graveyard for those unable to handle their addictions.

"This is the last stop for most of these folks," says Glenn McCaffrey, director of the Rescue Mission. "They're almost literally one yard from hell."

He says about half abuse alcohol, half abuse drugs.

This morning, the Mission houses seven regulars working off(打扫) their room and board and five other transients(临时人员).

"Most of these people get government checks of some sort, and when those checks run out later in the month, we begin to see them in greater numbers," says McCaffrey.

Breakfast is at 6 a. m. Today it's grits(粗玉米粉) and eggs, and clients are expected to help clean up the cafeteria and sweep out the dayroom before they head out.

"A few are actually looking for jobs," says McCaffrey, "but most of the professionals will be out collecting cans to get the money for alcohol or drugs."

"But we have a rule here—if you come in intoxicated(喝醉的), you forfeit(丧失) your bed."

8 A. M.

By county ordinance(法令), there can be no sale of alcohol between 2 a. m. and 8 a. m., so that's the earliest the bars can open. The old Maverick Bar in downtown Great Falls used to start its happy hour(减价供应啤酒时间) at 8 a. m. for the night shift workers and could be a rowdy(吵闹的) place in the early morning hours.

Some bars still open at this hour, including the Lobby Bar, the Prospector casinos and the Half Time Sports Bar.

8:15 A. M.

Tom Jerome, a former ranch hand(牧场工人).

from Miles City, is sitting on a bench in the Rescue Mission, already drunk and waiting for coffee at 9 a. m. Considering the Mission's rules, how did he spend the night there?

"I didn't," he says. "I usually spend the nights out."

But the gray-tiled dayroom can be a dry place, so Jerome periodically slips out into the alley where he has a cache(储藏物) of beer waiting for him.

"I pick up cans," he says. "If I go all day, I usually can get around 30 pounds."

That's $7.50, and Jerome says he spends most of it on drinking beer with his friends.

"Tom is what I call a suicidal drinker(自杀性喝酒者)," says McCaffrey. "He just drinks himself to death every day. I've watched him deteriorate over the past few years."

That's an unfortunate reality at the Mission, where success stories are rare and people are hitting bottom(降到最低点)at a younger age.

"One thing that really worries me is that we're beginning to see a lot of 18-to 25-year-olds here now," says McCaffrey.

8:30 A. M.

Officer Mark Thatcher of the police department's DARE squad is standing before Mrs. Figarelle's class at Blessed Trinity Catholic School, preparing to talk about the evils of alcohol, drugs and gangs.

But first, he opens a box of questions from the 19 fifth-graders:

Do you ever arrest anyone who doesn't want to be arrested?

Most people don't want to be arrested, responds Thatcher, remembering in particular a 16-year-old drunk who wanted to avoid being charged with minor in possession(未成年人酗酒).

"I put him up against the car to frisk(轻摇)him, but he took off and ran from me," he remembers. "I chased him and tackled him, but during the scuffle(混战), he bit me on the inside of the leg."

"Another officer joined me at the scene and we subdued him and threw him in the back of a police car," says the officer. "Then he spit in my face and kicked out the rear window of my police car."

Do many people abuse drugs and alcohol?

"I know quite a few people who take drugs and a lot of people who drink too much," says Thatcher.

How about police officers?

"I don't know of anyone who takes drugs, but I do know of a few people who drink a little too much," he responds. "I don't think they're alcoholics, but they may let the stress of their jobs get to them a little too much."

9 A. M.

The workday has started in Great Falls. All told, about 35,000 people hold jobs in and around the city.

Some, suffering from hangovers (宿醉) or other alcohol-related problems, won't make it to work today. Statistics say fewer than one American in 10 has a drinking problem, and two-thirds of them hold jobs.

Employees dependent on substances like alcohol have two to three times the normal absenteeism rate(旷工率), according to VRI, a company that contracts with businesses to provide counselors and programs to troubled employees.

9:15 A. M.

The Cascade County Tavern Association board of directors was to meet at the office of its executive director, John Hayes, on North Star Boulevard, but none of the board members show up.

Hayes has prepared a report, however, reporting that the association's major fund-raiser the week before had raised $12,000, most of which would go to support local charitable activities.

"We average 10 to 12 calls a week for donations," says Hayes. "Our board meets once a month to send checks to those we feel we should help."

"Our emphasis is on kids," he says. "For example, we usually help the St. Vincent DePaul Society with their annual outing that takes about 40 kids up to a camp near Monarch."

"That costs $1,500 to $2,000 each year, and we finance most of it," he adds. "They make the kids pay a buck apiece, and we make up the difference(差额)."

On this Friday, the tavern association received two requests for charitable donations, and it wrote checks for $250 to St. Vincent's and $400 to the food bank.

9:30 A. M.

Business is already booming at the Lobby Bar in downtown Great Falls.

Half a dozen folks are at the bar, a handful are gambling, and three people are locked in a serious discussion at a back table, with 12-ounce glasses of red beer in front of them.

"They're lined up at the door when I open at 8," says manager and former owner Tara Fatz.

"I have quite a few seniors who come in for coffee and some who come in to drink," she says. "We call it the 'Soaps and Suds Hour'(肥皂剧和啤酒时间) because we're all watching the big-screen TV."

Fatz is one of about 3,000 people employed by bars and restaurants in Great Falls. The annual payroll(薪水册) for these jobs? About $19 million.

10 A. M.

A dozen people meander(漫步) into a meeting room on the second floor of Opportunities Inc. for their weekly Alcoholics Anonymous session.

There are 63 meetings in Great Falls each week. They open with members introducing themselves by first name and admitting their alcoholism. Then they go around the room, discussing current problems and the 12-step recovery program.

At this meeting, members are nervous at the presence of a reporter and ask him to leave.

10:30 A. M.

At Gateway Recovery Center, a distraught(忧心忡忡的) mother shows up, asking center director Rod Robinson for "help and hope" in treating her 15-year-old daughter, hooked on(迷恋上) alcohol and marijuana.

A little while later, says Robinson, an alcoholism patient "just stopped in to say thank you" for helping him get his life and family back together again.

11 A. M.

Municipal Court is just winding down(绕道下去) in the basement of the Great Falls Civic Center(市府礼堂).

"I'd guess that more than half of the caseload is alcohol-related," says Kory Larsen, an assistant city attorney.

Of the 31 appearances this morning, he says 18 obviously involved alcohol.

11:15 A. M.

Paul Horning, a bartender with the Half Time Sports Bar who teaches a course in responsible alcohol consumption, visits with Viki Gallagher, owner of the Frontier Bar. He's explaining the TIPS program under which bars can get a 15 percent break(减少) on their liability insurance(责任保险).

"We're trying to promote responsible consumption of alcohol," says Horning, explaining that the classes cover how to deal with underage(未成年的) drinkers, fake ID cards and bar liability issues.

"One of the biggest problems our new bartenders have is how to tell someone they're cut off without creating a great big hassle(他们绝对不能引起激烈的争斗)," says Gallagher.

"It's never easy, and sometimes there will be hassles," Horning responds. "But we'll show your bartenders how to kill'em with kindness, and we'll do some role-playing to help them learn. We'll also show you some ways to slow customers' drinking down(比酒量)."

He said that can include giving the customers water along with their drinks, giving them non-salty snacks, and not being too quick to see if they need another round.

Gallagher agrees to enroll half the Frontier Bar's alcohol servers in the program, which is locally underwritten by Devine Brothers Distributing and Anheuser-Busch.

11:45 A. M.

At Largent School, Tammera Nauts is compiling a list of school district students who have been charged with being minors in possession of alcohol.

Through the end of October, 619 students have been written up for MIPs, compared with 491 at that time a year before.

"At the rate we're going, we're projected to have 766 MIPs this year," says Nauts. "Last year, we had 593."

NOON

Jack King, proprietor(经营者) of Bert & Ernie's Saloon and Eatery, is standing behind the bar, a glass of beer in each hand, pondering the question of how much alcohol his lunch crowd consumes.

"Give me a moment to think about that," he says and heads off to deliver the beers. When he returns, he has an exact count.

The restaurant has 45 tables, he says, and 40 are full. Only four of them have alcohol on the table, and retirees occupy two of those tables.

"People are drinking less, but that really doesn't affect us as much because this is a restaurant, not a bar," says King.

In the past, someone might have two drinks with lunch, he adds. "Now it's usually one."

1 P. M.

Two aides and one teacher are finishing feeding lunch to one student and beginning the afternoon special education class at Loy Elementary School.

The six students, ages 6 to 11, are severely and profoundly cognitively delayed, which is the new buzzword(时髦语) for mentally retarded.

One sits at a high chair, howling, another in an easy chair rocking, and the other four surround a teacher who is trying to help them pick out a picture of a tree in her textbook.

There are 1,327 special education students in Great Falls, with disabilities ranging from speech defects to severe retardation(智力迟钝).

The Centers for Disease Control in Atlanta has said that mothers' drinking during pregnancy is the leading cause of mental retardation. But only a few children in the school district have been formally diagnosed with Fetal Alcohol Syndrome(胎儿酒精中毒综合征).

"I suspect the problem is with the diagnosis," says Gail Cleveland, who is in charge of special education programs.

"It requires mothers to admit that they've been drinking during pregnancy," she explains. "So they deny it, and the physicians don't press the issue."

1:30 P. M.

At Benefis Healthcare, admissions records don't show the cases in which alcohol contributed to illnesses such as cirrhosis of the liver(肝硬化), heart problems, premature births or accidental injuries.

But the hospital does have a sophisticated program for treating alcoholism at its Addiction Medicine Center. A group session is winding up(结束) in a small conference room with a one-way-glass(单向玻璃) window that allows counselors to keep track of the half-dozen patients.

Benefis has a couple of padded rooms(软垫病室) for patients seriously out of control, but today they're empty.

In fact, there's no one in the detoxification(解毒) program or receiving inpatient(住院病人) care. Normally, there are three to five patients in detox and a couple more receiving inpatient treatment, says Dirk Gibson, the hospital's addictions abuse coordinator.

Nine patients are spending the day in the hospital for counseling, but go home at night, and an additional 44 adults and 15 adolescents are receiving outpatient(门诊病人) treatment for alcoholism.

There are also 32 people ordered by the courts to attend DUI classes at the hospital.

"We aren't the only ones offering these classes," Gibson adds. "There are probably 60 people in DUI school at any given time in Great Falls."

Dr. Dan Nauts, the program's medical director, says Montana's per capita alcohol consumption isn't so high, but that it's more concentrated.

"We have a lot of heavy drinkers," he says. "The levels on the breathalyzers(酒精测定器) far exceed what I was used to in Washington."

His frustration is evident.

"If all these problems are so obvious, why haven't we done more to solve them?" he asks.

3 P. M.

As schools get out, the H. A. N. D. S. (Heroes and Neighbors Down at the Schools) programs get going across town.

More than 900 elementary school children are enrolled in the program, designed to give students a safe learning environment from the end of school until their parents get off work.

"We're trying to provide a program that's better for the child than going home or being out on the streets," says its director, Ann Hagen-Buss, as she sits at a table in the Riverview School on the city's northwest side and plays a game of sequential numbers with 6-year-old Andrew Carter.

Later, a group of fourth-and fifth-graders join Hagen-Buss at the table. Asked if they are aware of teen-age drinking, all nod.

"My sister's in 12th grade, and she smokes and drinks," says one of the students.

The Department of Public Health and Human Services reports that 65 percent of Montana's adolescents experiment with alcohol before they reach 14 and that high school students binge drink(have five or more drinks at a single sitting)at twice the rate of adults.

For that reason, Hagen-Buss wants to expand H. A. N. D. S. into the middle schools.

"This would be a place for them to hang out, use the libraries or the computer labs or the sports equipment, or just do some of the activities that interest them," she says. "But if they just want to hang out and listen to music, that's better than being out on the streets."

4:30 P. M.

The Lobby Bar downtown is doing a thriving business by now, with drinkers shoulder-to-shoulder at the bar.

"We're just here to have a beer and gamble," says Loren Carrier, an out-of-work(失业)cook from Tacoma, Wash.

"I've only been here a month, but I hooked up with a woman who did me wrong, and I've been drinking for three weeks now," he says.

At a table near the front window, off-duty bouncer(保镖)Trevor J. Pasha is drinking with a friend and discussing the bar scene they both know.

"I've seen some people get about 10 feet tall and belligerent(好战的)when they drink," he says, "but other people kind of go into a coma and don't talk to anyone. Funny things get funnier and sad things get sadder."

"I've seen some bar fights, but not many injuries," he adds. "Most people are too drunk to do much damage to anyone. When you put those guys out, it's kind of like pouring out a kettle of chicken soup."

Up at the bar, Tara Fatz is preparing a tray of sandwiches and chicken wings to feed to anyone who's hungry. She figures it might slow the drinking down just a bit.

"I'm real proud that we've only had one DUI that I know in nine years of Friday nights," she says.

4:45 P. M.

With schools out, district administrators get some figures on drug and alcohol use in the schools.

There were 183 kids in group sessions, most of them for drug and alcohol dependency problems, and 84 more in individual counseling sessions.

Seven students were written up for illegal possession of alcohol on Friday, according to Tammera Nauts, and one was dismissed from school for using marijuana.

5:15 P. M.

Ellis and Ilse McLean are sitting at a table in Jaker's Restaurant, on 10th Ave. S., Montana's busiest street, finishing dinner on their 44th wedding anniversary.

"My husband doesn't drink anymore, but I'm having a glass of wine with my dinner," says Isle McLean with a captivating(迷人的) smile. "Two, in fact."

A native of Germany, she appreciates a good Riesling. And she has pronounced views on teaching young adults to drink responsibly.

"I think young people should learn to drink at home on special occasions," she says. "In Germany, we give children a little glass with water in it so they can join in the toasts. Later, we might add a little wine to their water."

"If children aren't allowed to have something, they automatically want it," she explains. "They should learn to drink responsibly at home."

5:40 P. M.

Police dispatchers(调度员) receive a call about a party in a home in which the owners were out of town. Officer Patrick Brinkman is sent to the scene.

"One of the people said he had permission to be in the house, but we couldn't verify that so we asked them all to leave and we secured the house," says Brinkman. "They were all pretty intoxicated."

That's relatively common for night-shift cops.

"On this particular shift, I would estimate that 70 to 80 percent of our business is alcohol-related, whether it be family disturbances, DUIs or parties," says Officer Mike Stimac.

6:55 P. M.

A middle school student walking up 5th Street North with his friends is shot with a pellet gun(粒丸枪) by a passing motorist.

Minutes later, another man is wounded slightly a few blocks away, jumps in his own car, gives chase, and gets a license plate number.

When officers make an arrest, they find beer in the car, but no indication either the driver or the alleged shooter had been drinking it.

8 P. M.

During an intensive outpatient alcohol dependency session at Gateway Recovery Center, one of the 11 patients told the group that she finally felt safe and hopeful that her life could change for the better.

8:28 P. M.

Officers are called to 504 41/2 Ave. S. W., where they find William Patrick Bailey bleeding profusely from the head and left eye.

"He and his friend had been drinking all day, and then they got to arguing so I hid all the knives," says his girlfriend, Shawna Odegard. "But the other guy grabbed a carving fork and just kept stabbing and stabbing and stabbing him in the head."

Stimac checks the home for the assailant(攻击者), finds no one, and begins working on Bailey's wounds. Bailey, sitting beside a half-consumed 18-pack of beer, wants no help.

"I don't want to press no charges," he declares repeatedly. "I just want to kill that boy."

As medics try to persuade Bailey to go to the emergency room so that he doesn't lose sight in his punctured(刺破的) eye, suddenly another man staggers into the kitchen.

"It's him," screams Odegard. "He's the one who did it."

Stimac is on him like a flash, whirling him against the doorjamb(门框两侧的直木), patting him down for weapons, and handcuffing(带上手铐) him.

"Are you going to arrest me?" asks the suspect, 31-year-old James L. Roach. "I just flipped out(神经错乱). He made me do it."

Roach bursts into tears as he's led to a squad car for booking(登记) on an assault charge.

"This is one of these houses where we come a lot," says Stimac on the way to the hospital. "And it's always alcohol-related."

Later, it turns out Bailey is a false name, the stabbing victim is identified as William Patrick Bird.

9:50 P. M.

Two teen-agers at a C. M. Russell High School winter prom(正式舞会) are charged with MIPs after one of them vomits on the dance floor and officers find an open 18-pack of beer in one of their vehicles.

10:15 P. M.

Two squad cars(警察巡逻车) scramble to the 1st Avenue Bridge after a caller advises the dispatcher that he saw a woman being chased down the street in front of the Lido Bar. The caller says the woman was abducted(绑架) and thrown in a blue and white pickup truck(敞篷小型载货卡车), which was heading for downtown Great Falls.

No truck matching that description crosses the bridge, and a bartender at the Lido says she knows nothing of an altercation(争吵) outside the bar.

11 P. M.

Police dispatchers begin receiving calls that vandals(故意破坏者) have spray-painted homes, cars and property in a four-block area on the West Side.

More than 30 people are victimized by the vandalism(破坏行为). When an 18-year old man is later arrested, he tells police he was intoxicated when he went on the spray-painting spree.

11:10 P. M.

Officer Stimac is still mulling(深思) the parting words of a Benefis emergency room technician, who had been complaining about the lack of a drunk tank(醉汉拘留所)in the city. As a result, the ER technician said, many drunks who can't be discharged are left occupying hospital beds until they sober up enough to allow them to be released safely.

"A lot of the bigger cities have drunk tanks," says Stimac, turning his squad car off Fox Farm Road onto 10th Avenue South, "but does that condone(宽恕)a drunk's actions?"

"There's no incentive to stay sober if you know you've got a warm place to stay for the night and maybe even breakfast when you sleep it off(睡掉忧愁等)."

"But it is a problem," Stimac adds. "What are we supposed to do with a drunk who really just needs to sleep it off?"

11:15 P. M.

There's a call to a teen-age drinking party in Prospect Heights. Three officers arrive with their lights off and park their squad cars around the corner from the party.

As they walk down the dark street, two young men—one with an open beer in his hand—leave the house. One officer stays with them and the other two sprint(疾跑)for the house, where the kids are already spreading the alarm(传出警报).

Officers suspect some of the teens—and probably some of the beer—escaped through a back door. Ultimately, there's not enough evidence to make any arrests.

11:45 P. M.

Four intoxicated males are reported fighting in an alley on the lower South Side, but they have left the scene by the time three squad cars get there.

11:55 P. M.

It's another call for a fork-stabbing at 504 4 1/2 Ave. S. W. Officer Stimac can't believe it, but he's rolling fast with lights flashing and siren sounding. There's an ambulance and EMT personnel in a fire truck right behind the squad car.

When he hits the scene, though, it's a different problem: two women brawling(喧嚷) in the doorway of the house he had left just a couple hours earlier.

"She got mouthy(饶舌) with me, and I punched(猛击) her," says one of the combatants.

The other woman asks an officer if he'll give her a lift to Cindy's Bar, just around the corner.

MIDNIGHT

Officer Stimac checks in briefly at the police station. In the first six hours of his shift, he has handled eight calls. All but one involved alcohol in some way.

"That's about the average I had anticipated," he says, "but the probability of alcohol-related calls increases as we get closer to closing time."

12:15 A. M.

Joe's Place on 9th Street across from Holiday Village Mall is tame(平淡的) by comparison. Several dozen people are drinking, chatting, gambling, but no one is out of control.

"It's been fairly quiet in here tonight," says bartender Tom Knutson.

12:30 A. M.

Just down the street a block, it's livelier at the Other Place. The music is a little louder and the crowd a little bigger. One patron(赞助人) with a point-and-shoot camera (傻瓜相机) wanders through the bar, capturing the action.

"Hey, cut that out(切掉)," snaps(突然地说) a guy in a baseball cap who has been hugging a woman by the bar. "Man, you're gonna get us both killed."

1:30 A. M.

The J-Bar-T is packed, and Alibi, a Billings band, is playing some old favorites.

The dance floor is full. One blonde is relatively formal in a low-cut, black velvet dress with a heavy silver necklace and high heels. Another is fashionably informal with her red vest unbuttoned to show her lacy black brassiere(黑色花边胸罩) and the elaborate tattoos on her chest and shoulders.

Hot off the dance floor, a young man in a white cowboy hat stands beside a woman perched on a barstool. She glances around, then begins unbuttoning his denim(粗斜纹棉布) shirt and nuzzling(用鼻爱抚) his chest. Embarrassed, he flushes and backs away.

Beside them, a middle-age man is asleep, the brim of his black cowboy hat just resting on the bar. Beside his head is his beer bottle.

"We're going to let him sleep until we close," says the barmaid, Laurene Lawson. "Then we'll escort him out of here, make sure he's OK and get him a cab if he needs one."

With that, the band winds it up for the evening and the lights come on.

"There's a point where you have to exercise self-control," says Page Lutes of Bozeman, looking down at the sleeper. "When you can't maintain control, you've lost it. And it takes a lot of control sometimes to maintain it."

Off the dance floor comes a younger couple. They begin to arouse the sleeper. Finally, they get him to his feet and begin to lead him out of the bar.

About halfway to the door, however, he lurches(倾斜) into a young woman and pinches her butt(捏她的屁股).

Without hesitation, she whirls him around, crouches down(蹲下), and bites the label off the rear pocket of his jeans. Laughing, she stands with the label between her teeth.

Outside the bar, the sleeping drinker comes to life in the chilly night air. He's Knute from Jordan, he announces.

As the parking lot is beginning to clear, Knute is asked if he is going to be driving home.

"It's too far to drive home tonight," says the young lady who has been helping Knute out of the J-Bar-T. "So we'll take him to a motel tonight."

"And tomorrow," she adds, "we'll probably start all over again."

For a distinguished example of explanatory reporting that illuminates a significant and complex subject, demonstrating mastery of the subject, lucid writing and clear presentation, Five thousand dollars($5,000). Awarded to Eric Newhouse of the Great Falls(Mont.) Tribune for his vivid examination of alcohol abuse and the problems it creates in the community.

Text C Desperate parents chase a stem-cell miracle

BY Gareth Cook
Boston Globe
September 26, 2004

导读：詹姆斯 5 岁时患了肌无力症（muscular dystrophy），其父母想尽一切办法给他治疗，最后把所有希望都寄托在使用胎盘干细胞药品上。但是，干细胞研究在美国一直受到限制。绝望的父母还能做什么呢？《波士顿环球报》记者加雷斯·库克以人文关怀为本，清晰明了地阐述了一个复杂的科学和伦理问题。

作者介绍

加雷斯·库克（Gareth Cook）：1999 年加入《波士顿环球报》，他先在市区新闻编辑部担任编辑，2000 年至今，一直担任科学报道工作。

1991 年，库克毕业于布朗大学，以优异的成绩获得国际关系和数学物理学两个学士学位。毕业后，他通过了外交工作人员的口笔试，但最后还是决定当记者。他先在《外交政策》杂志做了两年的编辑工作，后在《美国新闻和世界报道》做了一年的记者，接着又在另外两家报纸当过编辑。

他出生在密歇根州，现与妻子 Amanda 和儿子 Aidan 住在马萨诸塞州。

SUTTON—Many children have dreams about flying—soaring on wings, maybe, or zooming(急速上升) around like Superman. James Rossetti, a blue-eyed 15-year-old, says he doesn't have any of those. He dreams about walking.

James, who has his father Ray's dark hair, was a bustling toddler(忙乱的初学走路的孩子). He kicked around, Flintstones(美国动画电视剧《摩登原始人》中主人公)-style, in a bright yellow-and-red Little Tikes car. He loved baseball, just like his dad, and even with a fat Wiffle ball bat, Ray said, the kid had a beautiful swing(摆动).

But when James was 5, Ray and his wife, Karen, began to notice problems: an awkwardness to his gait(步态), trouble walking on the stairs, occasional complaints of "sore legs." They took James to the doctor for tests. The next day, Karen called Ray at work. She was sobbing so hard she could barely speak.

A nurse had just called, she said, and told her James had muscular dystrophy(肌无力症), a disease that destroys the muscles. First the legs go, then the upper body sags(下垂), and eventually, the lungs and heart stop working. There is no cure: Parents are left to watch as their children slowly fall apart(崩溃), and hope—against the odds(冲破困难)—that they make it past 25.

"It is just so unfair," said Ray, choking up(哽咽). "I kept thinking of all the things I have been able to experience that he will never get to do. I felt totally helpless."

Then, last year, with James in a wheelchair and getting worse, the Rossettis discovered what seemed an answer to many nights of praying.

The couple had been hearing about the fantastic promise of stem-cell(干细胞) research, about cells that might grow new hearts, rebuild wasted bodies, and lift suffering patients from the brink of death(死亡的边缘). They had also been listening to the increasing complaints about President Bush's restrictions on funding for embryonic stem-cell research in the United States. Ray and Karen, furious(暴怒) at the president, had vowed to go anywhere in the world to get help. "If it's Mongolia, then it's Mongolia," said Ray.

One day at lunch, a Polish friend of Karen's told her that she had been hearing about a clinic in Ukraine, called EmCell, that was giving "embryonic(胚胎) stem-cell" treatments to boys with muscular dystrophy. That night the couple looked through the clinic's website. It had a long discussion of the power of embryonic stem cells. It cited a number of scientific publications by the clinic's researchers. A single treatment cost an astonishing $15,000, but the results listed for muscular dystrophy were also astonishing.

"After transplantation of embryonic stem cells, patients show increase of muscular strength, improvement or even reappearance of lost reflexes(反应能力), improvement of functions of internal organs, and improvement of mental and physical activity," the website asserted.

The Rossettis immediately e-mailed EmCell. They were referred to another mother who had recently taken her son to the clinic, and was pleased with his progress. James's doctor warned the family that the clinic sounded suspicious, and that he had never heard of any treatment having the kind of results that EmCell claimed, but one doctor's caution couldn't stop them from chasing the first hopeful news they'd heard in years.

A few months after their first contact with EmCell, on a cold November afternoon last year, the Rossettis—Ray, Karen, James, and his younger brother Jonathan—piled into a van and headed to Logan Airport, beginning a journey from their town outside of Worcester to the distant city of Kiev, where the skyline is dotted with golden domes. They were also plunging into a world, fueled by the power of the Internet and by the rhetoric of stem-cell advocates(提倡者), where the potential cures of the distant future are being peddled(叫卖) as real treatments available today.

A frustrating battle

When James was first diagnosed, Karen and Ray began their quest for treatment conventionally, with muscular dystrophy specialists. But like many parents of children with muscular dystrophy, they soon became angry at the medical profession. In a time of seeming medical miracles—when renowned cyclist Lance Armstrong could beat cancer and go on to win the Tour de France—the Rossettis found themselves sitting in meeting after meeting as a doctor told them just how little could be done to help their son.

Despite some $50 million spent in research in the United States last year, and more than 30 years of Jerry Lewis telethons(长期连续电视节目), nothing approaching a cure exists. There are many forms of muscular dystrophy, but Duchenne muscular dystrophy, which affects James and about 15,000 other American children—almost all of them boys—is one of the most serious. The disease is caused by a genetic mutation(基因突变) that prevents the body from making a protein that protects muscles. The best treatments available can alleviate(减轻) some symptoms, but do little or nothing to lengthen a life.

As James got older, Ray recalled, his son's deterioration often surprised him. One year, James was able to keep up with his fellow Cub Scouts on a trip to Battleship Cove in Fall River. The next year, he was not. Ray bought toy bow-and-arrow sets for the brothers, but James could barely pull back the string(线). And eventually they had to stop playing baseball in the front yard: James couldn't hit the ball very far any more, while Jonathan, 3 years younger, could send it sailing across the street.

One day, when James was 10, the reality of the disease hit especially hard. The family was going to the Emerald Square Mall in North Attleborough, and James fell at the entrance.

"My stupid legs don't work," James screamed through frustrated tears. Shoppers walked through the doors around them, glancing at the boy sprawled on the floor(四肢伸开的坐在地上). "My stupid legs!"

The disease subjects(使屈从于) the parents to enormous pressure. In interviews, Karen, 48, a special education teacher in Worcester, and Ray, 51, a quality control manager at Fosta-Tek Optics in Leominster, spoke of the guilt they feel about James, even though they know his condition is not their fault. They worry about Jonathan and how he is holding up. They think about friends who don't call any more, and wonder if it is because the friends feel awkward. They imagine what might be on the horizon, but also worry about whether they are doing enough to enjoy the moments they have.

"I remember thinking, 'Either this is going to bring us together, or it is going to break us apart,'" Karen said.

The emotions are like riptides(激流), pulling the couple in different directions. When James was 10, Ray and Karen took him to buy his first motorized wheelchair. Ray remembers how happy he felt to see James scooting around(四处跑) so expertly, with a new independence.

Karen burst into tears at the sight of James and couldn't stop. Her mind filled with thoughts of milestones he will never experience, she recalled. First bike ride. First driver's license.

She looked at James, smiling up at her from his shiny wheelchair, and thought: "No, that is not what I wanted for my son."

Controversy clouds possible cure

What she wanted was a cure, and in embryonic stem cells she and Ray thought they might have found one.

The very idea of stem-cell medicine is an intoxicating(令人兴奋的) one. Stem cells are among the body's most versatile(多用途的) cells, with the power not only to replicate (复制) themselves, but also to transform into the more specialized cells that make up the body's blood, tissue, and organs. These rare, potent(强大的) cells play an essential role in the mystery of development—the entire human body makes itself from a single cell—and also play key roles in the body's amazing ability to regenerate.

What, scientists have wondered, if that power could be tapped(开发)?

Over the last six years, scientists have become particularly excited about stem cells taken from human embryos just days after conception (怀孕). First isolated in 1998, human embryonic stem cells have the potential to become any cell in the body. Such cells might one day be used to replace damaged cells, curing degenerative(退化的) diseases such as Parkinson's(帕金森病) or juvenile diabetes(青少年肥胖症).

But unlike many other promising areas of scientific inquiry, human embryonic stem-cell research has erupted into(爆发) a very public debate. For every new batch, or "line" of the cells(对每一个新的干细胞系的建立), scientists must destroy a human embryo. On Aug. 9, 2001, Bush announced that the government would only fund research on existing lines of human embryonic stem cells, ensuring that the government would not be encouraging the further destruction of embryos.

For anyone listening to the escalating fight over embryonic stem-cell policy, which has become an issue in the presidential campaign as well as the national divide over abortion, it is easy to conclude that the research is on the verge of delivering cures. Opponents of the Bush restriction—including former first lady Nancy Reagan—have pleaded for a change on behalf of loved ones. Even the president, in announcing the restrictions, spoke of the cells' power to help with Alzheimer's disease(阿尔茨海默病), Parkinson's disease, juvenile diabetes, and spinal cord injuries(脊椎损伤).

Yet the gap between the potential—the young field could revolutionize medicine—and the reality for patients is vast. Researchers can isolate the cells, but they do not know how to coax them to become many of the cells in the body. It is possible that the study of embryonic stem cells will yield knowledge that will lead to new drugs, but that is a long road, too. Today there is simply no embryonic stem-cell medicine.

But for patients and their families, these caveats(警告)can sound like an excess of caution.

"Because of all the hype(炒作), it makes stem cells seem like a secret that is not available to you," said Pat Furlong, executive director of Parent Project Muscular Dystrophy, an advocacy group.

Ray and Karen recall going to a talk by a Children's Hospital Boston stem-cell researcher. At one point, a parent asked how long it would be before his ideas might be ready for testing in patients. The answer: years, perhaps a decade.

Driving home, Ray and Karen felt disappointed and angry. "Why was he wasting our time?" Karen recalled thinking.

The Rossettis and other parents of children with Duchenne muscular dystrophy describe inaction(无为) as a toxin(毒素)that threatens their sanity(心智健全). Every day, they feel that there must be something more they can do. They feel the world does not understand the urgency of their situation. And these feelings, combined with the claims for stem cell's promise, make for a powerful concoction(导致).

EmCell, the clinic that attracted the Rossettis' attention, is just one of many clinics that have emerged around the world offering to bridge the wide chasm(差距)between stem cell hopes and today's proven medicine. The Globe found nine such clinics, including EmCell, all charging substantial sums of money. On patient-interest websites, there are rumors of many more.

EmCell, with its elaborate website, is one of the most sophisticated. The story it tells, of biological genius emerging from behind the fallen Iron Curtain, is one of the most compelling.

And this is how Karen and Ray came to board a plane with their sons, heading for a country they never dreamed of visiting, so a doctor they had never met could slide a needle into James and begin a series of injections. As their flight began to make its way over the Atlantic, the sun setting quickly behind it, Ray said he felt a little nervous, but also deeply relieved: Finally, he thought, I am doing something to fight the disease.

In Kiev, hopes rise

When the car ferrying the Rossettis pulled up to EmCell, in a mostly residential section of Kiev, they were met with a disturbing spectacle.

The clinic was located in one of the city's public hospitals, and the building looked abandoned. At the entrance drive, paint peeled from a white sign emblazoned with red Cyrillic letters. One of the Rossettis' family snapshots shows thick streaks of grime(厚厚的呈条状的尘垢)covering the aqua-and-cream colored exterior.

At a battered(损坏的)blue steel door, the Rossetti family was met by a man in a suit who pushed James into a dimly lit building. Inside, steel gurneys, decades old, lined the hallway. They followed the man around a corner and onto a slow, creaky(吱嘎作响的) elevator covered with posters of Orthodox religious figures and an ad for Orbit gum.

But then they stepped out on the seventh floor, passed through a gold-colored security gate, and felt they had arrived at another place entirely. The EmCell clinic was clean and well lit. In the waiting room there were flowers and an Iranian rug hanging from one wall. They were served tea, on saucers with doilies(装饰布), Karen said.

They were greeted by the clinic's founder and director, Dr. Alexander Smikodub, who told them that the "embryonic stem-cell" treatment would help their son—perhaps a great deal—but that it would not cure him.

Over three days of treatment, for several hours each day, James lay on a bed with bright white sheets, and the nurses treated him with a gentleness the Rossettis had never seen before, "like he was a crystal that could break," Ray said. On the first day, James received injections of a liquid suspension—the Rossettis never got a close look at it—in his arm. On two other days, he received injections in his abdomen(腹部).

Even before they left the clinic, Karen and Ray said that James seemed more flexible: He was able to move his legs and arms further than before without struggling. And there was something about James that just looked different.

"It was like he was glowing," said Karen. "His skin looked like a baby's."

When they returned home to Sutton, James said that he felt like he could think more clearly, an improvement Smikodub had told them they could expect. James said that he continued to feel this mental sharpness, but that the improved flexibility wore off(消失). Smikodub had also told them to expect this, that to feel the full benefits, James would need at least three treatments at the clinic. The price of a second treatment was $10,000, and Karen and Ray were encouraged enough that they went back in April.

To pay for these treatments, the Rossettis were helped by friends, relatives, and strangers. A columnist for the Worcester Telegram & Gazette wrote about James's plight, and readers sent money. His classmates at the Sutton Middle School organized a fund-raising dance.

After the second visit, when the Rossettis returned from Kiev, they watched James closely and pondered whether to go again. Everyone asked how James was doing. Except EmCell: The clinic did not contact them.

Mixed reports on treatment

Since first interviewing the Rossettis in late June, the Globe found 12 other patients who have visited EmCell with a variety of ailments(疾病).

Most of the families said their EmCell experiences were similar to the Rossettis'. Small improvements, at most, to begin with, and then their disease resumed its course.

Three of the patients have died of their disease since they were treated. Two reported lasting improvement.

One of them was the person to whom the clinic referred Karen when she first e-mailed: Maria Brodka, who has a son with Duchenne muscular dystrophy. Brodka said that her son grew stronger after one treatment, and then showed no improvement after a second treatment—but no deterioration either. (She has not taken her son for a third treatment.) Another Duchenne parent located by the Globe said that her child, who has had two treatments, seemed to be getting better, but is now getting worse. A third Duchenne parent said the one treatment their son was given had no effect.

Of the nine patients with other conditions, seven said it provided no benefit. One said that the treatment helped his multiple sclerosis (多重硬化症), but he has also been undergoing other treatments. Another said that his condition has continued to get worse, but that he believes the EmCell treatment has slowed its course.

It is hard to draw medical conclusions from these reports because EmCell does not conduct any scientific testing of its patients that would unambiguously show whether its treatment helps. None of the patients interviewed by the Globe said that EmCell regularly contacts them to chart their progress.

After more than a month of phone calls and e-mails, EmCell's director agreed to an interview with the Globe.

Smikodub's office sits at the end of the clinic's long central hallway. To American eyes, the room has a distinctly 1980s look—dark, shiny furniture, gray carpet streaked with little diamonds of color—combined with Eastern European touches, like a set of gold-gilt crystal goblets on display. Near the door is a large bust of Smikodub, draped in a handful of badges(徽章) from scientific conferences. Two tiny chandeliers(汁状吊灯) hang from the ceiling.

Smikodub, 55, has white hair, brown eyes, and dark eyebrows. He wears a white doctor's coat over a white Reebok shirt. The clinic's work, he said, began a decade ago with research he was doing into the properties of cells taken from aborted fetuses(流产的胎儿).

Smikodub, who said he is a physician and has a PhD, began injecting these cells into desperately ill people and seeing improvements.

"We started to notice tremendous effects," said Smikodub, speaking through a translator.

In a four-hour interview, he described the clinic's work and the more than 1,000 patients he has treated for dozens of conditions. He spoke with evident passion, conveying the sense that he believes he is helping his patients.

But when the discussion turned to the science underlying his treatments, his answers were amalgams(结合) of well-established principles and theories that wildly contradict scientific work in the rest of the world.

Several American scientists, experts in muscular dystrophy and stem cells, reviewed EmCell's claims for the Globe and said they found fundamental problems. Scientists said they would not consider implanting embryonic stem cells directly into a human because these cells are likely to develop into cancerous tumors(癌瘤). Diseases on EmCell's list—diabetes, cancer, "aging"—have causes and symptoms so different that it seemed impossible that a single clinic or technique could address them all, they said. And in the case of muscular dystrophy, any therapy based on injected cells would need to ensure the cells actually migrated from the bloodstream and helped create healthy tissue where they were needed—posing a set of obstacles that have frustrated the field's top scientists for more than a decade.

In his interview and in follow-up e-mails, Smikodub offered answers to these problems that did not convince the experts contacted by the Globe.

The cells used by the clinic are taken from the blood and other tissues of aborted fetuses between 2 and 8 weeks after conception, he said. Thus they are not, as the clinic claims, "embryonic stem cells," which have only been found well before the end of the second week of development and before the embryo implants in the wall of the uterus(子宫壁) and develops. Smikodub said he has not conducted any experiments that prove the cells can migrate from the blood, through the scars in a Duchenne patient's muscles, and then transform themselves into living, functioning muscle.

To this and other questions, he said the proof was not in scientific studies, but in the patients who improve and return for more treatment. He said he has treated more than 1,000 patients, but provided about 3,000 treatments.

"We think that many of the things we are doing will be explained by science in the very near future," said Smikodub. "My method of research is the clinical method, and it is impossible to explain many of these things."

But other scientists had harsh words. They said EmCell is a poorly documented operation that appears to be capitalizing on(利用) the excitement surrounding stem cells at the expense of desperate families.

"This is entrepreneurship (创业精神) at its very worst," said Dr. Jeffrey D. Rothstein, a professor of neurology(神经学) and neuroscience(神经系统科学) at Johns Hopkins Medicine, and one of several scientists who reviewed EmCell's claims for the Globe. "These are very expensive cure-alls(万灵药)."

For the Rossettis and others, the improvements brought by EmCell's treatments may not be illusory, but also may not be the long-term cures they most desperately want. Specialists said that the mere fact of believing in a treatment can have a powerful impact and lead patients to feel and even be better, at least for a while.

James says now that while he did feel a little better after the treatments, the long airplane ride was uncomfortable, and, if it were up to him, he wouldn't go back for another session.

Furlong, of Parent Project Muscular Dystrophy, said she would discourage anyone from considering EmCell, but understands the emotions that would send a family there. She lost two sons to muscular dystrophy, one at age 17, one just 15.

"I would have sold my soul for five more minutes," Furlong said.

Determination despite doubts

Twice a year, the Rossettis bring James to the Fegan building of Children's Hospital Boston for an evaluation. These are dispiriting visits, no matter how much they steel(使坚强) themselves. They serve as reminders that there is little the doctors can do.

Even seemingly little things are jarring(刺耳的), like the way the doctors talk about Duchenne muscular dystrophy patients, collectively, as "the boys." The boys sometimes stay the same between visits, but usually they get worse. The boys usually need a wheelchair by age 10 or 11. The boys eventually need a ventilator(呼吸器).

After a visit this month, Karen and Ray sat at a table in the hospital's main lobby, across from a fountain filled with coins. James had taken a test that day that showed his breathing was no worse than before his two visits to EmCell, which was good news of a sort. But they had let themselves hope that he would show some improvement. He had not.

Sometimes, Karen said, she looks at other couples and thinks that she should have a life more like theirs. Yet, she said, she is also profoundly thankful to be blessed with such a strong marriage. And, she said, having a son with muscular dystrophy has changed her perspective in ways she treasures. Once she dreamed of "material things"—the colonial house in the suburbs, the perfectly manicured lawn(修剪整齐的草坪).

"I have left that world," Karen said.

Eight thousand dollars, which is what EmCell has asked for a third treatment for James, is a lot of money for this family. But in another sense, she said, it is nothing.

Karen and Ray were not happy to hear what the Globe uncovered about EmCell—that scientists say the clinic's claims contradict what is known about stem-cell science, that the clinic has not shown its treatment can help, and that despite the hope, embryonic stem-cell treatments simply do not yet exist.

But Karen and Ray said they have not heard of any better alternatives. They will go for another treatment in November, during the children's Thanksgiving break. To help save money, the family skipped(跳过) their vacation this summer.

"I just don't know how we could live with ourselves knowing that we had this opportunity to try something and we didn't take it," Ray said.

They know some people will not understand this decision, they said. When they had told their doctor earlier that day how much they were paying, he had shaken his head.

Hands on the table, Karen looked over her shoulder to make sure James, who was off with his brother Jonathan, was out of earshot(没有听见).

At EmCell, Karen said, she met a quiet woman from Montenegro who watched her brother die of muscular dystrophy at age 16, only a year older than James. Now the woman's son has the disease.

Even through tears and the veil of broken English, Karen said, she and this woman shared a moment of sudden mutual understanding that made the world seem smaller and maybe a little less lonely. Three of "the boys," traveling the same rutted(有车辙的) path. Two families, hoping for a way out.

Ray leaned a little closer to Karen as she spoke; strollers(散步者) and wheelchairs slid across the hospital lobby.

"We're going to keep looking," Ray said.

Unit Eight　Commentary

专栏评论

单元导航

本单元我们将讨论专栏评论。本单元有三篇文章。课文 A 的主题涉及美国前总统克林顿与白宫实习生莱文斯基的绯闻。课文 B 的议题是美国的“特殊照顾政策”。课文 C 主要议论美国政府对沙特阿拉伯的暧昧态度。

Part One：Preparing to explore

一、专栏评论

1. 定义

专栏评论指在报纸固定的版面，特定的专栏中发表的评论，通常是针对现实生活中新近发生的、具有普遍意义的新闻事件和迫切需要解决的问题而发议论、讲道理、直接发表意见的一种论说形式。在西方报刊上，专栏评论一般发表在社论版对页（opposite editorial 或 op-ed）的评论版上，以示仅代表个人意见，不代表报纸立场。

普利策专栏评论奖从 1970 年开始颁发。评论文的议题非常广泛，从近十年来看，话题包括克林顿与莱文斯基绯闻、政治与政府、当权者和美国大选等政治问题，经济痼疾问题，弱势群体和社区问题，恐怖主义的影响问题，美国社会与文化问题，达尔夫尔问题。

2. 意义

早在 1921 年，首创了“社论版对页”（专栏评论版）的美国编辑和记者赫伯特·贝亚德·斯沃普（Herbert Bayard Swope）曾说：“如果观点有意思的话，没有任何东西比观点更有意思了……所以，我决定刊印言论，忽略事实”。首先，形式新颖、观点鲜明的个人言论因其趣味性而吸引受众；其次，专栏评论往往表达一个道理，阐发或者点拨新闻事实的内在意义，以事明理，思辨清晰，给大众以思想的启迪；再次，专栏评论的繁荣和发展体现了新闻言论空间的扩展，有利于创造一个良好健康的媒体生态环境；最后，让更多人的声音通过大众媒体传播出来，不仅可以吸引受众，提高其理性思维能力，尊重言论自由，还能够起到社会排气阀的功能。

3. 基本写作特征

从普利策奖评审委员会给予专栏评论获奖作品的赞词来看，优秀的专栏评论作品具有以下基本特点：

（1）就选题而言，提供大量有关信息（informative）。

（2）具有新鲜独到的观点（fresh and insightful）。

（3）表述方式清晰、流畅和优雅（clear，eloquent and graceful）。

（4）风格上富有个性，与众不同（against-the-grain）。

二、课前讨论

1. According to the opinion poll of Quinnipiac University in 2006, Clinton was regarded as the second best post-war president after Reagan. However, in the same poll, Clinton was also regarded as the third worst post-war president after Nixon and George W. Bush. Why do you think this discrepancy occurred?

2. Should morality play a part in politics? Give your comments.

Part Two: Exploring the text

Text A The wizard（磨法师）of is

BY Maureen Dowd

New York Times

September 16, 1998

WASHINGTON—The quintessential(典型的)Bill Clinton moment can be found in footnote 109 of *The Starr Report*(斯塔尔报告).

The President was asked before the Starr grand jury about Robert Bennett's assertion during the deposition(庭外采证)for the Paula Jones case that "there is absolutely no sex of any kind" between the President and Monica Lewinsky.

Mr. Bennett was right, Mr. Clinton said, because he was using the present tense. "It depends on what the meaning of the word 'is'," the President explained helpfully.

The same footnote offers three other Clintonian gems(精华)before the grand jury: "I have not had sex with her as I defined it." "It depends on how you define alone." And, "There were a lot of times when we were alone, but I never really thought we were."

Mr. Clinton's double-talk(模棱两可的话)had a contagious(传染的)effect on Betty Currie. "I don't want the impression of sneaking(偷偷地进入)," the secretary said, about Monica, "but it's just that I brought her in without anyone seeing her." And, "The President, for all intents and purposes(实际上), is never alone."

Mr. Clinton's greatest sin is not sex or dissembling(掩饰)about sex, as the heavy-breathing(说话喘粗气的)Kenneth Starr believes. His greatest sin is swindling(欺骗)and perverting(歪曲)the American language. He is like the cursed girl in the fairy tale: Every time he opens his mouth, a toad(蛤蟆)jumps out.

His problems stem from his instinct(本能), when he runs into trouble, to shroud(遮盖)rather than illuminate(阐明、解释).

He tries to make words subjective, insisting they mean only what he wants them to. Just as he made the Democratic Party about himself, and the Democratic Conventions about himself, and the Presidency about himself, he tries to make the language about himself.

But he can't. Laws are composed of words. The President is in charge of our laws. When he drains(提取)meaning from words, he jeopardizes his ability to govern. He has made Washington Orwellian(奥威尔式的，指像作品描述的高度集权的状态). His corrupt language corrupts thought.

In order to escape the noose (套索), the President is admitting and denying at the same time, and forcing his lawyers and aides to go out and behave like crazy contortionists(柔术体操演员).

Even Democrats are ashamed of the chuckle-headed(愚蠢的)"hairsplitting," as Tom Daschle calls it.

The President admits trying to mislead Paula Jones's lawyers, but denies lying under oath. He admits Monica had sex with him, but denies he had sex with Monica. He denies that oral sex(the second word of which is sex)is sex. The President, David Kendall says, committed "interpretations of contorted definitions," not perjury(作伪证).

Once I went to Elizabeth Arden and they tried to sell me some soap. I told them that soap dried out my skin. "But," said the saleswoman, "this is the soap that isn't a soap." I bought it. It dried out my skin.

A friend of mine once picked up a purse at a counter in Saks(位于纽约曼哈顿萨克斯第五大道的精品百货店)and observed that it felt like plastic. "No," the saleswomen told her contemptuously, "it's Plastique(塑料，是法语)."

The Clinton world is full of soap that isn't soap and plastic that isn't plastic.

"The great enemy of clear language is insincerity," George Orwell wrote in a famous essay on politics and language.

Mr. Clinton's supporters are upset that he did not give his groveling(背躬屈节的) prayer breakfast speech 25 days earlier, on the night he made his defiant(挑衅的) television address.

But the petulant(暴躁的)and angry TV address was the authentic(真正的)Clinton moment. The repentant(后悔的)and lip-biting prayer breakfast speech was the contrived (人为的，不自然的)Clinton moment.

We no longer expect this President to be sincere. We just expect him to fake better, fake sooner.

I don't think the President should be pushed from office. For his transgressions(违法,罪过),he should have to perform 28 months of community service. He can join his National Service corps. Let him put aside his risky and challenging sex life and take up a risky and challenging public life. Let him cash in on(利用)his popularity, and do something wonderful for the country in return for all the slop(污水)he's put us through. As Rhett Butler said,"If you have enough courage you don't need a reputation."

But if he wants to move past "the adversity of the moment," as he so delicately calls it, Mr. Clinton must stop ducking(躲避), and find a way to reconnect words and meaning.

If he can't, he'll be in big trouble.

Depending on what you mean by the word "be".

一、作者背景

莫林·多德(Maureen Dowd):1983年进入《纽约时报》,最早从报道市内事务开始,1995年成为该报专栏作家。她同时也在《纽约时报杂志》上开辟了题为"关于华盛顿"的专栏。作为专门负责报道白宫的记者,她曾两次报道了总统选举活动,报道风格以睿智尖锐著称,成为许多人仰慕和模仿的对象。在报社工作期间,她获得过无数奖项,包括哥伦比亚大学"女人、男人和媒介"突破奖(1991年),普利策提名奖(1992年),纽约传播界女性巨阵奖(1994年),年度最耀眼女性奖(1996年)。

在《纽约时报》工作之前,她曾在其他报社工作过,写过体育专栏和特稿等。

多德生于1952年1月14日,1973年毕业于位于华盛顿的天主教大学,获得英语文学学士学位。

二、课文背景

1992年11月,克林顿当选为美国第42任总统。1996年11月,克林顿再次当选为美国总统。1995年11月—1997年3月,克林顿与白宫实习生莱文斯基保持了近两年的不正当关系。1998年2月,莱文斯基案初起,克林顿在多种场合一口咬定与莱文斯基没有不正当关系。1998年8月6日,莱文斯基正式出庭向大陪审团承认与克林顿有染,同年8月17日,检察官斯塔尔传唤克林顿出庭作证,同日晚上,克林顿向全国发表电视讲话,承认与莱文斯基有"不恰当关系",并承认他和莱文斯基的关系是错误的,他对此将承担全部责任。美国舆论大哗,纷纷责骂克林顿"下流、无耻、伪君子、撒谎",要求克林顿下台。

《纽约时报》专栏作家莫林·多德就此事连续发表个人评论,其中的10篇文章因观点新颖(fresh)、见解深刻(insightful)而获得普利策专栏评论奖。

三、主要观点

1. What is the writer's main point of view concerning the Clinton-Lewinsky affair? Do you think that Clinton may restore his reputation by "performing 28 months of community service" as suggested by the author? If not, what do you think is the best way to regain his popularity?

2. What does the author mean by saying that "His corrupt language corrupts thought."(para. 9)

四、写作风格与手法

1. What has intrigued you most about the article in term of its writing style?

2. How much would this article interest the average reader? Why?

3. What is the constructive purpose of the writer?

4. Do you think the writer has provided a fresh and insightful view on the Clinton-Lewinsky affair? Explain.

4. How is the writer's argument presented?

5. Do you think the article is written in clear style? If so, find out evidence to support your view.

6. What do you think of the words used in the commentary? Original or hackneyed?

7. Is there variety in sentence length and sentence construction?

Part Three: Further exploring the text

一、语言点讲解

1. *The wizard of is* (title)

本文题目可译成"Is 的魔法师"。

该文题目暗讽克林顿玩文字游戏，像巫师一样玩鬼把戏。为什么这么说呢？克林顿律师 Robert Bennett 说总统与莱文斯基现在绝对没有任何性关系。克林顿狡辩说他没错，因为他用的是现在时，指的是现在，他还进一步解释道：这取决于"is"这个词是什么意思。克林顿强词夺理，说一些模棱两可的、毫无意义的话，以此掩饰过去的所作所为。所以，作者认为他像巫师一样在愚弄公众。

该题目来自美国童话《绿野仙踪》(*The Wizard of Oz*)，也翻成《Oz 国的巫师》。作者借用童话素材，并根据实际需要，稍做改动，恰到好处地表达了自己的观点，不能不说是新颖独到。

2. *The Starr Report* (para. 1)

即《斯塔尔报告》。

这是美国独立检察官肯尼斯·W·斯塔尔 (Kenneth W. Starr) 起草的有关克林顿

性丑闻案的调查报告。该报告长达 11 万字，历时近一年完成，耗资上千万美金，被称为有史以来最昂贵的报告。该报告惊爆克林顿艳情，指控克林顿在隐瞒绯闻时，曾发假誓、阻碍司法、影响证人和滥用总统职权四项罪名，并列出可能弹劾克林顿的依据以及大量的旁证和物证。

1998 年 9 月 9 日，该报告提交国会，10 月 8 日，共和党控制下的众议院表决通过了对克林顿总统展开弹劾调查的决议案。同年 10 月中旬，40 多名美国历史学家发表联合声明，认为弹劾调查可能使总统的职权受到“永久的破坏和削弱”。同年 10 月下旬，有不少社会团体发表声明，表示反对议会对克林顿总统的弹劾调查，认为“一味追着总统的一次不检点行为不放，对美国精神将是一种损伤”。1999 年 2 月 12 日，美国参议院最终裁决：众议院针对克林顿的两项弹劾罪名均不成立。克林顿将继续担任总统，弹劾审讯就此结束。

据说，斯塔尔本人并不想让克林顿被弹劾下台，而且弹劾不弹劾不是他说了算的。只要克林顿老老实实地承认错误，并接受某种形式的惩罚也就行了。调查报告只是为了彰显正义和公正。

3. Every time he opens his mouth, a toad jumps out(para. 6).

这句话出自美国作家简·约伦（Jane Yolen）的童话《睡丑人》(*Sleeping Ugly*)。故事的主人公是米萨雷拉公主（Princess Miserella)，她虽然美丽，但生性狂妄自大。她踩小狗，踢小猫，驱奴使婢，更糟糕的是，她还说谎。有一次，她对仙女连骂了三声“愚蠢”，仙女举起魔杖警告道：“再说一次愚蠢，我就让你的嘴里跳出蛤蟆。”她不信，便又骂了一声，结果一只蛤蟆从她嘴里跳了出来。蛤蟆是公主最讨厌的动物，所以她再也不骂了。

在文章中，作者认为克林顿在扭曲和滥用美国语言，他说的话就像蛤蟆一样，令人生厌，因为毫无诚意。这种表达让读者感到很新鲜，很有趣。

4. In order to escape the noose, the President is admitting and denying at the same time, and forcing his lawyers and aides to go out and behave like crazy contortionists.

在这句话中，作者把克林顿的律师和助手们比喻成“疯狂的柔术体操运动员”，因为克林顿出尔反尔，他们也就不得不左右摇摆，像做体操一样，而且还是柔术的、疯狂的那一类。此表达非常形象新鲜，给人留下了深刻印象。

5. The Clinton world is full of soap that isn't soap and plastic that isn't plastic. (para. 15)

这句话主要批评克林顿的虚假性。在克林顿的世界里，充满了“不是肥皂的肥皂，不是塑料的塑料”。这种说法确实让人有耳目一新的感觉。

6. Depending on what you mean by the word “be”.

这句话的上文是：如果克林顿继续采取躲避的态度，玩文字游戏的话，他将会陷入麻烦，但作者最后又加上一句：这取决于“be”这个词是什么意思。这是作者模仿克林顿狡辩时用的一个句型。作者想再次加深读者对“典型的克林顿瞬间”（the quintessential Bill Clinton moment）或“虚假的克林顿瞬间”（the contrived Clinton moment）的印象，突出克林顿的“精华”之处（Clintonian gems）。

这不仅起到了幽默讽刺的作用，同时也加强了评论文的中心观点，点到了克林顿的“死穴”，令读者感到畅快淋漓。

二、中西文化比较

1. 论“真诚”

课文中有这样一句话：We no longer expect this President to be sincere. We just expect him to fake better，fake sooner（para. 19）

“我们不再期望这位总统（克林顿）能够真诚。我们只是期望他伪装得更好，更加不择手段。”这是一句带有讽刺性的话。作者觉得克林顿最可恶之处是犯了错误后还企图掩盖事实，不但对公众缺乏坦诚，而且简直变成了一个伪善之人（fake 或 sham）。这是最不可饶恕的错误。可见，“真诚”是作者非常看重的一个价值观，从一定程度上说也代表了美国的核心文化价值观。

其实，无论在美国文化，还是在中国文化里，真诚待人、不说假话都是非常重要的价值观。真诚的人往往容易得到别人的好感。下面是一些中西方有关真诚的格言。

（1）What is uttered from the heart alone，will win the hearts of others to your own.（Johann Wolfgang von Goethe）

（2）No man can produce great things who is not thoroughly sincere in dealing with himself.（James Russell Lowell）

（3）However much we may distrust men's sincerity，we always believe they speak to us more sincerely than to others.（François de la Rochefoucauld）

（4）Always be sincere，whether you mean it or not.（Graffiti）

（5）Sincerity is the highest compliment you can pay.（Ralph Waldo Emerson）

（6）Sincerity makes the very least person to be of more value than the most talented hypocrite.（Charles Haddon Spurgeon）

（7）人而无信，不知其可也。（孔子《论语·为政》）

（8）君子养心莫善于诚。（《荀子·修身》）

（9）真者，精诚之至也，不精不诚，不能动人。（《庄子·渔父》）

（10）见其诚心而金石为之开。（《韩诗外传》）

（11）世上的言语，本无所谓“奇警”与“平凡”。一句话所以成为奇警或成为平凡，视其与真实的内容相符与否而定。（徐懋庸）

（12）千教万教教人求真，千学万学学做真人。（陶行知）

三、语言练习

1. 请用英文解释下列短语或句子。

（1）The same footnote offers three other Clintonian gems before the grand jury.

（2）Mr. Clinton's double-talk had a contagious effect on Betty Currie.

（3）His greatest sin is swindling and perverting the American language.

(4) He tries to make words subjective, insisting they mean only what he wants them to. Just as he made the Democratic Party about himself, and the Democratic Conventions about himself, and the Presidency about himself, he tries to make the language about himself.

(5) When he drains meaning from words, he jeopardizes his ability to govern.

(6) The Clinton world is full of soap that isn't soap and plastic that isn't plastic.

(7) Mr. Clinton must stop ducking, and find a way to reconnect words and meaning.

2. 请将下列短语翻译成英文，并比较中英文表达方式的异同。

(1) 歪曲语言

(2) 利用

(3) 负责

(4) 由文字组成

(5) 模棱两可的话

(6) 堕落的语言

(7) 扭曲的定义

(8) 愚蠢的"强词夺理"

(9) 挑衅性的发言

(10) 事实是

3. 请将下面句子或段落翻译成中文，并比较中英文表达方式的异同。

(1) His problems stem from his instinct, when he runs into trouble, to shroud rather than illuminate.

(2) He tries to make words subjective, insisting they mean only what he wants them to. Just as he made the Democratic Party about himself, and the Democratic Conventions about himself, and the Presidency about himself, he tries to make the language about himself.

(3) But he can't. Laws are composed of words. The President is in charge of our laws. When he drains meaning from words, he jeopardizes his ability to govern. He has made Washington Orwellian. His corrupt language corrupts thought.

(4) I don't think the President should be pushed from office. For his transgressions, he should have to perform 28 months of community service. He can join his National Service corps. Let him put aside his risky and challenging sex life and take up a risky and challenging public life. Let him cash in on his popularity, and do something wonderful for the country in return for all the slop he's put us through. As Rhett Butler said, "If you have enough courage you don't need a reputation."

Part Four：Exploring beyond the text

一、自我反思

1. 我学到了什么？我要如何改进？

2. 一篇高质量的专栏评论的基本标准是什么？我能清楚地告诉别人吗？该篇报道的作者莫林·多德是如何达到这些标准的？我能向别人解释清楚吗？

二、知识扩展

1. 阅读其他 9 篇莫林·多德的获奖作品。在阅读前，思考一下你会如何去评论总统绯闻中的女主角莫尼卡·莱文斯基。

2. 迄今为止，美国历史上有 44 位总统。如果感兴趣的话，不妨多些了解，看看哪些总统最受欢迎？为什么？从而可以总结出美国人民对其元首的最大期待是什么？哪些是永恒的期待？

三、能力扩展

1. 围绕一点展开，就此文写一篇 500 字左右的新闻评析。

2. 就当下你关注和感兴趣的时事写一篇专栏评论。

Text B　To irate（激怒）readers：race has always benefited whites

BY Leonard Pitts Jr.

The Miami Herald

October 20，2003

导读：在美国，为了防止种族和性别歧视，加强社会公正的建设，政府实行了一系列的“反歧视行动”（affirmative action），使少数民族、妇女、残疾人和退伍老兵等社会弱势群体在就业、入学等方面能够得到照顾。但是，该政策也引起了一些争议。反对者认为这是一种基于集体主义理念的政策，会导致另一种歧视，使合格者失去学习或工作的机会。因此，此政策曾引发了数起法庭纠纷。就此，《迈阿密先驱报》记者以热情的态度、同情的笔触向普通老百姓说出了自己的看法。

作者介绍

小李奥纳多·匹慈（Leonard Pitts，Jr.）生于 1957 年 10 月 11 日，15 岁进入南加利福尼亚大学，4 年后以优异的成绩获得英文学士学位。1991 年，匹慈加入《迈阿密先驱报》，任流行音乐评论家，现为该报专栏作家。他曾做过兼职记者和一份娱乐小报的编辑，有大量作品刊登于各类报纸杂志上，包括《读者文摘》等。他还参与过许多广播节目的录制。

匹慈成绩斐然，获得过无数奖项，其中包括普利策评论奖提名（1993 年）、两度获绿眼罩评论奖二等奖（1997 年和 1990），以及 ANSE 评论奖（2002）。

I guess I touched a nerve(触动了神经).

That much seems apparent from the dozens of responses to my recent column about a hospital in Abington, Pa., where a white man asked that no black doctors or nurses be allowed to assist in the delivery of his child. The hospital agreed, a decision I lambasted (抨击).

Which has produced the aforementioned(上述) dozens of critical e-mails. The tone varies from spittle-spewing(唾沫星四溅的) bigotry(顽固，偏执) to sweet reason, but they all make the same point: that affirmative action(反歧视行动) entitles white people to question black people's competence.

As a reader who chose to remain nameless put it, many people wonder if a given black professional "is there because of his/her skills and abilities, or because of affirmative action. Unfortunately, affirmative action policies leave many unanswered questions about a black person's education and training, as well as skills and abilities.... How do we answer these questions?"

I will try my best to answer them with a straight face. It's going to be difficult.

Because there's an elephant in this room, isn't there? It's huge and noisy and rather smelly, yet none of these good people sees it. The elephant is this simple fact:

White men are the biggest beneficiaries of affirmative action this country has ever seen.

That's not rhetoric or metaphor. It's only truth.

THE NATION'S CUSTOM

If affirmative action is defined as giving someone an extra boost based on race, it's hard to see how anyone can argue the point. Slots for academic admission, for employment and promotion, for bank loans and for public office have routinely been set aside for white men. This has always been the nation's custom. Until the 1960s, it was also the nation's law.

So if we want to talk about achievements being tainted(使受影响) by racial preference, it seems only logical to start there. After all, every worthwhile thing African Americans achieved prior to the mid-60s—Berry Gordy's record label, John Johnson's publishing company, Alain Leroy Locke's Rhodes scholarship, Madame C. J. Walker's hair care empire, Dr. Daniel Hale Williams' pioneering heart surgery—was done, not just without racial preference, but against a backdrop(背景) of open racial hostility.

By contrast, nothing white men have ever achieved in this country was done without racial and gender preferences. Affirmative action.

I know that will be hard for some folks to hear. I know it will leave some white brothers indignant(愤怒). And I expect many recitations of "up by my bootstraps" and "know what it's like to be poor." We all want to feel that we made it on our own merits, and it's not my intention to diminish the combination of pluck, luck, hard work and ability that typically distinguishes success, whether white, black or magenta(品红).

On the other hand, there's a word for those who believe race is not a significant factor in white success: delusional(妄想的).

UNLEVEL PLAYING FIELD

It is not coincidence, happenstance(偶然事件) or evidence of their intellectual, physical or moral superiority that white guys dominate virtually every field of endeavor worth dominating. It is, rather, a sign that the proverbial(众所周知的) playing field is not level and never has been.

My correspondents feel they should not be asked to respect the skill or abilities of a black professional who may or may not have benefited from affirmative action. They think such a person should expect to be looked down upon. But black people have spent generations watching white men who were no more talented, and many times downright (绝对的) incompetent, vault(跳跃) to the head of the line based on racial preference.

So, here's my question:

Would African Americans be justified in looking down on white professionals? In wondering whether they are really smart enough to do the job? In questioning their competence before they had done a thing?

Yeah, you're right. That would take one hell of a nerve.

Text C The Saudi sellout

BY Colbert I. King
Washington Post
January 26, 2002

导读：无论在经济、外交还是军事领域，美国都对沙特阿拉伯做出了种种让步，甚至牺牲了人权这个传统的原则和价值观。《华盛顿邮报》记者对此发表了一番睿智而坦诚的议论，并对美国政府提出了独到的建议。

作者介绍

考伯特·I·金（Colbert I. King）：1939年9月20日生于华盛顿。1961年，他毕业于哈佛大学，获得文学学士学位。他还在哈佛大学学习了公共管理学的硕士课程。

1990年，他加入《华盛顿邮报》编委会，2000年被提拔为该报社论版副主编。

在加入该报前，金曾做过许多不同种类的工作，有着丰富的经验。

20 世纪 60 年代，他当过军官（commissioned officer）；20 世纪 70 年代，他在位于华盛顿市的里格斯国家银行任职，主要从事国际银行和联邦金融方面的事务；1979 年卡特任总统时，提名金担任世界银行美方总裁；金曾任财政部部长助理、参议院哥伦比亚特区委员会主任；他还在美国驻德国波恩使馆工作过。

The folks at Starbucks can be downright(绝对地)fussy about their world-famous logo: You know, the one depicting a longhaired mermaid with a crown on her head, encircled by a band of green. When, for instance, a San Francisco cartoonist created a not so nice parody(滑稽模仿)of the Starbucks trademark in 1998, he found himself sued by Starbucks for copyright(版权) infringement(侵害). And two years ago, Starbucks Coffee Japan Limited went to court to seek an injunction against a Japanese coffee chain operator for coming up with a logo that was similar to Starbucks'.

You don't mess with the mermaid, pure and simple. That is unless you want to do business in Saudi Arabia, where the display of the female figure—even in the form of a mermaid—is regarded as porn(色情).

Starbucks' solution to a Saudi selling stumbling block (绊脚石)? "Bye-bye, mermaid."

In a further bow(屈从) to Saudi male sensitivities(Starbucks, along with McDonald's and other U. S. fast-food shops, already practices gender segregation, providing separate entrances, service and seating) the Starbucks logo found on coffee cups, signs, aprons and napkins in the kingdom is reportedly triangular shaped with a crown, but without a sign of that—wash my mouth out—woman.

Asked about this alteration of its jealously guarded trademark, Peter Maslen, president of Starbucks Coffee International in Seattle, said in a statement:

"As a company that is entering many international markets, we are very sensitive to, and highly respectful of, local religious customs, social norms and laws." He declared further that Starbucks won't impose its will and values in countries where it does business. Describing his company as a "responsible, respectful and caring corporate citizen," Maslen said: "In the kingdom of Saudi Arabia, Starbucks customized its company's logo on the advice of our Middle East business partner."

Said the observer in Saudi Arabia who brought the censored Starbucks logo to my attention: "It appears that like apartheid in South Africa, U. S. businesses are willing to sacrifice just about anything in pursuit of riyals (Saudi currency)—even their corporate identities."

But sacrifice in Saudi Arabia isn't limited to American businesses and their principles. Consider the situation at the American Embassy.

If the embassy's political counselor(领事) or the administrative chief wishes to run out in the evening for a quick meal, it's a simple matter to get behind the wheel of a car and drive. But if the deputy chief of mission—the embassy's second in command—or, say, the economic counselor should wish to do the same, those seasoned diplomats must call the motor pool and wait for someone to drive them, because they happen to have been born female.

There's another cost. Since Saudi law prohibits women from driving, the embassy maintains a 24-hour motor pool in case female staffers require transportation.

Female American military in Saudi Arabia fare no better. Until this week, it was mandatory(必须的)for them to wear abayas(黑袍), the black head-to-toe gowns covering the face that are worn by Saudi women, when leaving their posts or bases. That is, until Air Force Lt. Col. Martha McSally, America's highest-ranking female fighter pilot, launched her protest. Until then, it mattered not to the Pentagon, according to McSally, that the religious freedom of nearly 1,000 American women stationed in Saudi Arabia was being violated by forcing them to wear the clothing of another faith.

But even with this latest Pentagon concession(让步)to American values, the Defense Department still can't see its way clear to drop regulations barring American military women from sitting in the front seats of cars or from leaving their bases only in the company of men. As for allowing U. S. female diplomats and military personnel in Saudi Arabia to behave like adult males and drive themselves? Now hear this from(1)the Army brass, (2)the Foggy Bottom set and(3)the Saudis: "Fugged about it!"

But should we?

Gender segregation(性别隔离)in U. S. fast-food restaurants and sexist restrictions (性别限制) imposed on female American officials are only a small part of the Saudi problem.

We're talking about a country where, reports the Saudi Institute, a Saudi woman must get the permission of a male relative before she can have surgery, go to college, seek a job, accept a marriage proposal, buy a mobile phone or go to court—even when accused of murder. Now substitute "African American" for "Saudi woman" and "white male" for "male relative." Get the picture?

For the United States to profess(公开宣称)deep respect for human rights and deplore(表示悲哀)the Taliban's persecution of women, and then regard the treatment of women in Saudi Arabia as a matter of no consequence, is hypocrisy at best and cowardice at worst.

It's hypocritical because the Saudis' segregation of women in schools, public transportation, workplaces and restaurants—coupled with their trampling on freedoms of speech, assembly, religion and press—are the antithesis of everything that we as a nation profess to hold dear. How dare the United States lecture Africans, Asians and the rest of the world about democracy and human rights but then turn a blind eye to the Saudis.

It's cowardly because, at bottom, we are scared to death of getting on the wrong side of an oil-producing monarchy that provides 20 percent of the total U. S. crude oil imports and 10 percent of U. S. consumption.

So we let them play us for chumps(傻瓜).

The kingdom publicly boasts of its proselytizing(使改变信仰) in America under King Fahd, heralding the fact that it has spent millions of dollars funding an Islamic academy in Washington, 15 mosques and Islamic centers, and nine Islamic research institutes across the length and breadth of America.

Okay, that's fine by me.

But get this. If an American shows up in Saudi Arabia carrying a Bible, wearing a cross or a Star of David—or if he or she gathers with a handful of like-minded Christians, Jews, Sikhs, etc., for the express purpose of holding public worship—he or she will be subject to harassment or worse by Saudi authorities.

In short, U. S. respect and tolerance for Saudi Arabia's promotion of its official religion in America is reciprocated with contempt when non-Muslim Americans seek to observe—not propagate, simply observe—their faith on Saudi soil.

And yet we are the ultimate guarantor of Saudi security, propping the Saudis up with Patriot and Hawk missiles, F-15s, AWACS and UH-60 Blackhawks, tanks, smart bombs, infantry fighting vehicles plus the training in how to use them.

Washington should abandon its human rights double standard and get serious about producing an energy policy that makes this country less dependent on Saudi oil. It should also quit doing a "Starbucks"—bowing, scraping and selling out time-honored principles to Saudi princes.

Unit Nine Editorial Writing

社论写作

单元导航

本单元我们将讨论社论写作。本单元有三篇文章。课文 A 的中心议题是同性婚姻；课文 B 的选题是美国“9·11”后救援人员的健康问题；课文 C 涉及美国俄勒冈州一家几乎被人遗忘的精神病院。

Part One：Preparing to explore

一、社论

1. 定义和历史发展

社论是代表报刊编辑部就当前重大事件和迫切问题发表的权威性评论，是最为重要的新闻评论和舆论工具。

在美国，报刊社论的兴起和发展可以大致分为以下四个阶段：

萌芽阶段。18 世纪初美国报纸刊登的来自公众的评论文章可视为现代社论的雏形。到了美国革命时期（1775—1783），政治作家成为报纸评论文的主要撰稿人。他们写的政论文章往往在报刊上连续发表，对美国的历史进程产生了深远影响。如英裔美国政治活动家、作家托马斯·佩恩（Thomas Paine，1737—1809）写的题为“危机”的系列文章对美国革命战争时期败多胜少的美军产生了激励作用，鼓舞了美军士气。他还与其他政论作家一起写了题为“联邦党人文集”的系列文章，强烈呼吁制定美国宪法。可以说，美国革命危机带来了报纸社论的兴起和发展。

党派报纸阶段（1783—1833）。1783 年 10 月 28 日，《康涅狄格报》（*Connecticut Courant*）首次刊登了美国报人诺亚·韦伯斯特（Noah Webster）写的有关州议会通过的一项动议的评论，并发表在该报的社论专栏“哈特福德专栏”上。这篇评论文章被认为是现代意义上的美国第一篇报刊社论。此后，以汉密尔顿为首的联邦党和以杰弗逊为首的共和党都把报纸视为他们的政治工具和舆论阵地，在报纸上发表社论文章以维护其党派利益。著名联邦党报人有《合众国报》（*Gazette of the United States*）发行人和编辑约翰·芬诺（John Fenno）、《豪猪报》（*Porcupine's Gazette*）发行人威廉·科贝特

(William Cobbett) 以及《纽约晚报》编辑威廉·科尔曼 (William Coleman); 著名共和党报人包括费城《曙光女神报》(*Aurora*) 创办者本杰明·富兰克林·贝奇 (Benjamin Franklin Bache)、《国民报》(*National Gazette*) 创办人菲利普·弗伦诺 (Philip Freneau) 和《美国公民报》(*American Citizen*) 编辑詹姆斯·奇汉姆 (James Cheetham) 等。19 世纪初，社论的地位在许多报纸已得到确立，并对美国政党体制运作发挥了巨大影响。

大众化报纸阶段 (1833—1900)。在这一时期，报刊不再被视为政治工具，而被普遍认为是促进人类文明发展的公器，政党控制逐渐削弱并消失，社论发展从而进入了一个成熟阶段，成为报纸的灵魂。从 1833 年大众化报业产生到 1861 美国内战爆发，这段时期被称为社论的"黄金时代"。报刊编辑不受政治和经济的束缚，享有充分的言论自由，成为公众利益的代言人，社论在公众中的影响力和信誉度空前提高。这一时期有三位著名的社论员值得一提：《纽约论坛报》(*New York Tribune*) 编辑赫雷斯·格里利 (Horace Greeley)、《纽约时报》(*New York Times*) 的创办人亨利·雷蒙德 (Henry Raymond) 和《纽约世界报》(*New York World*) 业主约瑟夫·普利策 (Joseph Pulitzer)。他们的社论各有特色，格里利因胸怀为人类进步事业而奋斗的理想和立场鲜明的社论风格而著称；雷蒙德的文章虽然没有格里利的冲击力，但对事物的把握较为客观全面，为当今客观、理性而冷静的社论风格开创了先河；出于竞争的压力，普利策一方面采用煽情主义和耸人听闻的新闻来吸引普通读者，另一方面注重用严肃的社论抨击时弊，反映民情，提倡改革，其社论面向大众，语言简洁而有力。

专业化报纸时期 (1900 年至今)。20 世纪初出现两大报业趋势：报纸产业化和报纸专业化。社论也由此受到两方面的影响。一方面，报业变成了产业，报纸被视为个人财产，以赢利为目的。在无激烈党派竞争的环境下，客观报道被证明是报纸赢利的有效方法，因此，客观新闻成为报纸的灵魂，社论的地位逐渐下降；同时，20 世纪三四十年代的自由派批评受雇佣的报纸社论员都是在报业主的授意下而写作，以增加报纸销量和提高利润为最终目的，社论日趋保守，也是导致影响力下降的原因。另一方面，在 20 世纪，以"公共服务"为信念的新闻专业主义有所加强，自由派社论并没有完全被保守派淹没，而且这个时期的社论无论在内容深度上还是在语言上都更加成熟，有代表性的社论家包括沃尔特·李普曼 (Walter Lippmann)、宾汉·兰普曼 (Ben Hur Lampman) 和拉尔夫·麦吉尔 (Ralph McGill) 等，还有当今的保罗·格林伯格 (Paul Greenberg) 和詹姆斯·基尔帕特里克 (James Kilpatrick) 等。他们充分意识到报业商业化对社论地位的挑战，建立了"全国社论家协会"。他们坚守理想，也经常反思自我，以继续维护社论的地位，发挥社论的影响力。

2. 普利策社论奖

自 1917 年开始颁发普利策奖以来，就设有社论奖。但出于各种原因，该奖分别于 1919 年、1921 年、1930 年、1932 年、1935 年、1981 年，以及 2008 年出现空缺。

从普利策奖网页上可以查阅到的历年获奖社论内容来看，文章题材广泛，涉及政治、经济、法律、社会、文化等话题，并且每个时代的社论获奖作品都从某一侧面反映了该时代的特征。

1917 年第一篇获奖社论涉及世界著名沉船事件，即英国海军舰队卢西塔尼亚号 (RMS Lusitania) 于 1915 年被德国鱼雷击中而沉没海底的事件；20 世纪 20 年代的社论关注私刑、鞭刑、黑社会、种族和宗教迫害等问题；20 世纪 30 年代的社论文章主要讨论国内国际问题；20 世纪 40 年代的社论主题包括种族、宗教、经济以及新闻自由等问题；20 世纪 50 年代社论的主题有种族、教育、劳工、军事、宪法和美苏关系等；20 世纪 60 年代的社论谈及的话题有住房改善问题；20 世纪 70 年代的社论反映了教育、司法、种族和政府丑闻的问题；20 世纪 80 年代的获奖文章触及过度开发、移民、宪法等问题；20 世纪 90 年代的社论涉及的话题包括地方政府的腐败、税收、土地、妇女、儿童福利、环境、文化等问题。进入 21 世纪，有大量文章关注社会弱势群体，呼吁加强社会公正建设，如同性恋者的结合问题、智障流浪者的解决问题、精神病患者的医疗条件问题、死刑犯的公正问题、“9・11”救援人员的健康恢复问题等等。

3. 意义

社论是意见与事实结合的精确、合理而有系统的言论，它不仅可以解释新闻，使读者愉悦，还能影响公众。如果说新闻是报纸的身体，代表报纸的形状和形式，那么社论就是报纸的灵魂。没有了灵魂，身体就等于一具失去活力的躯壳。可以说，社论是表达报纸立场的基本手段，是报纸存在的基本理由。

4. 基本写作特征

从普利策奖评审委员会给予获奖社论作品的赞词来看，优秀的社论文章具有以下基本特点：

（1）观点深刻、平衡、全面（incisive，even-handed，comprehensive）。

（2）深入调研，用证据说话，内容丰富（deeply-researched，richly-reported）。

（3）文风优雅清晰（gracefully written）。

（4）具有权威性，能够影响舆论（powerful，persuasive）。

二、课前讨论

1. Should people of the same sex be allowed to get married?

2. What are civil rights? Discuss.

Part Two：Exploring the text

Text A Yes to civil unions

BY David Moats

Rutland Herald

March 12, 2000

The House this week is due to take up the bill establishing legal recognition for the civil union of same-sex couples(同性伴侣的民事结合), and more than a few legislators face the prospect of voting contrary to the expressed view of their constituents(选民).

About 50 towns voted at town meeting on same-sex marriage. Voters nowhere approved marriage for gay and lesbian couples, but 11 towns out of 49 voted in favor of domestic partnerships(家庭伴侣).

The aggregate(总的)vote total on the issue was about 15,000 opposed to benefits for same-sex couples and about 10,000 in favor.

Some opponents have vowed to take revenge against representatives who disregard the vote of the people by voting to support civil unions. It is by no means clear, however, that the margin of difference is so vast that defeat of anyone based on this issue is assured.

Politicians frequently face criticism because they pay attention only to the polls. Those who do so are accused of being followers rather than leaders.

A sort of poll has now been taken on the issue of same-sex marriage. Are our politicians supposed to surrender their judgment so as to mirror the town meeting ballot (投票) results? On that question the famous quote from Edmund Burke is in order(适宜): "Your representative owes you, not his industry only, but his judgment; and he betrays instead of serving you if he sacrifices it to your opinion."

Moreover, the ballot questions faced by voters on Town Meeting Day were not the best reflection of the realities to be faced by the House members. Voters were asked whether they favored same-sex marriage or domestic partnerships. House members face a different question, which might be phrased as follows: Do you favor civil unions in light of the fact that the Supreme Court has said that civil unions or marriages are necessary to redress injustice and in light of the fact that if you don't approve civil unions the court will probably impose same-sex marriage?

In addition, most of those who voted on Town Meeting Day were probably not aware that the bill before the House contains a paragraph stating that marriage exists only between a man and a woman. Would all those town meeting voters have voted no to a proposal defining marriage in that manner and extending benefits to same-sex couples as well?

These imponderables(难以准确判断或估量的事物)show only that the town meeting vote was not definitive. Whether or not it was definitive, House members now must do what elected representatives are meant to do. They have listened to testimony and studied the question. And in many cases House members inclined to oppose civil unions were persuaded that the bill before the House is fair and necessary.

The raw numbers(原始数目,指选民的投票数)may scare some representatives who fear their political future. Others are determined to vote their consciences, knowing that their duty is not merely to follow the numbers but to exercise leadership. The House should support the bill establishing civil unions. It is an honorable compromise between the requirements of the law and the cherished institutions of the people.

一、作者背景

大卫·墨茨（David Moats），1947年出生于犹他州盐湖城。1969年，他毕业于加利福尼亚大学，获得英语学士学位，毕业后即刻赴阿富汗担任“和平队”志愿者。

之后，他写过剧本，其中四个剧目曾由佛蒙特剧团上演。1988年，一个题为“硬新闻”的剧目获得佛蒙特剧作家奖。

墨茨于1992年起担任佛蒙特州《拉特兰先驱报》（*Rutland Herald*）的社论版编辑。在此之前，他曾在该报做过网络编辑、州发行部编辑、总编助理和城市发行部编辑。

二、《拉特兰先驱报》

RUTLAND HERALD

Multiple problems in reactor shutdown

Vt. Scout parents anxious about Va. tragedy

With a bang

Entergy, NRC slam teeth study

Vermont ranks 2nd in nation for well-being of children

《拉特兰先驱报》创建于1794年，是一个家族报业，在佛蒙特州的拉特兰城发行。目前，该报是佛蒙特州第二大日报，日发行量为22,000份，仅次于《柏林顿自由报》（*Burlington Free Press*）。

该报发行人R·约翰·米薛尔说，墨茨承继了他父亲罗伯特·W·米切尔的正直勇敢的报人精神；米切尔是1942年到1993年《拉特兰先驱报》的主编兼发行人。民事结合法的主要起草人之一的共和党议员汤姆斯·李托（Thomas Little）说，《拉特兰先驱报》的编辑“是振奋士气的人，而且有时还提供给我们一些点子。”该报的成功应正了“小报常常在关键时刻扮演重要角色”的这句话。

三、课文背景

1997 年，佛蒙特州的两对女同性恋伴侣和一对男同性恋伴侣到政府部门申请登记结婚，遭到拒绝后他们便到法庭上告州政府。案子的主要原告是斯坦·贝克，“贝克起诉佛蒙特州”一案开始。

1999 年 11 月 20 号，贝克起诉佛蒙特州案告终，佛蒙特州最高法院大法官的裁决虽然承认了同性恋伴侣应该享受与异性伴侣一样的权利和义务，但是，裁决并没有给予同性恋伴侣结婚的权利，而是指示州议会研究讨论同性伴侣享有已婚待遇的可行性。于是，从 1999 年 12 月起，长达一年的辩论开始了，各种民意调查纷纷出笼。本文作者墨茨力排众议，在 2000 年 1 月至 2000 年 4 月，撰写了 20 多篇社论，积极提倡保护同性伴侣民事结合权，其中 10 篇获得了 2001 年第 85 届普利策社论奖。由于墨茨的公正性和民权意识而得到普利策奖评审委员会的青睐，认为其文章客观公正（even-handed）、而且影响力大（influential），在最后决选时脱颖而出，击败了《纽约时报》与《亚利桑那共和报》，为《拉特兰先驱报》赢得了历史上的第一个普利策奖。

在本文中，墨茨勇敢地提出州议员不应该盲目跟从选民的投票结果，而应该成为意见领袖，起到领导舆论的作用，推动同性伴侣民事结合法的建立。作者的说理角度和强烈的道德感值得我们关注和学习。

四、作者主要观点

1. Why do you think the author supports the civil union of same-sex couples?

2. What reasons does the author give when he suggests that the House members should vote for civil unions?

五、写作风格与手法

1. What has intrigued you most about this article in terms of its writing style?

2. How much would this article interest the average reader? Why?

3. What is the constructive purpose of the writer?

4. Do you think the author gives an even-handed presentation of the opposing views? Explain.

5. How dose the author display his sense of moral purpose?

6. In what way does the author persuade the House members to support the bill establishing civil unions? Is it effective? Explain.

7. Do you think the article is written in clear style? If so, find out evidence to support your view.

8. Does the first groups of words at the beginning of each paragraph attract you as your eye glances down the article? If not, could any of the paragraph beginnings be made more effective? How?

9. Is there variety in sentence length and sentence construction?

Part Three：Further exploring the text

一、语言点讲解

1. *Yes to civil unions*（title）

这是本文的题目，相当于“say yes to civil unions”，可译成“同意民事结合”。该题目简单明了，很口语化，但观点鲜明，容易给读者留下深刻影响。

2. Domestic partnerships（para. 2）

“家庭伴侣关系”提供了不同程度的权利和义务，通常要少于婚姻所提供的权利。美国一些地方承认这种关系，目的是使同居者（包括同性伴侣）享有与已婚者相似的权利。该称呼主要在加利福尼亚等州使用。在佛蒙特和马萨诸塞等州，人们往往称同性婚姻为“民事结合”。它比前者享受的权利和义务要多一些。

目前，虽然同性婚姻在美国13个州及首都华盛顿市获得了合法地位，但是，保守派组织“美国价值观”的主席、前总统里根的国内政策总顾问加里·鲍尔认为，大多数美国人反对同性婚姻，也反对同性伴侣享有与异性伴侣同等的权利。

3. It is by no means clear, however, that the margin of difference is so vast that defeat of anyone based on this issue is assured(para. 4).

这句话的意思是：民调中显示的意见差别是否如此之大以至于逆民意而行的人就肯定会失败呢？这一点尚不明确。

作者是想告诉议员们支持民事结合虽然表面上违反了多数选民的意见，但民意差别其实并不算大，总体情况是有15,000人反对，10,000人支持。所以，站在支持者一面并不意味着你就会被打败。

作者从现实角度出发，规劝议员支持民事结合。这是他提出的第一个支持的理由。他还提出了其他三个理由。请把它们一一找出来并分析是从那个角度来说服议员的。

4. Your representative owes you, not his industry only, but his judgment; and he betrays instead of serving you if he sacrifices it to your opinion(para. 6).

“你们的代表不仅仅用他的勤勉工作来感谢你们，还有他的判断力；如果他为了你们的意见，放弃自己的判断，那么他就不是在为你们服务，而是背叛了你们。”这是18世纪英国政治思想家埃德蒙·伯克（Edmund Burke）说的一句话。

作者用伯克的话强烈呼吁那些支持民事结合的政治家坚持自己的判断，不要盲从民意。他认为只有这样，才是真正地为民众服务。

作者从政治家职责的角度来规劝议员支持民事结合。

5. Vote their consciences（para. 10）

“凭良心投票”。在文中，作者首先从民调的两派意见差距不大、什么是真正服务于大众的政治家、用问题误导议员以及议员本身四个方面规劝并呼吁议员不要盲目跟从选民的投票结果，而要凭自己的良心投票，支持同性伙伴结合法律的通过，从而真正为大众服务。可以说，此短语充分显示了作者强烈的道德感。

二、中西文化比较

1. 司法体系

课文中提到“the supreme court”（para. 7），指佛蒙特州的最高法院。

美国是联邦制国家，美国法院机构的基本框架分为联邦法院和各州地方法院两个完全独立的系统。联邦法院由联邦最高法院、联邦上诉法院、联邦地区法院及联邦特别法院组成。联邦最高法院由美国宪法设立，是联邦上诉法院的终审法院和美国司法系统的最高一级法院。联邦上诉法院和地区法院则由国会决定设立。美国的州法院是指由各州设立的独自完整的司法组织系统。大多数的州法院由三级构成，也有四级法院，一般没有统一的称谓，且名称比较复杂。美国州法院设置三级组织系统的分别为州最高法院、中级上诉法院和初审法院。

在中国，根据《中华人民共和国宪法》及《中华人民共和国人民法院组织法》，司法体系由最高人民法院、地方各级人民法院、军事法院及其他特别人民法院组成。地方各级人民法院由基层人民法院、中级人民法院及高级人民法院组成。基层人民法院由民事、刑事、经济及行政法庭组成。中级人民法院与基层人民法院的结构类似，并进一步分成其他特别法庭，如知识产权法庭等。高级人民法院对基层人民法院及中级人民法院进行监督。人民检察院亦有权对同级及下级人民法院的民事诉讼行使法律监督权。最高人民法院为中国的最高司法机构，具体监督所有人民法院的司法工作。

2. 论“良心”

在本文中，墨茨呼吁议会代表要“凭良心投票”。在墨茨眼里，“良心”是一个非常重要的价值观。

所谓良心，乃“良善之道德存乎于心”。良心体现了人类的勇气，可以避免人类痛苦，带来和平，也可以说是人类最后的家园，如果失去了它，就没什么值得我们拥有的了。在中西文化中，都有许多关于“conscience”的名言。如：

(1) Conscience is the root of all true courage; if a man would be brave let him obey his conscience. (James Freeman Clarke)

(2) When will our consciences grow so tender that we will act to prevent human misery rather than avenge it? (Eleanor Roosevelt)

(3) While conscience is our friend, all is at peace; however once it is offended, farewell to a tranquil mind. (Lady Mary Wortley Montagu)

(4) The person that loses their conscience has nothing left worth keeping. (Izaak Walton)

(5) 天凭日月，人凭良心。

(6) 人靠良心树靠根，走路纯靠脚后跟。

(7) 天地良心，到处通行。

三、语言练习

1. 请用英语解释下列短语或句子。

(1) The House...is due to take the bill

(2) yes to civil unions

(3) voting contrary to the expressed view of their constituents

(4) The aggregate vote total on the issue was about 15,000 opposed to benefits for same-sex couples and about10,000 in favor.

(5) Those who do so are accused of being followers rather than leaders.

(6) Your representative owes you, not his industry only, but his judgment; and he betrays instead of serving you if he sacrifices it to your opinion.

(7) The House should support the bill establishing civil unions. It is an honorable compromise between the requirements of the law and the cherished institutions of the people.

2. 请将下列短语翻成英文，并比较中英文表达方式的异同。

(1) 开始从事

(2) 投票赞成同性婚姻

(3) 报复某人

(4) 纠正不公正现象

(5) 凭良心投票

(6) 行使领导力

(7) 趋向于反对民事结合

(8) 根据事实

(9) 承认民事结合的法案

(10) 不确定的投票

3. 请将下面一个段落翻译成中文，并比较中英文表达方式的异同。

(1) Politicians frequently face criticism because they pay attention only to the polls. Those who do so are accused of being followers rather than leaders.

(2) Moreover, the ballot questions faced by voters on Town Meeting Day were not the best reflection of the realities to be faced by the House members. Voters were asked whether they favored same-sex marriage or domestic partnerships. House members face a different question, which might be phrased as follows: Do you favor civil unions in light of the fact that the Supreme Court has said that civil unions or marriages are necessary to redress injustice and in light of the fact that if you don't approve civil unions the court will probably imposed same-sex marriage?

(3) In addition, most of those who voted on Town Meeting Day were probably not aware that the bill before the House contains a paragraph stating that marriage exists only between a man and a woman. Would all those town meeting voters have voted no to

a proposal defining marriage in that manner and extending benefits to same-sex couples as well?

Part Four: Exploring beyond the text

一、自我反思

1. 我学到了什么？我要如何改进？

2. 一篇高质量社论的基本标准是什么？我能清楚地告诉别人吗？该篇社论的作者大卫·墨茨是如何达到这些标准的？我能向别人解释清楚吗？

二、知识扩展

1. 阅读墨茨其他九篇关于同性伴侣民事结合的获奖文章。

2. 了解更多对墨茨的不同评论。

三、能力扩展

1. 围绕一点展开，就此文写一篇500字左右的新闻评析。

2. 选择一个当下激烈讨论的话题，并写一篇500字左右的社论。

Text B Abandoned heroes

BY Arthur Browne, Beverly Weintraub and Heidi Evans

Daily News

Sunday, July 23, 2006

导读："9·11"事件过去近5年后，美国媒体开始关注在救援中幸存下来但备受病痛折磨的大批救援人员。纽约《每日新闻》的三位记者用饱含同情的笔触以及大量的事实向读者展示了一群被人遗忘的英雄。

作者背景

亚瑟·布朗（Arthur Browne）（中）：《每日新闻》社论版编辑。他已在该报工作了30多年，做过许多不同的工作，如当过送稿件的工友（copy boy）、记者、主任调查记者（chief investigative reporter）、市政厅新闻部主任（City Hall Bureau chief）、本地新闻编辑（city editor）、都市新闻编辑（metropolitan editor ）、执编助理（assisting managing editor）、执行编辑（managing editor）、高级执行编辑（senior managing editor）。

2002年至2003年期间，他加入彭博新闻社，担任高级编辑，曾负责新闻社对安然公司丑闻的报道工作。

布朗毕业于波士顿学院和圣约翰大学法律学校，也是位不执业的律师（non-practicing attorney）。1985年，他与人合写了关于纽约前任市长爱德华·柯奇的传记。

比佛莉·温特劳布（Beverly Weintraub）（右）：1990年进入《每日新闻》报社，当过送稿件工友、标题作家、新闻编辑部主任，现为编委成员。她擅长对教育、无家可归和移民等社会问题的报道。之前，她曾在社区报、杂志等许多家新闻单位工作。

海蒂·伊万斯（左）已在《每日新闻》报社工作了14年，主要报道健康和社会问题。她曾获过多次地方和国家级新闻奖，包括乔治·伯克奖。

她于1984年毕业于哥伦比亚大学，获得新闻学硕士学位。1993年获得哈佛大学纽曼记者奖学金。

12,000 brave souls who worked in this toxic cloud(有毒云雾) after Sept. 11 are sick. For too long, their suffering has been ignored. This must end now. (Photo credit: Greg Semendinger /NYC Police Aviation)

Forty-thousand-strong, they labored at Ground Zero(废墟中心) under miserable conditions in a time of crisis, working 10 and 12 hours a day to search for the lost, extinguish underground fires and haul off 2 million tons of rubble. As a direct result, well over 12,000 are sick today, having suffered lasting damage to their respiratory systems (呼吸系统).

In increasing numbers, they are the forgotten victims of "9·11". The toll has risen steadily over the past five years, yet no one in power-not Gov. Pataki, not Mayor Bloomberg, not the state and city health commissioners, not the U. S. government-has acknowledged the epidemic's scope, much less confronted it for the public health disaster that it is.

They cough.

They wheeze(气喘).

Their heads and faces pound with the pressure of swollen sinuses(因肿胀的鼻窦所压而剧烈跳动).

They lose their breath with minor exertion(稍微用力就喘不过气来).

They suffer the suffocation of asthma(哮喘) and diseases that attack the very tissues of their lungs.

They endure acid reflux(硅酸的流入),a painful indigestion that never goes away.

They are haunted by the mental and emotional traumas(受精神和感情创伤的折磨) of having witnessed horror.

Many are too disabled to work. And some have died. There is overwhelming evidence that at least four Ground Zero responders-a firefighter,two police officers and an Emergency Medical Service paramedic(紧急医疗服务护理人员)-suffered fatal illnesses as a consequence of inhaling the airborne poisons(空气传播的毒气)that were loosed when the pulverized(摧毁的)remains of the twin towers erupted seismically (地震般地)into the sky.

The measure of how New York and Washington failed the "9 · 11" responders starts with the fact that after a half-decade, no one has a grip on the scope of the suffering. The known census of the ill starts at more than 12,000 people who have been monitored or treated in the two primary medical services for Ground Zero workers,one run by the Fire Department,the other by the World Trade Center Medical Monitoring Program based at Mount Sinai Medical Center.

In the Fire Department, more than 600 firefighters—soon to be 700—have been forced into retirement because they were deemed permanently disabled. Most suffer from asthma that disqualifies them from battling blazes. And fully 25% of the FDNY's active fire and EMS forces have lung-related conditions—more than 3,400 people in all.

At the Mount Sinai program,where physicians are monitoring the health of 16,000 cops,construction workers and others, Dr. Stephen Levin estimates that from half to two-thirds of the patients are similarly sick. That works out to at least 8,000 people and pushes the tally of the ill over 12,000.

The count goes up from there among the thousands of responders who are not enrolled in either program. How far up,nobody knows. But doctors are all too aware that the general prognosis for the sick is not good. While treatment has helped many to improve,few have regained their health.

"I think that probably a few more years down the road we will find that a relatively small proportion will be able to say,'I am as good as I was back on Sept. 10,2001,'" said Levin.

Officer Steven Mayfield patrolled Ground Zero for more than 400 hours. Now he has sarcoidosis,shortnesss of breath,sinusitis and sleep apnea(睡眠休克症). "My lungs are damaged;They will never be the same," he said.

Officer Steven Mayfield patrolled Ground Zero for more than 400 hours. Now he has sarcoidosis, shortnesss of breath, sinusitis and sleep apnea. "My lungs are damaged;They will never be the same," he said. (Photo credit:Craig Warga/*Daily News*)

Typical is the case of NYPD Officer Steven

Mayfield, who logged(花时间) more than 400 hours at the perimeter(周边) of what became known as The Pile(世贸大厦的废墟) and suffers from sarcoidosis(肉类瘤病), a disease that scars the tissues of the lungs; shortness of breath; chronic sinusitis, and sleep apnea. "My lungs are damaged; they will never be the same," said Mayfield, 44.

Still more frightening: Serious new conditions may soon begin to emerge. Top pulmonary specialists(肺病专家) say lung-scarring diseases and tumors generally begin to show up five to 20 years after toxic exposure, a time frame that's about to begin.

Some responders have received excellent care. The FDNY's medical service, led by Dr. Kerry Kelly and Dr. David Prezant, has delivered first-rate monitoring and treatment to more than 13,700 active(现任的) and retired firefighters and EMS workers. But the rest of the Ground Zero responders have not been nearly so well served.

Most of them-from police to construction workers-are eligible for monitoring and treatment through the Mount Sinai program. The center's leaders, Dr. Robin Herbert and Levin, are among the world's experts in occupational health, but they have been badly hobbled(束缚) by a lack of funding. The wait for treatment is four months, and doctors are able to schedule follow up appointments less frequently than they would like.

In even worse shape are an estimated 10,000 federal workers who participated in the Ground Zero effort. The government promised to create a program specially for them, and then reneged(违约). The federal workers are on their own.

The big lie

The betrayal of the "9 · 11" responders began with a lie that reverberates(回荡) to this day. When the twin towers collapsed, the remains of 200,000 tons of steel, 600,000 square feet of window glass, 5,000 tons of asbestos(石棉), 12,000 miles of electric cables and 425,000 cubic yards of concrete crashed to the ground and then spewed into the air. To the mix were added 24,000 gallons of jet fuel burning as hot as 1,300 degrees.

At The Pile, the air was "darker than a sealed vault and thicker than pea soup," in the description of one deputy fire chief. But officials pronounced that would-be rescuers were safe.

As then U. S. Environmental Protection Administrator Christie Whitman put it in a press release on Thursday, Sept. 14, 2001: "Monitoring and sampling conducted on Tuesday and Wednesday have been very reassuring about potential exposure of rescue workers and the public to environmental contamination." Two weeks later, Mayor Rudy Giuliani said rescue workers faced minimal risk because the air quality was "safe and acceptable."

In truth, those who rushed to the scene were at the epicenter of "the largest acute environmental disaster that ever has befallen New York City," according to a 2004 analysis by several dozen scientists in the journal Environmental Health Perspectives. In truth, every breath at Ground Zero was noxious(有毒的) to health and even to life.

A cauldron of toxins(沸腾的一锅毒气)

The Environmental Health Perspectives report cited the presence in the air of highly alkaline concrete dust(碱性石灰), glass fibers and cancer-causing asbestos, as well as particles(分子) of lead(铅), chlorine(氯), antimony(锑), aluminum(铝), titanium(钛), magnesium(镁), iron, zinc and calcium. The flaming fuel and burning plastics released carcinogens(致癌物) including dioxins(二恶英), polycyclic aromatic hydrocarbons(多环芳烃), polychlorinated biphenyls(多氯联苯) and polychlorinated furans(多氯呋喃).

Almost immediately, the toxic cloud began burning the lungs of the responders because most were not provided with, or did not wear, proper respiratory protection. Hundreds soon started coughing up pebbles(卵石) and black or gray phlegm(痰), and, for most, symptoms steadily worsened. The false assurance of safety and the failure to adequately equip the workers has opened the city and its construction contractors to potentially huge liability. More than 8, 000 responders have joined a lawsuit that has targeted a $1 billion federal insurance fund established after "9 • 11" to facilitate the recovery work. So the lawyers, not the doctors, have taken charge.

The city's chief attorney, Corporation Counsel Michael Cardozo, says, for example, that he is confident Ground Zero workers have been provided with appropriate medical attention and disability benefits. This may be wise to argue for the purpose of limiting liability, but it's destructive denial as a public health strategy.

Never did the state health commissioner, Dr. Antonia Novello, or the city health commissioner—Dr. Neal Cohen in the days immediately after "9 • 11", Dr. Thomas Frieden since January 2002—step forward to lead a crusade that marshaled the resources of New York's vast public and private health systems.

Nor did Cohen or Frieden ever issue protocols advising physicians on recognizing and treating syndromes generated by World Trade Center exposures. Inexcusably, Cohen failed to disseminate advisories at a time when the Giuliani administration was declaring all was safe at The Pile, and Frieden's staff is only now getting around to completing its first bulletin.

Nor did the Police Department establish a system for tracking the prevalence of illnesses such as asthma among the thousands of cops who worked at The Pile. The police surgeon, Dr. Eli Kleinman, says he believes there hasn't been more than "a blip" in lung-related ailments which would be a truly remarkable outcome compared with the 25% of the Fire Department that is counted as having "9 • 11" aftereffects.

The city Health Department in 2003 did establish the World Trade Center Health Registry, inviting people who worked at Ground Zero or lived in the area to report their health conditions. More than 71,000 provided information, and the department is in the midst of conducting a followup survey. The data are likely to prove highly valuable when the department finishes crunching the numbers. But that milestone is planned for next year, astonishingly long to wait when the unaddressed needs of the sick have been building since 2001 and are so large at this very moment.

Frustrated by the response to "9 • 11"-related illnesses, Reps. Carolyn Maloney and Vito Fossella in February won the appointment of Dr. John Howard as federal Ground Zero health coordinator. Howard's valuable presence should be taken as a rebuke to all the local officials who allowed this health crisis to fester(逐渐恶化)a decade.

But Howard is hardly the solution. As director of the National Institute for Occupational Safety and Health, the doctor has a schedule that is quite booked. Nor does Howard have the capacity to do a great deal. He has no special budget and no special staff, and he can only study and recommend. Far more is required.

A cry for leadership

What's urgently needed is dynamic leadership by someone with the muscle and brains to tackle the World Trade Center health crisis on all fronts-medical, legal, social, political and more. The person who best fits the bill today is Michael Bloomberg.

As the 108th mayor of the City of New York, Bloomberg commands vast municipal resources, occupies an unparalleled bully pulpit(一流的专栏论坛)from which to prod(敦促)other levels of government, has a deep, long-standing commitment to public health and, most important, knows how to get things done. And it is simply inconceivable that he would not act were he to inquire deeply into the facts.

Were the mayor to ask Herbert and Levin, he would find out that Mount Sinai's doctors succeeded only this year in getting the okay for the first federal funding for treatment, that patients frequently arrive at Mount Sinai after being misdiagnosed or improperly treated by family physicians and that Ground Zero responders are seeking help in increasing numbers because they haven't gotten better with time or have developed new illnesses.

Were the mayor to speak with Dr. Alison Geyh, assistant professor at his namesake Johns Hopkins Bloomberg School of Public Health in Baltimore, he would learn that a program aimed at tracking the health of Ground Zero's "invisible" recovery workers—heavy equipment operators, sanitation workers, truck drivers and laborers—stopped for lack of money after less than two years.

"It took a year to get this labor-intensive project up and running, only to have its funding stream cut off 18 months later," said Geyh. "It's been frustrating and a lost opportunity."

Were the mayor to talk to Kelly and Prezant at the Fire Department, or to Herbert and Levin at Mount Sinai, or to their colleague Dr. Alvin Teirstein, an eminent lung specialist, he would hear calls for long-term monitoring for cancers and other diseases that could emerge among Trade Center responders in the coming years.

And, were the mayor to spend time with any of the 8,000 responders who are suing the city, he would hear the voices of fury and fear. Their anger is well grounded in that they were lied to, but it is far less clear that each of their illnesses, among them brain and blood cancers, is attributable to Ground Zero exposures. Still, lacking authoritative, trustworthy information, they live under agonizing shadows.

It is vitally important for *Bloomberg*(彭博新闻社)to take charge.

To take the full measure of this growing epidemic.

To devise appropriately funded treatment programs so that all "9 · 11" responders have access to the quality of care provided to firefighters.

To establish monitoring systems that can detect swiftly the emergence of new diseases or improved treatments.

To create a clearinghouse that would inform workers and physicians about illnesses and proper treatments, and keep them up to date on the latest developments.

To begin to acknowledge that service after "9 · 11" did, in fact, cause fatalities, rather than let city officials keep insisting that there is no absolute, total scientific proof that anyone died from illnesses contracted at Ground Zero.

To galvanize the federal government into supporting long-term monitoring and treatment programs.

To review disability and pension benefits afforded to "9 · 11" responders with an eye on eliminating gross inequities. While firefighters and cops have been granted extremely liberal, even overly liberal, line-of-duty retirement benefits, thousands are trapped in a workers' compensation system that is ill-suited to treat them fairly.

When the call came, the instant the first hijacked jet knifed into the north tower of theWorld Trade Center, the Ground Zero recovery army surged to the aid of their fellow human beings without a thought as to their own safety. After the buildings collapsed, they worked long and hard to bring New York back from the worst attack on U. S. soil. But they were lied to and they were badly equipped, and then, when they became sick, as many physicians predicted they would, far too many were abandoned. Decency demands better.

Text C All the lonely people

BY Rick Attig and Doug Bates

The Origonian

Sunday, January 09, 2005

导读：俄勒冈是位于美国西北海岸的一个州，州名是印第安语，意为“美丽之水”。但是，在这块美丽的领土上发生了不该发生的故事。《俄勒冈人报》的两位记者以详尽的事实和有说服力的语言描述了被人遗忘的一家精神病院和一群社会上最脆弱的人，敦促并呼吁立法者采取行动，改善现状。

作者背景

瑞克·阿提格（Rick Attig）：《俄勒冈人报》副主编和编委成员，也是该报的主要社论作家，关注州政府、政治和环境问题。

迄今为止，他获得过许多新闻奖，包括40多项州和地区报纸奖，7次最佳社论奖。

1983年，他毕业于俄勒冈大学，以优异的成绩获得新闻和政治学学士学位。

道格·贝慈（Doug Bates）：《俄勒冈人报》副主编和编委成员。他曾在许多家新闻单位工作过。

贝慈写过两本书，其中较著名的一本是《普利策新闻奖：美国最高声誉奖的内幕故事》。

他于1968年毕业于俄勒冈大学。目前，他与妻子住在波特兰，有四个成年孩子。

A room stacked with the unclaimed remains of patients（堆满了无人认领的病人遗物的房间）symbolizes what's wrong with the Oregon State Hospital.

Eva York died in a bathtub in 1896 at the Oregon Asylum for the Insane（精神病院）. After an inquest（审讯）, which absolved（宣布免除）the hospital staff of any blame, no one claimed her corpse（尸体）, so she was buried in the asylum cemetery（墓地）and forgotten.

Eighteen years later Eva's remains were exhumed（发掘）, cremated（火化）, placed in a copper urn（铜制的骨灰盒）and forgotten all over again. Today the corroding canister（腐蚀的小罐）containing her ashes sits on a plain pine shelf in what's called the "Cremains Room"（骨灰存放屋）at the 122-year-old Salem institution, now known as the Oregon State Hospital.

Eva York is one of about 5,000 patients whose cremains are neatly stacked in that stark（荒凉的）, lonely room like cans of paint in a well-stocked hardware store. Her story, one of the rare stories that can be told, thanks to the inquest into her death makes her a perfect symbol for what's wrong with the way Oregonians treat some of the most frail（最脆弱的人）among us. The 2005 Legislature（立法机构）, which convenes（集合）Monday, must address this shameful truth.

The state hospital was a dumping ground（垃圾堆积场）in Eva's day, and to some extent it still is today. Even its administrators admit they're housing patients who don't belong there.

Wards（病房）are overcrowded. Staffing is inadequate（工作人员不足）. Patients whose psychoses（心理）have been stabilized by medication are being warehoused（储存）in the hospital for lack of smaller community-based mental health centers that would be far better for them.

The grim(简陋), sprawling(杂乱无章的) hospital is no place for juveniles(青少年), yet Oregon houses about a dozen frightened, troubled kids there. Some of the girls, often prior victims of sexual abuse, pull their mattresses out into hallways to sleep in safe view of staff. During the day, adolescents pass time outdoors in plain view, through concertina and barbed wire(蛇腹型铁丝网和带刺铁丝网), of maximum-security adult patients.

These kids are left there, however, because Oregon has no proper facility for them. There's really nowhere else they can go.

Out of sight, out of mind(眼不见,心不烦). It's an age-old story of neglect for Oregon's most unfortunate. In fact, it was Eva York's story more than a century ago.

Today we know far more about Eva than any of her forgotten companions in the Cremains Room. That's because her death led to a story in Salem's Daily Capital Journal on Nov. 25, 1896.

Eva was a 36-year-old Marion County woman who probably wasn't even mentally ill. According to the old newspaper clipping, she was an epileptic(癫痫患者), confined to the hospital's asylum-era epileptic ward five years before her death. In those days her malady(疾病), like depression and alcoholism, was viewed as akin to insanity(类似于精神病).

Eva died between 2 and 3 p.m. on a Tuesday, "bath day" in the epileptic ward. While left unattended in a tub, she had a seizure and died from it, a coroner ruled (验尸官作出裁决). He found no evidence of drowning. An inquest jury declared the hospital to be "in no way responsible."

The news account went on to say the hospital telegraphed word of Eva's death to "a brother residing near Hubbard." Her remains, however, were never claimed.

The entire asylum cemetery was exhumed in 1913-1914 when the state decided it needed the land. Many of the headstones(墓碑) were unceremoniously(随便地) dumped on a nearby hilltop. All unclaimed remains, including Eva's, were cremated and stored in a basement.

By 1976 that bleak collection of urns exceeded 5,000. That year, in a long overdue act of respect, they were placed underground in a modest memorial on the hospital grounds. But water seeped into the vaults, damaging the copper containers and destroying most of their paper labels. A few years ago, the cash-strapped(经费紧缺的) institution unearthed(掘出) the urns and stashed(隐藏) them in the Cremains Room, next to the incinerator(焚尸炉) where all the patients had been cremated.

If Eva York is a symbol of Oregon neglect, the hospital itself, its physical hulk, is a full-blown metaphor(医院楼体是典型的象征). The tub that she died in is still there, gathering mold(霉菌) and rat droppings(老鼠屎) in an abandoned wing that's creepier(令人毛骨悚然的) than any haunted house one might imagine.

Occupied spaces of the hospital are cheerier only by comparison. They comprise a foreboding(有不祥之兆的), ramshackle(摇摇欲坠的) collection of additions to the original 1883 structure along with several decrepit(衰朽的) satellite buildings(附属的楼群),the newest of which is more than a half-century old.

Patients spend their hours locked in jam-packed day rooms connected by long,dreary corridors to their prisonlike sleeping quarters,crammed with more bodies than they were designed for. They gaze out windows covered with oppressive security screens,and they stare at visitors coming and going on balky(停止不前的),creaky(叽叽嘎嘎的)old elevators. No wonder the makers of "One Flew Over the Cuckoo's Nest,"(飞越疯人院) the Oscar-winning movie based on Ken Kesey's novel,chose to film it at the Oregon State Hospital. It was a fright (惊骇)30 years ago,and the place still looks the same today.

Unlike the cinematic "Cuckoo's Nest" villains(恶棍),however,the administrators and staff at today's Oregon State Hospital aren't the bad guys. They're pretty much doing the best they can with deplorable(糟糕的)resources provided by a state with a long history of giving short shrift(忏悔)to its mentally ill.

Those running the institution,in fact,say they want change. They also voice support for a fledgling movement(新生运动)in the Legislature to create that change.

One man Senate President Peter Courtney,D-Salem lit the flame. Fed up with the state pouring money and crowding patients into the hospital,he engineered a $467,000 emergency appropriation last month to start a process that ought to lead to replacement of Oregon's disgraceful relic(不光彩的遗迹).

That emergency money will pay for stopgap measures(权宜措施)to relieve overcrowding. It also will launch work on a master plan that will give lawmakers a blueprint for a new,more humane way of caring for these patients.

On Monday,when the 2005 Oregon Legislature convenes,all 90 members should mark May 16 on their desk calendars. That's the deadline for presentation of this blueprint. It will likely call for a years-long project requiring tens of millions of dollars to build a smaller,modern hospital and an enlarged network of community mental health centers that would be less costly to operate and more effective at treating patients.

Every legislator must commit right now to moving Oregon mental health care out of the dark shadows of its 19th-century roots. And while they're at it,they should spend some money on a suitably dignified memorial for the earthly remains of Eva York and her fellow lost souls in the Cremains Room.

Unit Ten Criticism

文艺批评

单元导航

本单元我们将讨论文艺批评。本单元有三篇课文。课文 A 对美国前副总统迪克·切尼（Dick Cheney）的着装给予批评；课文 B 是对当代美国摄影师阿伯拉多·莫瑞尔（Abelardo Morell）作品的评论；课文 C 涉及对美国中餐馆里南京盐水鸭的评论。

Text A Dick Cheney, dressing down（穿着随便）
Parka, Ski Cap at Odds With Solemnity of Auschwitz Ceremony
（风雪大衣和滑雪帽与奥斯威辛集中营解放纪念仪式格格不入）

BY Robin Givhan

Washington Post

January 28, 2005

At yesterday's gathering of world leaders in southern Poland to mark the 60th anniversary of the liberation of Auschwitz, the United States was represented by Vice President Cheney. The ceremony at the Nazi death camp was outdoors, so those in attendance, such as French President Jacques Chirac and Russian President Vladimir Putin, were wearing dark, formal overcoats and dress shoes or boots（正装皮鞋或皮靴）. Because it was cold and snowing, they were also wearing gentlemen's hats. In short, they were dressed for the inclement weather（恶劣的天气）as well as the sobriety and dignity（严肃性和尊严）of the event.

The vice president, however, was dressed in the kind of attire one typically wears to operate a snow blower（开除雪机）.

Cheney, flanked by his wife and Israeli President Moshe Katsav at the Holocaust memorial event.

Cheney stood out in a sea of black-coated world leaders because he was wearing an olive drab（色调灰暗的）parka with a fur-trimmed hood. It is embroidered with his name. It reminded one of the way in which children's clothes are inscribed with their

names before they are sent away to camp. And indeed, the vice president looked like an awkward boy amid the well-dressed adults.

Like other attendees, the vice president was wearing a hat. But it was not a fedora(浅顶软呢帽)or a Stetson(斯泰森帽,美国西部牛仔戴的阔边高顶毡帽)or a fur hat or any kind of hat that one might wear to a memorial service as the representative of one's country. Instead, it was a knit ski cap, embroidered with the words "Staff 2001". It was the kind of hat a conventioneer(会议代表)might find in a goodie bag(会务袋).

It is also worth mentioning that Cheney was wearing hiking boots(远足靴)—thick, brown, lace-up(系带子的)ones. Did he think he was going to have to hike the 44 miles from Krakow—where he had made remarks earlier in the day—to Auschwitz?

His wife, Lynne, was seated next to him. Her coat has a hood, too, and it is essentially a parka. But it is black and did not appear to be functioning as either a name tag or a billboard. One wonders if at some point the vice president turned to his wife, took in(注意到)her attire and asked himself why they seemed to be dressed for two entirely different events.

Some might argue that Cheney was the only attendee with the smarts to dress for the cold and snowy weather. But sometimes, out of respect for the occasion, one must endure a little discomfort.

Just last week, in a frigid, snow-dusted Washington, Cheney sat outside through the entire inauguration without so much as a hat and without suffering frostbite(冻疮). And clearly, Cheney owns a proper overcoat. The world saw it during his swearing-in as vice president. Cheney treated that ceremony with the dignity it deserved—not simply through his demeanor(行为), but also through his attire. Would he have dared to take the oath of office(宣誓就职)with a ski cap on? People would have justifiably considered that an insult to the office, the day, the country.

There is little doubt that intellectually Cheney approached the Auschwitz ceremony with thoughtfulness and respect. But symbolism is powerful. That's why the piercing cry of a train whistle marked the beginning of the ceremony and the glare of searchlights signaled its end. The vice president might have been warm in his parka, ski cap and hiking boots. But they had the unfortunate effect of suggesting that he was more concerned with his own comfort than the reason for braving the cold(勇敢地面对寒冷)at all.

Part One: Preparing to explore

一、文艺批评

1. 定义

文艺批评是新闻评论大体系中一个重要的分支。

文艺批评（Criticism）指对文学艺术现象的分析和评价，既有批评，也有对优缺点的分析。它可分为两类：一是学术性文艺批评（scholarly criticism），通常发表在专业刊物或出现在专业研讨会上，侧重于分析判断，具有学术价值；二是新闻性文艺批评(journalistic criticism)，通常发表在报纸、大众杂志或广播电视上，侧重于论述评价，或对事件的深度解读，讲究新闻性和时效性。本单元的文艺批评属于后者。

普利策文艺批评奖自1970年开始颁发。从往届获奖作品的内容来看，大部分都是针对音乐、电视、文学、艺术、舞蹈、建筑等方面的文学艺术性评论，但也有少数作品触及其他话题，比如汽车文化（2004），服饰文化（2006），餐饮文化（2007）等。普利策奖文艺批评文章所涉及的内容似乎有从传统的文学艺术等高雅文化（high culture）逐步向衣食行等大众文化（popular culture）方向扩展的趋势。

2. 意义

作为一种重要的新闻评论形式，文艺批评具有多重价值。

首先，新闻性文艺批评是针对文化类新闻的阐释分析和价值评判，所以能使受众获得有效的文化信息；其次，它对新闻事件的分析需要具备一定的深度，要主动对读者表明立场、观点，发表导向正确且有说服力的评论，所以，还能使媒体工作者不断提升自己的思想水平、理论水平和业务水平，从而提升媒体竞争力；再次，文艺批评也是进行文化论争的有效途径，可以对文化思想和文化倾向产生很大的影响，更重要的是，新闻性文艺评论的价值在于其审美价值和意识形态价值。文艺批评通过对文化内涵的解析和辨识，以主流价值观作为精神向度进行思想引领，能够帮助人们建立起先进的文化观念，识别并自觉抵制不良文化，深化并提高审美能力和思想道德修养。

值得一提的是，由于网络的崛起，特别是博客和微博的流行，媒介商业化的压力以及当今的文化大众化和反智化趋势等综合因素，文艺批评的影响力有所削弱。

3. 写作基本特征

从普利策奖评审委员会给予获奖文艺批评作品的赞词来看，优秀的文艺批评作品具有以下基本特点：

（1）作者具有细致敏锐的观察力和智慧（astute and close observation，wit）。

（2）观点新鲜、独到、深刻（fresh，insightful and penetrating ideas）。

（3）叙事手法高超，生动幽默（dramatic and humorous storytelling）。

（4）文字表达清晰明了（lucid writing）。

（5）给人启迪，并能够影响舆论（luminous writing and influential effect）。

二、课前讨论

1. Attire reflects attitude. Do you agree? Explain.

2. Charles Dickens once said: “Great men are seldom over-scrupulous in the arrangement of their attire.” What does it mean? Do you agree? Explain.

Part Two: Exploring the text

一、作者背景

罗宾·基凡（Robin Givhan）：生长在美国芝加哥底特律。她于1986年获普林斯顿大学英语学士学位，1988年获密歇根大学的新闻硕士学位。毕业后，她在《底特律自由报》（*Detroit Free Press*）工作，从报道夜总会或二流电影新闻的娱乐版的小记者成为时装界新闻专题记者。她曾在《旧金山纪事报》（*San Francisco Chronicle*）工作过，但时间不长。1995年，基凡到《华盛顿邮报》供职，专跑时装界。2000年基凡曾在《时尚》（*Vogue*）杂志担任副主编，同年9月又回到《华盛顿邮报》。

二、《华盛顿邮报》

The Washington Post

Clinton and McCain Rebound to Take N.H.

Redskins' Gibbs Resigns As Coach

《华盛顿邮报》是美国首都华盛顿哥伦比亚特区（Washington D. C.）最大、最老的报纸，以报道美国国内政治新闻而著称，与擅长报道综合性新闻和国际新闻的《纽约时报》以及重点报道财经新闻的《华尔街日报》齐名，是美国最大的三家报纸之一。

在130多年的办报历史中，该报经历了曲折的发展道路。《华盛顿邮报》于1877年由斯蒂尔森·哈钦斯（Stilson Hutchins）创办，早期曾几易其手；1933年《华盛顿邮报》由于经营不善而倒闭，由尤金·迈耶（E. Meyer）接管后，又恢复了该纸的声誉和经济状况；1946年尤金出任世界银行董事长后，该纸由其女婿格雷厄姆（P. Graham）接任；1963年格雷厄姆因精神分裂症自杀，其妻凯瑟琳·格雷厄姆（Katharine Graham）成为该报发行人和董事会主席，全面主持报纸工作；1979年儿子唐纳德·格雷厄姆（Donald Graham）接替其母位置，并于20世纪90年代初担任董事会总裁和主席；目前，该报的发行人和总裁是前发行人凯瑟琳的外孙女凯瑟琳·韦姆斯（Katharine Weymouth）。

20世纪70年代初，《华盛顿邮报》因揭露水门事件并迫使理查德·尼克松总统退职而获得国际威望。

该报坚持采取新闻与观点分立的架构，大力支持自由贸易、人权、政府职责在于帮助最穷苦人群的理想，反对死刑等。在政治上一般多支持民主党。其最大读者群是大学及以上学历的专业人士。

截至2013年，这份报纸共获得58次普利策奖，在2008年第九十二届“普利策奖”中，该报独揽十四个新闻奖项中的六项大奖，成为该届“普利策奖”的最大赢家。

三、课文背景

二战期间，为了实施犹太种族灭绝政策，纳粹德国建立了1000多座集中营，其中奥斯威辛集中营（Auschwitz Concentration Camp）是最大的一座。在这里有100万左右的犹太人被德国法西斯杀害，因此，又被称为“死亡工厂”。1945年1月27日，苏联红军解放奥斯威辛集中营时，只有7000名幸存者。2005年1月27日，德国在此地举行了集中营解放60周年纪念仪式。参加活动的有世界各国领导人，幸存者和苏联老红军。美国副总统切尼携夫人也参加了这次纪念活动，但是，切尼因着装不合时宜而引起媒体关注。他身穿带毛边兜帽的橄榄色风雪大衣，头带滑雪帽，脚穿厚实的棕色登山鞋，与穿戴庄重的其他领导人极不相称。

《华盛顿邮报》记者罗宾·基凡女士敏锐地观察到这种反差，并进行了细致的描述，幽默机智地对切尼的装束作了一番评说。基凡在《华盛顿邮报》上刊登的10篇评论文章使她获得了2006年普利策文艺批评奖。这些文章基本上都涉及对服饰尤其是对名人服饰的评价，除了本篇对美国前副总统迪克·切尼的装束进行评论外，还有对美国前国务卿康多莉扎·赖斯的着装以及英国王子查尔斯现任妻子卡米拉·罗斯玛丽·尚德的服饰进行点评等。基凡具有非凡的洞察力和判断力，她把对服饰的看法转化成了文化评论，突出了服饰的社会文化功能，透过穿着挖掘人的心理状态和价值观念。基凡的诙谐机智（wit）和细腻的观察（close observation）尤其值得我们关注和学习。

四、作者主要观点

1. What is the author's main point of view concerning the way Dick Cheney dressed at the 60th anniversary of liberation of Auschwitz? Does the author seem to be fair or unbiased?

2. What do you think is one of the qualities in state leaders that the author values most?

五、写作风格与手法

1. What has intrigued you most about the article in terms of its writing style?

2. How much would the article interest the average reader? Why?

3. What, if any, is the constructive purpose of the writer?

4. Are the detailed descriptions about Dick Cheney's dress effective? Why?

5. How are the details arranged in the body of the essay?

6. What is the average length of the paragraphs?

7. What is the average length of the sentence?

9. Are informal expressions found in the essay? What is the effect of them?

10. In the last paragraph, the author wrote that "...intellectually Cheney approached the Auschwitz ceremony with thoughtfulness and respect" . What does the word "intellectually" imply?

11. In what way can the article be described as "witty"?

Part Three: Further exploring the text

一、语言点讲解

1. Dress down (title)

这是动词短语，非正式用语，有两个意思，一个是"穿着随便"，如：The staff are allowed to dress down on Fridays；另一个是"批评、谴责"，如：She dressed me down for being late. 在本文中，作者没有用"wear casually"，而选择了"dressing down"，可以起到双关语的作用。本题目表面上是取第一层意思，但也暗含了第二层意思，传达了另一种信息，即迪克·切尼在奥斯威辛集中营解放纪念仪式上穿戴的风雪大衣配滑雪帽和远足靴的行装很不得体，理应受到批评。此外，这与题目下面的小标题也很好地呼应了起来。一箭三雕，显得颇有智慧。

2. ...he was wearing an olive drab parka with a fur-trimmed hood. It is embroidered with his name...it was a knit ski cap, embroidered with the words "Staff 2001"...Cheney was wearing hiking boots—thick, brown, lace-up ones. (paragraphs. 3,4,5)

作者对切尼的衣服、帽子和靴子逐个进行了细致的描写，连大衣帽兜上的字和帽子上的字都没逃过她的眼睛，作者还清楚地交代其靴子是系鞋带的那种。这种丰富的描写把我们带进了一个视觉画面，让我们很真切地看到了切尼当时的着装。

3. Did he think he was going to have to hike the 44 miles from Krakow—where he had made remarks earlier in the day—to Auschwitz? (para. 5)

这句话批评切尼不应该在如此庄重严肃的场合穿靴子，这显得对当时的场合很不尊重。但作者没有直接批评，而是抱着一种开放的态度，说得幽雅风趣，耐人寻味。

4. One wonders if at some point the vice president turned to his wife，took in her attire and asked himself why they seemed to be dressed for two entirely different events. (para. 6)

"Take in"是动词短语，非正式用语，意思是：to spend some time looking at something，即观赏，观看。该词有"轻松地看"的含义。如：We sat there taking in the scenery. 我们坐在那里欣赏风景。可见，作者用此短语，而没有用 see 或 notice 这样的中性词，暗含了当时切尼敷衍了事的精神状态。

5. Without so much as a hat (para. 8)

相当于 even without a hat，甚至不戴帽子。该短语与中文表达方法相差很远，需要经常用才能掌握好。如：He took my umbrella without so much as asking.

(他问都不问一下就把伞给拿走了。)

6. And clearly，Cheney owns a proper overcoat. (para. 8)

"Own"，"拥有"的意思，一般后面跟"房子"、"汽车"、"饭店"等庞然之物。而这里与"大衣"搭配，形成鲜明反差，让人觉得很风趣。

二、中西文化比较

1. 服饰文化

在中国，尤其在改革开放以前，无论在学校还是在家里，我们从小接受的传统教育都是艰苦朴素，不要讲究穿衣打扮，因为那是资产阶级的生活方式。所以，一旦我们走出国门，特别是第一次参加人家的宴会时，难免会因着装不合适而遭遇一些尴尬。

着装礼仪是西方文化中非常重要的一部分，强调不同场合穿不同服装，是自我修养的体现，也是对别人的尊重。在大多数情况下，宴会或舞会的请贴上一般都会注明着装要求（Dress Code)，基本上分以下几种：

(1) White tie 或者说是 Ultra－formal（白色领带或超正装）

这是最正式的场合，如授勋仪式、宫廷晚宴等。男士要穿燕尾服（tailcoat)，配套的是白色马甲，白色衬衫，白色领结。裤子两侧有两道笔直的竖条。裤子不用皮带用吊带。女士要穿大裙摆的长晚礼服。

(2) Black tie 或者说是 Formal（黑色领带或正装）

这是最常见的正规着装要求，男士要穿晚礼服（英国叫 lounge suit，美国叫 Tuxedo)，前襟领子是黑缎面的，配白衬衫，黑领结，黑腰带，黑袜子，黑鞋。裤子两侧夹缝有和领子同面料的黑缎夹条。女士穿晚礼服（evening gown)，低胸露肩，相配小包和鞋子。项链、耳环等首饰的真假无所谓，但是要闪亮，戴手镯而不是手表。而且妆化浓一些比较好，灯光下不会显得惨淡无光。中国女士则可穿面料好的剪裁得体的旗袍或改良过的旗袍，并把头发挽起来配上头饰，效果一定不错。

(3) Semi-formal（半正式装）

男士穿深色西服，女士穿短礼服（cocktail dress）或考究的套装（women's suit）。

（4）Smart casual/dressy casual（优雅时尚便装）

男士穿比较讲究一点的便装，像西装上衣配休闲裤，衬衣休闲西裤等。女士则穿连衣裙，漂亮上衣配裤子，毛衣配裙子等可以自由发挥。

（5）Business casual（商务休闲装）

比 smart casual 再随便一些，但是不能穿牛仔裤。

（6）Casual 或 Informal（便装或非正式装）

可以随便穿，但还是要避免短裤、凉鞋。女士化点淡妆，穿一件质地普通的连衣裙肯定比穿牛仔裤雅致。总之，比别人穿的相对正式一点比穿的随便要好。

四、语言练习

1. 请用英语解释下列短语或句子。

（1）Dress down

（2）At odds with

（3）The Nazi death camp

（4）They were dressed for the inclement weather as well as the sobriety and dignity of the event.

（5）One wonders if at some point the vice president turned to his wife, took in(注意到)her attire and asked himself why they seemed to be dressed for two entirely different event.

（6）...out of respect for the occasion, one must endure a little.

（7）But they had the unfortunate effect of suggesting that he was more concerned with his own comfort than the reason for braving the cold at all.

2. 请将下列短语翻译成英文，并比较中英文表达方式的异同。

（1）穿着随便

（2）与……不一致

（3）那些出席的人

（4）恶劣的天气

（5）突出

（6）带毛边的兜帽

（7）穿黑色上衣的人

（8）穿正装的人

（9）甚至没戴帽子

（10）出于对……尊重

（11）雪尘覆盖的城市

（12）位于 A 和 B 中间

（13）在他就任副总统的宣誓仪式上

（14）宣誓就职

（15）顶着寒冷

3. 请将下面几个段落翻译成中文，并比较中英文表达方式的异同。

（1）Some might argue that Cheney was the only attendee with the smarts to dress for the cold and snowy weather. But sometimes, out of respect for the occasion, one must endure a little discomfort.

（2）Like other attendees, the vice president was wearing a hat. But it was not a fedora or a Stetson or a fur hat or any kind of hat that one might wear to a memorial service as the representative of one's country. Instead, it was a knit ski cap, embroidered with the words "Staff 2001." It was the kind of hat a conventioneer might find in a goodie bag.

（3）There is little doubt that intellectually Cheney approached the Auschwitz ceremony with thoughtfulness and respect. But symbolism is powerful. That's why the piercing cry of a train whistle marked the beginning of the ceremony and the glare of searchlights signaled its end. The vice president might have been warm in his parka, ski cap and hiking boots. But they had the unfortunate effect of suggesting that he was more concerned with his own comfort than the reason for braving the cold at all.

Part Four: Exploring beyond the text

一、自我反思

1. 我学到了什么？我要如何改进？

2. 一篇高质量的文艺批评的基本标准是什么？我能清楚地告诉别人吗？该篇文章的作者罗宾·基凡是如何达到这些标准的？我能向别人解释清楚吗？

二、知识扩展

1. 收集更多有关美国前副总统迪克·切尼的信息，并了解其他人是如何评价他的。

2. 如果你是迪克·切尼的助手，你会如何帮助他面对和处理媒体的批评？

三、能力扩展

1. 围绕一点展开，就此文写一篇500字左右的新闻评析。

2. 就周围人衣着的得体度进行评论，并写一篇500字左右的评论文章，最好配有照片。

3. 就你关注和感兴趣的某一文化现象写一篇评论，可以是书评或影评等。

Text B　Ordinary becomes extraordinary

BY Mike Feeney

Boston Globe

November 2,2007

导读：阿伯拉多·莫瑞尔（Abelardo Morell）是古巴籍美国摄影家，曾先后在美国鲍登学院和耶鲁大学学习摄影，现为马萨诸塞艺术和设计学院（Massachusetts College of Art and Design）教授。他以倒置的“暗箱摄影”（Camera Obscura）而饮誉世界。他把房间当作暗箱，只剩一个拇指盖大的进光孔，让窗外的风景穿过此孔，落在屋内的背墙上，使内部和外部画面奇怪相遇，造成超现实的荒诞感，赋予平凡的日常事物以全然陌生的形象。莫瑞尔的独特视角也迫使观赏者变换角度重新审视自己的立场，体验和发现蕴藏在平凡事物中的不平凡特性。

2007 年 9 月至次年 1 月，位于美国马萨诸塞州的著名文理学院艾姆赫斯特学院的米德艺术博物馆举办了莫瑞尔的个人摄影作品展。《波士顿全球报》（*Boston Globe*）记者马克·菲尼（Mike Feeney）对此次作品展给予了高度评价。

作者介绍

马克·菲尼（Mark Feeney）：出生于 1957 年 7 月 28 日，他于 1979 年获得哈佛大学历史和文学优等学位。

毕业后他开始在《波士顿环球报》的图书馆工作，后来为该报写书评，并成为图书编辑。从 1991 年起，他任该报周日版“焦点”版面编辑，负责编辑分析和评论性文章。1993 年 9 月，他利用半年的学术休假时间为《波士顿环球杂志》写稿，次年又回到“焦点”，一直供职于《波士顿环球报》。目前，他是该报艺术版面的作家和编辑。他的文章刊登在许多报纸杂志上，如《新共和》、《纽约观察家》、《华盛顿月刊》、《洛杉矶时报》、《新闻日报》等。

此外，他还是布兰德斯大学的兼职讲师，并在普林斯顿大学教授写作。

菲尼在《波士顿环球报》上发表的 10 篇有关摄影、绘画和电影题材的评论文章获得了 2008 年第 92 届普利策文艺评论奖。普利策奖委员会称赞他“透彻并全面的把握了电影、摄影和绘画类的视觉艺术（penetrating and versatile command of visual arts）”。

AMHERST-Abelardo Morell straddles the uncertain border between dislocation and enchantment(跨越了移动错位和摄人心魄的美之间的模糊界限). He transforms the everyday, exalting it. He tames the exotic, domesticating it. And in his best-known photographs, which show camera obscura images(暗箱摄影影像) superimposed on blank walls, he turns the world literally upside down.

“A Room With a View: The Photography of Abelardo Morell,” which runs at Amherst College's Mead Art Museum through Jan. 20, isn't all that big a show just 32 images. Many are quite large, though, which gives the show a certain heft(给摄影展增添某种分量). Greatly increasing that heft are the quality and variety of the images. Career retrospectives are rarely this small. That's all right, since career retrospectives are rarely this good.

Born in Cuba in 1948, Morell came to this country with his family in 1962. The Morells moved to New York, and one can see the city's influence in the two earliest photographs here. "Central Park, Skating Rink" seems conventional, even touristy(为了吸引观光客的), until one realizes Morell was barely into his teens when he took it. Conversely, "Twins," which shows a pair of identical young men standing in front of a Greyhound bus, could have been taken anywhere. But the sensibility is pure—which is to say impure—New York street. Diane Arbus (twins) meets Robert Frank (bus). It's a picture taken by a young man waiting for something to happen who was also a photographer waiting for a sensibility to emerge. For all that "Twins" is a memorable picture, most of the memorableness derives from other, better photographers. Soon enough, the memorableness would be Morell's own.

The title "A Room With a View" is both witty and inadequate. It's witty because for some 15 years Morell has followed a distinctive procedure in many of his photographs. He'll set up shop in an interior space—often, but not always, a hotel room-that overlooks an impressive exterior. Morell will then reduce all incoming light to a single small source, in effect turning the room into a supersize pinhole camera, which projects an inverted image of what's outside. He then takes an actual camera to photograph the result.

Morell's recurring use of the camera obscura could seem like a gimmick(魔法), little more than a visual calling card, like the black frame lines on an Avedon portrait. Morell uses the device for so much more, though-and by no means does he use it exclusively (hence the inadequacy of the show's title). These camera obscura images collapse differences-not just inside and out, but rich and plain, familiar and novel-and give Morell a stage of his own making on which to induce the unexpected.

The range of effects Morell produces with the camera obscura is great. "Camera Obscura Image of Umbrian Landscape over Bed, Umbertide, Italy" is strange and unsettling. What's more mundane(普通的，世俗的) than a bed-yet what's it doing seemingly in the middle of an Italian field? Conversely, the patent unreality of "Camera Obscura Image of Times Square in Hotel Room" reinforces the dizzying effect the actual place can have. The pair of camera obscura images from a 2002 trip to Havana, Morell's first visit to Cuba in 40 years, carry a weight of profound emotion: the woman's portrait, the two roses, the inviting chair, in one; the cracked, scarred, and chipped plaster(剥落的灰泥), flecked with feeling(充满了无数情感), in the other.

Morell, who teaches photography at Massachusetts College of Art and Design, can also use the technique for comedy. "Camera Obscura Image of Manhattan View Looking

West in Empty Room" is a study in incongruity(对不协调状态的研究). Amid the forest of skyscrapers projected from outside, one can make out a stepladder and electric plug inside a sly reminder that construction comes in all shapes and sizes. Even better is "Camera Obscura Image of the Empire State Building in Bedroom." The sight of the tower's limp phallic immensity sprawled across the bed, tired perhaps after a long day spent skyscraping, is hilarious. It also nods to Andy Warhol's marathon film "Empire" and, more distantly, Lewis Hine's noble chronicling of the building's construction.

The presence of others' art is a near-constant in Morell's work(几乎是经久不变的莫瑞尔作品). They range from Lewis Carroll and Edward Hopper to Irving Penn and William Henry Fox Talbot. Sometimes that art is front and center. "King Philip IV by Velasquez, Gardner Museum," a distorted photograph of the kingly portrait, functions as shrewd commentary on its subject: It's artifice(photograph) about artifice(painting) about artifice(costume, pose, monarchy). "Tim and Rembrandt, Gardner Museum" shows a young man next to the canvas resembling the painter on the canvas. It might just as well be called "Time and Rembrandt," as it folds together past and present, art and life, here and there.

One of three color images in the show, "Camera Obscura Image of the Philadelphia Museum of Art, East Entrance in Gallery 171 with a de Chirico Painting" is nearly as spectacular as its title is long. The shades of orange and dun in both painting and facade chime lusciously. The painting itself works as a window within the frame, letting Morell play vertiginous games with depth and perception.

Art in his photographs need not take the form of great paintings. Morell delights in objets trouvees(天然艺术品): paper bags, maps, boxes. The more banal the item, the more pleasure he takes in its metamorphosis. The thumb indentations of the thick volumes stacked high in "Six Dictionaries" take on an almost geological solidity. "$7 Million," a real crowd-pleaser, is just what its titles say it is: that much cash in elastic-band-held blocks(a few bucks here, a few bucks here-it does add up).

In "Slide", Morell shoots the piece of namesake playground equipment so that it looks horizontal, receding into the picture plane (descent as depth). He's wild about light, yes (what photographer isn't?), but Morell revels in the sheer thing-ness of objects, too. The raised metal letters of the manufacturer's stamp on the slide take on a monumental quality.

A different sort of monumentality is on display in "My Eyeglasses". Making the optical sculptural, he declares how much his work is a tribute to the act of seeing. Seeing is believing?

For Morell, seeing is loving, too.

Text C The great white duck

Jonathan Gold
La Weekly
March 15,2006

导读：南京盐水鸭又叫板鸭，久负盛名，已有一千多年的历史。其特点是皮白肉嫩、肥而不腻、香鲜美味，久食不厌。跨洋过海到了美国的板鸭又是什么样的？美国人作何评价呢？

作者介绍

乔纳森·古德（Jonathan Gold）：《洛杉矶周报》的评论家，主要写餐饮方面的评论文章。他也是《反侦察：在真正的洛杉矶去何处觅食》一书的作者。自1984年起，他就开始为该报撰写有关饮食方面的文章。

他也为许多其他报纸杂志提供有关饮食的评论文章，如《洛杉矶时报》、《洛杉矶》和《美食家》等杂志。他因此曾获得过美食世界的最高奖"贝尔德美食写作奖"。

他还经常给《滚石》、《名利场》等杂志写音乐和大众文化方面的评论文章，同时也写广播剧。

古德在《洛杉矶周报》上发表的10篇有关美食的评论文章获得了2007年第91届普利策文艺批评奖。普利策奖委员会称这些文章体现了"一位饱学食客的愉悦之情"(pleasure of an erudite eater)。

A Nanjing duck is cold and ghostly white(煞白),a seemingly goose-fleshed fowl that has been pressed,cooked and brined until the meat firms,becomes scented with mild spice,and is fatless. When you press your finger into it,the flesh springs back almost as quickly as hard rubber,but the texture of the flesh is fine and delicate,yet with little of the immediate pleasure you might associate with Cantonese roast duck(广州烤鸭),air-dried Beijing duck(北京风干鸭)or even duck confit(油封鸭). Nanjing duck may be the least-likely candidate for duck-dish greatness in the world.

Nanjing duck is very difficult and time-consuming to prepare. It began as a preservative process,so did sushi,bacon and confit. And yet upon seeing a Nanjing-style duck leg,pale and frigid,whomped into neat slices with a cleaver and served absolutely plain,your first impulse might be to dream about the Shanghainese braised duck(焖鸭) you might have had for dinner last week,or at least to look ahead to the noodles to come.

Nanjing Kitchen, the local specialist in Nanjing duck, is a bare, tiny restaurant plunked down in a San Gabriel pocket mall,finished with jazzy tile that suggests a rural diner. When you hear the occasional lonely moan of a train whistle from the tracks that run a few blocks south of here, it seems exactly right, as if you are eating your lunch at some railroad-station restaurant a hundred miles out in the countryside instead of in the middle of multicultural San Gabriel.

Presiding over Nanjing Kitchen is John Zhang, a rumpled, erudite man, his English as inflected with British idiom as by the accent of his native Nanjing, who seems very much like a Graham Greene character devoted to protecting the integrity of his spare, precise Nanjing dishes from the wild spices and lush, tropical Southeast Asian cooking in the storefronts surrounding his own.

The ducks in California are terrible, he says. Food for nothing but roasting. I have to get special ducks all the way from Indiana.

His restaurant is dominated by a huge refrigerator running the entire length of the dining room, displaying neat arrays of boxed appetizers behind its glass doors. On my first visit to the restaurant, I had cold boiled peanuts, a delicate salad made from slivered pressed tofu, and a seaweed salad. Zhang plucked a container of Nanjing-style simmered meatballs from the cold case, tawny orbs about the size of golf balls, much firmer and much plainer than Shanghainese lion's-head meatballs (狮子头), which they superficially resembled. There was a bowl of fragile won ton in a strong chicken broth(鸡汤混沌), each dumpling stuffed with minced pork and a green vegetable Zhang imports from China. We had a couple bowls of the jingsu noodles(净素面)(No. 8 on the minimalist menu), spaghetti-thick strands tossed with bean sauce, steamed bok choy(白菜) and either spicy braised pork shank or chewy pork ribs. It was a delicious meal, a meal with no duck at all.

Nanjing duck does not appear on the menu. There are no obvious ducks in the cold case. When we had finished, surprised to find a Nanjing-style restaurant that didn't seem to serve the most famous Nanjing-style dish, I asked Zhang whether his restaurant served Nanjing duck.

He snorted. If you were able to read Chinese, he said, you would see our sign advertising Nanjing duck in characters 1 foot high. If you look in the refrigerator, you will see Nanjing duck wings, Nanjing duck legs, Nanjing duck gizzards(鸭胗), Nanjing duck feet and Nanjing duck neck, which is most delicious. We have Nanjing duck whole, half or quartered. Our specialty is in fact Nanjing duck.

There are millions of people who think Nanjing duck is the single greatest duck dish in the world. I am not one of them. But Zhang's Nanjing duck, if you are into austere cuisine(节制饮食), is in fact pretty delicious once you get past the salt: complex and flowery, with an almost vanilla-like undercurrent to the taste. It is a dish for connoisseurs (美食家), the caviar of the duck world(鸭中极品). If you are of a certain mind, Beijing duck, Shanghainese braised and Cantonese roast duck may seem unspeakably vulgar.